The United States and Japan
in the Postwar World

The United States and Japan
IN THE POSTWAR WORLD

Edited by Akira Iriye and Warren I. Cohen

THE UNIVERSITY PRESS OF KENTUCKY

This book is based upon papers presented at a conference
sponsored by both the Japan Society for the Promotion
of Science and the Joint Committee on Japanese Studies
of the Social Science Research Council and the American
Council of Learned Societies.

Scholarly publisher for the Commonwealth,
serving Bellarmine College, Berea College, Centre
College of Kentucky, Eastern Kentucky University,
The Filson Club, Georgetown College, Kentucky
Historical Society, Kentucky State University,
Morehead State University, Murray State University,
Northern Kentucky University, Transylvania University,
University of Kentucky, University of Louisville,
and Western Kentucky University.

Editorial and Sales Offices: Lexington, Kentucky 40506-0336

Library of Congress Cataloging-in-Publication Data

The United States and Japan in the postwar world / edited by Akira
    Iriye and Warren I. Cohen.
        p. cm.
    "Based upon papers presented at a [1984] conference sponsored by
both the Japan Society for the Promotion of Science and the Joint
Committee on Japanese Studies of the Social Science Research Council
and the American Council of Learned Societies"—P. iv.
    Includes index.
    ISBN 0-8131-1652-X (alk. paper)
    1. United States—Foreign relations—Japan—Congresses. 2. Japan—
Foreign relations—United States—Congresses. 3. United States—
Foreign economic relations—Japan—Congresses. 4. Japan—Foreign
economic relations—United States—Congresses. I. Iriye, Akira.
II. Cohen, Warren I.
E183.8.J3U723   1989   88-38372
327.73052—dc19

Contents

Tables

Preface

In 1984 a group of distinguished American and Japanese scholars met under the auspices of the Social Science Research Council—with the support of the Ford Foundation, National Endowment for the Humanities, and the Japan-United States Friendship Commission—to examine relations between their countries in a historical and global context. They recognized that the constantly growing issues between the two countries, which were becoming so complex that many across the Pacific were warning of a "drifting apart," if not a rupture, of two of the closest allies since the war, could only be understood if examined historically—in relation to the overall themes and trends in the past several decades—and globally—in the context of changing world and regional affairs.

Such an effort is, if anything, needed even more today when one hears talk of a serious conflict, crisis of confidence, or misunderstanding between the United States and Japan that threatens to erode the Pacific alliance. The editors, therefore, have assembled some of the papers presented at the 1984 gathering to make them available to concerned citizens as well as to the specialists.

The editors would like to express special thanks to the Social Science Research Council for its support of the initial gathering and to the University Press of Kentucky for its willingness to publish the essays in book form. The editing of the papers has been facilitated by the cheerful and efficient help of graduate assistants at the University of Chicago and Michigan State University, in particular Alexa Hand and Barbara Welke.

Abbreviations

ANZUS	Pacific Security Treaty [Australia, New Zealand, United States]
ASEAN	Association of Southeast Asian Nations
ASPAC	Asian and Pacific Council
CHINCOM	China Committee
COCOM	Coordinating Committee for Export to Communist Areas
DSP	Democratic Socialist party (Japan)
ECA	Economic Cooperation Administration
ECAFE	Economic Commission for Asia and the Far East
EEC	European Economic Community
ESB	Economic Stabilization Board
FIDA	Foreign Investor Deposit Account
FYA	Free Yen Account
FEC	Far Eastern Commission
GATT	General Agreement on Tariffs and Trade
GDP	Gross Domestic Product
GNP	Gross National Product
IMF	International Monetary Fund
JCP	Communist party (Japan)
JSP	Socialist party (Japan)
LDP	Liberal Democratic party (Japan)
MITI	Ministry of International Trade and Industry
NATO	North Atlantic Treaty Organization
NDA	Nonresident Deposit Account
NIC	newly industrialized countries
NSC	National Security Council
NYDA	Nonresident Yen Deposit Account
OECD	Organization for Economic Co-operation and Development
OIR	Office of Intelligence Research (U.S. Department of State)
OMA	orderly market agreement
OPEC	Organization of Petroleum Exporting Countries
PRC	People's Republic of China
ROC	Republic of China
SEATO	Southeast Asia Treaty Organization
SITC	Standard International Trade Classifications
Sōhyō	General Council of Trade Unions (Japan)
VER	voluntary export restraint

The United States and Japan
in the Postwar World

PART ONE

U.S.-Japanese Relations since 1945

As the basic framework of international affairs since the end of World War II, Robert Gilpin proposes the concept of the "American System." According to this analysis, the postwar world was characterized by America's military, political, and economic predominance, and it continued to define the international system until the 1980s. Western European countries and Japan basically accepted this definition and generally fitted themselves into it. The American System, however, had two components—the U.S.-European and the U.S.-Japanese axes, each buttressed by security alliances and close economic ties—but these two were not always well coordinated, The third possible axis, the European-Japanese connection, was very tenuous.

Gilpin shows that the American System faces a crisis in the mid-1980s not only because the supremacy of the United States in the strategic and economic fields has been undermined by the ascendance of Soviet military power and the challenge of European, Japanese, and NIC (newly industrialized countries') economies, but also because the tension between the two axes is reaching a near-breaking point, forcing upon Washington difficult choices in its dealings with its allies. In the meantime, the third axis, the European-Japanese connection is, if anything, more ridden with conflict than ever. The current state of U.S.-Japanese affairs, Gilpin argues, must be put in this broader context.

The next five essays narrow the focus to East Asia, to United States efforts to integrate Japan into the American System. Two basic themes emerge: the development of a more equal relationship between Japan and the United States, referred to by Cohen (chapter 3) as "normal" and by LaFeber (chapter 6) as the end of an "aberration"; and the persistent asymmetry of American political, and Japanese economic, concerns.

Not surprisingly, China loomed large in U.S.-Japanese relations from the preparations for the peace conference in 1951 to Japan's recognition of the People's Republic of China in the aftermath of the "Nixon Shock." Cohen, Hosoya (chapter 2), and Aruga (chapter 4) all note competing pressures on the Japanese government and the way in which policy toward China became enmeshed in Japanese as well as American domestic politics, including the factional struggles within the ruling Liberal Democratic party. Hosoya underscores the strains engendered by the rigidity of the American posture toward the People's Republic, and Aruga describes the price Japanese leaders paid for accepting American leadership. Cohen, on the other hand, stresses the ease with which Japan circumvented American strictures—and the acquiescence of American leaders in Japan's course. He offers a novel interpretation of the "Yoshida Letter" (in which the Japanese prime minister promised to conclude a peace treaty with the Nationalist Chinese government in Taiwan), contending that it was a device by John Foster Dulles to prevent Dean Acheson from yielding to Yoshida's hope for more leeway in Japan's relations with the People's Republic.

All of these essays point to the unequal partnership of the 1950s, and Aruga analyzes widespread Japanese discomfort with this state of affairs as a key to the security treaty crisis of 1960. Japanese leaders needed a new, less blatantly unequal treaty and found the United States responsive. He attributes the crisis that nonetheless came to Prime Minister Kishi's maladroit handling of the Diet. Aruga also explains the restructuring of Japanese politics consequent to the crisis of 1960.

Southeast Asia is the focus of attention in the essays by Watanabe (chapter 5) and LaFeber. Watanabe examines Japanese and American maneuvering relative to that region in the 1950s, while LaFeber looks more sharply at Vietnam as an irritant in those relations in the 1960s and 1970s. Both note the preeminence of Cold War strategic concerns in American thinking and the preeminence of economic concerns in Japanese thought. Watanabe perceives American efforts to direct Japanese trade and the Japanese search for raw materials toward Southeast Asia. Some American planners clearly saw this strategy as central to a plan to create a strategic crescent to contain China. Others were determined to focus Japan's economic attention on Southeast Asia, not only as an alternative to China but also as a means of protecting American markets. Japanese planners always intended to find a global solution, and it is clearly their vision that has been realized.

LaFeber, noting tensions over trade, Okinawa, and China, focuses on America's war in Vietnam as an immediate and long-term source of friction between the two allies. Despite Prime Minister Satō's support for American policy in the face of widespread Japanese disgust, the Americans were not satisfied. From Washington's perspective, the Japanese, instead of aiding in the strategic effort to contain communism, were taking advantage of American distress to seize markets, including an enormous share of America's domestic market.

These essays offer a series of case studies of the shift in relative power between the United States and Japan since 1945, of the erosion of the American System. As LaFeber demonstrates—and as revealed in the "Japan bashing" of the 1980s—few Americans have accepted the loss of American dominance. The generous hegemon of the 1950s often behaved like an irritable supplicant in the 1970s and 1980s. The ability of Americans in the twenty-first century to adapt to their country's status as a possibly declining power will determine whether Cohen's optimism about the future of U.S.-Japanese relations is justified.

1

The Global Context

ROBERT G. GILPIN

The future of American-Japanese relations must be analyzed in the larger context of the evolving relationships among the United States, Western Europe, and Japan. The interactions and tensions among these three industrial democracies cannot be isolated from one another. Because the United States has been the linchpin of these crucial relationships since 1945, this article will refer to them as the "American System" and will argue that this system is in a state of crisis that necessitates difficult policy choices.

This essay defines the American System as the political understandings, military alliances, and economic agreements that the United States has entered into with its principal allies since the end of the Second World War. One set of relationships is based on the American-Japanese Treaty of Mutual Cooperation and Security, signed in 1960, in combination with America's economic and political relations with Japan. The other set consists of the North Atlantic Treaty Organization (NATO), established in 1949, in addition to America's political and economic relations with its Western European allies. Together these ties between the United States and Japan, on the one hand, and between the United States and Western Europe, on the other, not only have provided the basis of American foreign policy over the past several decades, but also have defined the fundamental relationships among the industrial democracies.

The political, strategic, and economic foundations of the American System have withstood numerous assaults, but deepening fissures are embedded in each of these foundations. To understand the present difficulties among the allies and their consequences for American-Japanese relations, one must first analyze the foundations of these relationships and the sources of conflict now growing in significance in the 1980s.

The first, and by far the most important, link among the industrial democracies has been a common political assessment of the Soviet threat. Primarily as a consequence of Soviet behavior following the collapse of the wartime alliance against the Axis, the Soviet Union has been regarded as an expanding imperial power whose intentions are inimical to the interests of the United States and its allies. This Soviet challenge has been seen as political, military, and ideological. It has involved internal subversion through the use of domestic Communist parties and the external threat of the Red Army. In response to these perceived dangers, agreement about the necessity of the policy of Soviet containment has provided the political cement of the Western system of political and military alliances.

Yet almost from the very beginning of these alliance relationships, there have been significant differences between American and allied perceptions of the nature and scope of the Soviet threat, differences that arise principally from the contrasting geographical circumstances, political interests, and assumed responsibilities of the United States and its European and Pacific allies.

The United States has regarded the Soviet threat as primarily military in nature and global in scope. Yet until recently, the United States had not given high priority to the Soviet military threat in Asia. Asian events have been viewed in the context of Europe. For example, the United States regarded the Korean War more as a possible forerunner to Soviet adventurism elsewhere, particularly in Western Europe, than as a direct threat to the security of Asia, and based its "swing" strategy on the assumption that, in the event of a war with the Soviet Union, the United States would shift its military forces in Asia to the European theater. America believed the major threat in Asia was the Communist Chinese and, in fact, entered the Vietnamese civil war to contain what was perceived to be an expansionist China. The Vietnam War itself and America's estrangement from Communist China put a heavy strain on relations between the United States and Japan, which did not wish to be involved. With American-Chinese rapprochement and the growth of Soviet power in East Asia, however, the political situation has begun to change. Both the United States and Japan are more concerned than in the past about the expansion of Soviet influence in the Pacific and Southeast Asia, but a profound conflict continues to divide the two allies. Whereas the United States desires that Japan increase its role in the containment of Soviet power, the Japanese remain wary of remilitarization and of being drawn into a conflict of the superpowers over which they have little or no control.

The West Europeans have also differed from the United States' view of the Soviet threat. They have considered the threat to be primarily political and have focused their concerns on regional problems. Thus, although the United States worries about the Middle East, Asia, and South America, Western Europe worries mainly about itself and the effect of superpower collisions on its own security.

The second foundation of the American System has been the set of parallel military alliances formed in the 1950s that have connected the United States with Japan and with Western Europe. Although Western Europe and Japan have no direct military or security ties with one another, indirectly they have been linked through their respective military ties with the United States. In effect, in these alliances the United States placed Western Europe and Japan under its nuclear umbrella. This so-called policy of extended deterrence has been the real foundation of both alliances and has united the industrial democracies militarily. The United States, with its commitments in both the Atlantic and the Pacific regions, has provided the keystone for the global alliance system directed at the containment of the Soviet Union.

As in the case of their political relations, inherent differences have existed among the allies over strategic issues, and consequently in the nature of the two sets of military alliances. In the first place, a fundamental premise of the initial American military commitment to both Western Europe and Japan was that it was a limited commitment. For example, American leaders assumed that, as Europe recovered economically from the devastation of the war, it would assume an ever-increasing share of the financial and military burden of containing Soviet power in the European theater. Although the policy of extended deterrence would stay in place, the conventional defense of Europe would become primarily a responsibility of the West Europeans themselves in the NATO division of labor. In the case of Japan, the nuclear umbrella by itself was deemed to be sufficient to deter the Soviets, and little need was seen for a major Japanese military role in containing Soviet conventional power in Northeastern Asia.

The third foundation of the American System has been the so-called Bretton Woods System of economic cooperation. At the end of the Second World War this system was established between the United States and Western Europe and was later expanded to include Japan. Under American leadership and operating through a set of international institutions—the International Monetary Fund (IMF), the General Agreement on Tariffs and Trade (GATT), and the World Bank—the industrial democracies and other members of the Organization for Economic Co-operation and Development (OECD) have cooperated to eliminate barriers to trade and other forms of economic nationalism. Further, these economies have been tied together by the central role of the dollar in the international monetary system and, with some major exceptions, increasingly by the freedom of capital movements. Within this monetary and financial framework, the United States and its economic partners have tried to liberalize trade through successive rounds of trade negotiations.

Despite this general commitment to the creation of a system of multilateral free trade, the past several decades have witnessed three major departures that have become sources of intensifying interallied conflict. One has been a high level of Japanese protectionism against a wide range of products from other countries. Another was the formation of the European Economic Community (EEC), or Common Market, that has simultaneously lowered trade barriers among the West European countries and maintained certain barriers toward external economies. The third has been a tendency of the United States to protect selected threatened industries, a practice that has grown in recent years. This combination of the broad movement toward liberalized trade and restrictive, protectionist practices has produced the main features of the world trading system. These features in turn embody a number of asymmetries that increasingly endanger the future of the contemporary world economy.

One prominent feature of the postwar international economy has been the American-Japanese relationship. Largely for security reasons, the United States in the early postwar years took a number of steps to facilitate the reconstruction of the war torn Japanese economy. It opened the American economy to Japanese exports and encouraged the transfer of U.S. technology to Japan, put pressure on the European colonial powers to open their colonies in South and Southeast Asia to the Japanese, and, over strong European opposition, secured Japanese entry into the IMF, the GATT, and other international organizations, thus ensuring Japan's full participation in the world economy. Within this favorable framework, the Japanese have been able to pursue their highly successful policy of export-led growth and advance to the position of an economic superpower.[1]

The American-Japanese relationship has been characterized by a basic asymmetry that has increased over the years and has become a major source of tension between these allies. The United States, as it sponsored the reentry of Japan into the world economy, made a number of economic concessions to the Japanese without seeking an economic quid pro quo. As a consequence, the Japanese were able for a number of years to enjoy unimpeded access to the American market and American technology while giving little economically in return. The Japanese home market has been relatively closed to American exports and to American direct investment as well. Further, both American and European financial institutions have been kept out of Japan's government-manipulated, low interest rate capital market. A major objective of American and European policy toward Japan in recent years has been to make the economic relationship with the Japanese more symmetrical. Translated into specific demands, this means at the least a Japanese economy more open to foreign goods, the internationalization of the yen, and increased access to Japanese technology for American businesses and military.

Another prominent feature of the contemporary world economy has been the rapid growth of a high level of economic interdependence between the United States and Western Europe. Although the Europeans have discriminated against American agricultural and manufactured products, the rapidly expanding European market, as the distinguished economist Jacob Viner had predicted, proved to be more trade-creating than trade-diverting.[2] American exports to the EEC soared while the Europeans themselves were able to expand economically through the lowering of trade barriers. Of equal importance, American multinational corporations found the rapidly growing and partially closed European market a fertile soil for foreign expansionism. Thus, the growth of both trade and investment rapidly linked the two sides of the Atlantic.

Inherent in this situation, however, was a potential source of serious disagreement. From its very beginnings, the EEC, with its trade restrictions and other departures from a liberal economic order, was regarded by the United States as a temporary expedient. As Europe regained its competitive strength, American decision makers assumed that the barriers to free trade would come down. West Europeans, on the other hand, have had more ambiguous feelings on this matter. Whereas the West Germans have tended to favor the lowering of trade barriers, the French have been actively hostile to the dismantling of the external tariff barriers and especially of the common agricultural policy. These conflicting views have resulted in a stalemate and have frustrated the creation of what president John F. Kennedy called a "grand design" for the economic and political integration of the industrial democracies. In recent years, the tension between American and European conceptions of the global economic order have increased and now threaten the unity of the transatlantic economy.

The third significant feature of the contemporary world economy is a direct consequence of the other two features. In the economic as in the security realm, the United States plays a pivotal role in the relations among the industrial democracies. Western Europe and Japan are tied to one another principally through their respective associations with the United States. In contrast to the intimate and extensive American-European and American-Japanese linkages, the Europeans and the Japanese have few formal relations, and the Europeans for their part would undoubtedly like to keep it that way.

Because of opposition on both sides, trade and investment between the EEC and Japan until recently have been very slow in developing. From the early postwar period, the EEC and Japan have discriminated against one another's goods. West European exasperation with the Japanese has intensified because of Japan's large trade surplus with the EEC and what the Europeans perceive as continuing Japanese discrimination against European goods. More ominously, a growing and powerful strain of European thought has become increasingly xenophobic regarding Japanese competition. This line of thought argues that Japanese "tribal" culture and "unfair" government policies separate Japan from the liberal Western trading system. Hence, it is argued that Japan should be ostracized by the United States and Western Europe; the Japanese, it is claimed, are really not like us and should be drummed out of the club. Individual West European countries and the Common Market acting as a bloc have begun to take more strenuous measures to close off the West

European market to the Japanese. With the parallel growth of American protectionism over the past decade, especially with respect to Japanese goods,
this third asymmetry of the world economy, i.e., the absence of close European-Japanese political and security ties that might moderate economic conflicts, has become a major problem, which magnifies the fundamental issue
of where Japan and, more generally, the newly industrializing countries (NICs)
of Asia fit into an increasingly protectionist world economy.

Since World War II, the political, security, and economic relations among
the United States and its principal allies have provided the foundations of the
American System and of American foreign policy more generally. Although
these relations have proven to be highly durable, inherent differences in perception and interest among the allies have existed for a long time.[3]

Political relations between the United States and Japan and those between
the United States and Western Europe have moved in diametrically opposed
directions since the founding of the two sets of alliances. Despite a number
of severe crises and the ever-present deep conflicts over economic and security
matters, American and Japanese political relations have improved in many
respects since the late 1960s and early 1970s. However, although the United
States does continue to give primacy to the European connection, the strains
in this relationship have grown ever greater with the passage of time.

The deterioration of American-West European relations that began with
the Vietnam War has continued because of contrasting attitudes toward East-
West détente and the Soviet Union. For the West Europeans, a major priority
is the reunification of the continent and the closing of the split between Eastern
and Western Europe, especially for the Federal Republic of Germany whose
ultimate objective is the reunification of the nation. From this perspective,
détente and the East-West discussions begun at Helsinki in 1975 are fundamental. Nothing must interfere with the slow and long-term healing of the
cleavage dividing Eastern and Western Europe.[4]

Although relatively few Americans reject the ideal of détente and the easing
of East-West tensions, most would no doubt characterize the results of détente
as disappointing if not as a failure. The Reagan administration and important
currents in American public opinion believe that the United States has gained
little from détente in terms of overall relations with the Soviet Union. Most
West Europeans, on the other hand, believe that they have gained much and
do not wish to see those gains jeopardized by American actions such as the
invoking of economic sanctions against the Soviet Union over its role in Poland
and Afghanistan. Among these perceived gains are the political stability of
the continent, the decline of the internal communist threat, and the growth
of East-West trade.

These differences in interests and perceptions reveal that a profound psychological distancing is taking place between the United States and Western Europe. This crisis of mutual confidence can be observed in many different ways. For example, many West Europeans exhibit a strong tendency to equate the United States and the Soviet Union as immoral, imperial, and irresponsible superpowers. Statements by high-ranking Europeans have proposed that Europe position itself equidistantly between the superpowers and play a middle role between the two giants.

Americans are also criticizing the West Europeans in new and more fundamental ways. West Europeans are seen as thinking only of their own immediate concerns, failing to support American policies vis-á-vis the Soviet Union, and leaving the defense of Western interests solely up to the United States. West Europeans also are criticized for not being willing even to defend themselves. Furthermore, the United States is frustrated with the European opposition to American policies in the Middle East and elsewhere. Thus, despite frequent demonstrations of unity, this political and psychological estrangement between the United States and Western Europe is significant and widening. It is in part a generational conflict and, therefore, promises to become worse as the younger generation of West Europeans and Americans comes to power. In combination with security and economic issues, these political differences, if they are not resolved, threaten the future of the alliance between the the United States and Western Europe.

Turning toward the Pacific, despite a general improvement in American and Japanese economic and political relations, profound conflicts exist over trade and other economic issues. Resentments also abound on both sides in the security area, especially the Japanese response to American pressures on Japan to assume a larger defense burden. Nevertheless, American and Japanese policies toward the Soviet Union have moved closer together. The Japanese have taken a very serious view of the Soviet invasion of Afghanistan, despite their reluctance to follow the American lead in applying economic sanctions. The fact that the first use of the Red Army outside the postwar boundaries of the Soviet sphere of influence occurred in Asia was more ominous for the Japanese than for the West Europeans. More generally, the continuing expansion of Soviet power in Asia threatens the Japanese most seriously, at least in the short run. It was undoubtedly in recognition of this that the Japanese, over strong Soviet protests, signed the 1977 bilateral Treaty of Peace and Friendship with China containing the implicit condemnation of Soviet hegemonism.[5] Like the Chinese, the Japanese deeply resent continued Soviet occupation of their territory and are profoundly concerned over Soviet expansionism in East Asia.

Despite these growing concerns over Soviet policy, however, the Japanese remain very reluctant to follow American political leadership, particularly when the latter pursues a confrontational policy toward the Soviet Union. For the Japanese, the more prudent course of action is one that avoids unnecessary generation of Soviet wrath. Japan is in no position to challenge Soviet power directly; Japanese worry that the United States may provoke a conflict into which they will inevitably be drawn. This leads to American charges that the Japanese, like the West Europeans, are failing to take a stand and carry their share of the responsibility for containing Soviet power in the Pacific. By the same token, however, American pressures on Japan to increase its military role in the Pacific for American (and not necessarily Japanese) reasons cause deep resentments.

The fundamentally differing attitudes of the two countries toward their relationship constitute a powerful potential for a serious breakdown in American-Japanese relations. For Americans, security and economic issues are intimately related; for the Japanese, they are not. Although the United States benefits economically from its partnership with Japan, American economic policy is strongly conditioned by American security interests in the Pacific. Whereas the Japanese believe that the security and economic spheres should be kept totally separate from one another, Americans tend to regard their concessions in the economic realm as the necessary price for present or future Japanese security concessions. Consequently, more recent American demands in the economic realm as well place a double burden on the Japanese and, at the same time, intensify American resentments over Japanese economic and security policies. Possibilities of intense ill will are inherent in this situation.

The differences between European-Japanese political relations and American-Japanese relations are worth noting. The political and psychological gap between Western Europe and Japan has widened over the past several decades.[6] Although for Americans the phenomenal economic success of the Japanese is one to be studied and if possible emulated, for West Europeans it is a darkly looming and mysterious threat of gigantic proportions. Western Europe appears to want as little as possible to do with Japan and has made little effort to understand or learn from Japan's economic success.[7] Moreover, intensifying anti-Japanese resentments and the West European fear of Japanese competition are not leavened by common security concerns as they are with the United States. Contrary to the pronouncement of Prime Minister Nakasone Yasuhiro at the Williamsburg Summit (1983) that the defense of the West was indivisible, the opposite may very well be the case.[8] For example, in the negotiations over intermediate missiles, an important trade-off for the Soviets was the deployment of SS 20s against Asian targets to balance those removed from Western Europe. Rather than see their fate tied to that of Asia, many West Europeans might actually prefer the Soviet Union to turn its attention and massive military machine eastward. Thus, perhaps even more than in the earlier postwar period, the United States finds itself allied to two sets of nations, one of which wants as little as possible to do with the other.

On the other hand, American response toward Japanese protectionism and trade expansionism may be more damaging in its effects. European trade restrictions deny the Japanese what they have never had, but recently imposed American barriers, on the other hand, are taking away something that they have enjoyed. More important, the Japanese can tolerate West European protectionism more easily than they can American pressures to liberalize their economy and change their traditional ways of conducting business. It is possible, then, that American economic and security policies toward the Japanese could undercut the political basis of the relationship.

Over the past several decades, the security relations among the allies have changed dramatically. The primary cause of this transformed environment is the tremendous growth of Soviet military power in the nuclear, conventional land, and naval spheres. This profound shift in the international balance of power underlies the changes in political attitudes and perceived national interests already discussed.

With the growth of Soviet nuclear and conventional power, the West Europeans have vacillated between contradictory fears. The first has been that the United States would not use its nuclear weapons to protect them if it meant risking a Soviet nuclear attack on the United States. The second fear has been that the United States *would* use its nuclear weapons, thus precipitating a totally destructive nuclear war. This second concern requires that the United States constantly reassure the West Europeans of its nuclear prudence through the pursuit of détente and arms control talks with the Soviet Union. Unfortunately, as Soviet military power has expanded, the inherent contradiction between the task of convincing West Europeans of the credibility of extended deterrence and the task of reassuring them of American prudence has become increasingly sharp and is driving a psychological wedge between the United States and Western Europe.

A second, and in some ways greater, challenge to the policy of extended deterrence has also developed in the United States itself where the American public has discovered nuclear war. The "nuclear war fighting" rhetoric of the Reagan administration and the growth of Soviet nuclear capability have made Americans aware of the logic of the policy of extended deterrence as applicable to themselves. As French president Charles De Gaulle predicted, Americans are changing their collective mind regarding their willingness to risk the destruction of their own country in order to safeguard Western Europe. This discovery by Americans of the terrible dangers of nuclear war has given rise to a powerful peace movement in the churches, in the middle classes, and in all sections of the country. Consequently, despite the resistance of the Reagan administration, the national consensus appears to be moving in the direction of abandoning, or at least drastically modifying, the policy of extended deterrence.

The solution to the problem of West European security proposed by an increasing number of American strategic experts is the outright abandonment of the policy of extended deterrence in favor of a conventional defense of Western Europe. Unfortunately, this course of action is strongly rejected by West European political leadership. It would be very expensive, and, perhaps more important, it raises the other West European fear that a weakening of extended deterrence would increase the probability of a limited war fought in Western Europe. For West Europeans, a third world war on their continent, even if fought only with conventional weapons, would be an unmitigated disaster.

In the Pacific area as well, the growth of Soviet military power has had important consequences for political relations. Over the past decade or so, the Soviet Union has greatly increased its land forces along the Chinese border. Soviet naval and air power have expanded, establishing a strong presence in both Northeast and Southeast Asia. Although these developments do not yet threaten the American position in the Pacific, they have undercut the policy of extended deterrence and have raised substantially the cost of containing the growth of Soviet power in that part of the world. Furthermore, the Pacific area is increasing in political and economic importance to the United States so that it cannot overlook the Soviet challenge in Asia or continue an overall military strategy that assumes the abandonment of Asia in the event of a war with the Soviets.[9]

The fundamental problem caused by the growth of Soviet military power is an increasing disjuncture between America's overseas commitments and its ability to meet these commitments. Until recently, reliance upon the policy of extended deterrence enabled the United States to meet its global commitments vis-à-vis Japan and Western Europe at a relatively low cost. Now increasing numbers of influential Americans support abandonment of the policy of extended deterrence and a shift to a conventional defense of these commitments. Such a change in strategy would be very expensive, assuming continuing growth of relative Soviet power. Therefore, more and more Americans argue that either greater assistance must be forthcoming from America's allies or the United States must considerably reduce its overseas commitments.

April 15, 1971, marked the end of the postwar era of international economic relations. On that date President Richard Nixon announced a new foreign economic policy for the United States. He imposed a surcharge on American imports, suspended the convertibility of the dollar, and took other remedial actions, thus dramatically altering the relationships and understandings that had characterized the world economy since the establishment of the Bretton Woods System.

President Nixon's decision was both cause and consequence of a profound transformation in the structure and functioning of the world economy. A series of far-reaching changes in the areas of trade, money, and technology are eroding the postwar foundations of the Bretton Woods System and threatening to pull the three poles of the postwar economy farther and farther apart. The most significant structural change is the altered position of the United States in the world economy. An important shift has taken place in the distribution of economic and industrial power among the United States, Western Europe, and Japan. Western Europe and Japan have regained the economic and industrial positions that they lost because of the destruction and distortions of the Second World War, and there has been a general decline in the economic and industrial preeminence of the United States. Moreover, this relative economic decline and the consequent increase in the size of the foreign sector in the American economy have made the United States more sensitive to imports and are undermining the domestic free trade alliance, giving rise to increased protectionism.

A second and related structural change is that the economies of the OECD countries and certain other developing economies have become increasingly similar in their industrial sectors and the composition of exports. Western Europe, Japan, and the NICs (Taiwan, South Korea, Singapore, Brazil, Mexico, etc.) can now engage in import-substitution and can export goods once available only from the leading industrial countries, especially the United States. As a consequence, a global overcapacity exists in a number of important industrial sectors: steel, petrochemicals, automobiles, textiles, consumer electronics, shipbuilding. This surplus capacity is leading to the cartelization of international markets and other forms of market-sharing arrangements. An increasing portion of international trade is characterized by what the French euphemistically call organized free trade. With trade patterns and the distribution of world market shares becoming more and more a function of intergovernmental bargaining, the crucial question for economic and foreign policy is who is to be included, who excluded, from these market-sharing arrangements.

A third structural change is the energy revolution that occurred initially during the winter of 1973 and repeated itself in 1978-79. Effective control over the supply and pricing of world petroleum (and by implication other forms of energy) was transferred from American and other multinational oil companies to the producing countries themselves as represented by the Organization of Petroleum Exporting Countries (OPEC). The cost of petroleum increased multifold. And the United States, for the first time in its history, became dependent upon foreign suppliers for a vital resource. The energy revolution also increased global inflationary pressures and economic insecurity, made much of the world's industrial plant obsolete, and reversed the terms of trade for most energy-importing economies. The cost of adjusting to these profound changes and the massive financial redistribution wrought by the energy revolution have imposed an immense burden on the world economy. This transfer of global wealth and power have in turn intensified protectionism and international competition as individual countries seek to cushion the effects on their economies.

Yet another major change in the world economy is the increasing role of the state in the economy and the consequent growth of interstate economic competition. The reasons for this greater government participation in the private sphere range from the increased importance of welfare concerns to the perceived need to finance research and development. This change in the role of government has numerous economic consequences; it tends to politicize international economic relations. The tendency is for the free market to give way to interstate negotiations regarding such matters as orderly marketing agreements and market shares for domestic industry.

An additional structural change is that inflation, or at least the fear of inflation, has become an inherent feature in most OECD economies, especially the United States and Western Europe. Several inflationary factors are embedded in most economies today: energy cost concerns; an enhanced capacity of workers to raise real wages faster than advances in productivity; the increasing concentration of industry and the substitution of administered for market-determined prices; rising expectations with respect to social welfare, housing, medical care, environment; and the leveling off of increases in industrial and agricultural productivity. Such inflationary pressures, it is feared, cannot be kept in check by traditional Keynesian techniques, and therefore economic growth must be constrained. Too rapid a rate of economic growth could trigger a new wave of double-digit inflation. This contraction of the growth rates of the major industrial economies is encouraging a retreat from the postwar trend toward increasing global economic interdependence.

Another structural change is that the factors and assumptions underlying America's postwar commitment to liberalized trade have been greatly eroded. The American industrial, technological, and financial superiority upon which this commitment rested has been weakened and in certain important areas actually eliminated. The domestic political alliance behind America's free trade policy has also been weakened. Large sections of organized labor and import-sensitive businesses are now actively opposed to free trade. Further, the assumption that a strengthened Europe and Japan would make greater contributions to the anti-Soviet alliance is increasingly questioned. Some believe that an economically strong Europe and Japan have made it more difficult and costly for the United States to compete politically and militarily against the Soviet Union. Also, the fact that China is no longer considered to be an enemy is leading to a reassessment of policies fashioned in an earlier era. All of these political and economic changes encourage the forces of protectionism in the American economy.

Perhaps the most important cause of the powerful resurgence of protectionism taking place in the United States and Western Europe is that the technologies that previously propelled economic growth and international trade are decreasingly able to do so, at least in the developed countries. Comparative advantage in steel, consumer durables, and other areas is shifting to the developing countries. For the developed countries, economic growth and exports must increasingly depend on the development of new products in emergent areas of high technology. It is precisely in these areas that Japan is staking its claim to world economic leadership and posing a powerful challenge to the United States and particularly to the West European economy. This Japanese challenge and the West European response to it are of crucial importance for global economic interdependence and for the future of the American System.

During the 1950s and 1960s, the formation of the European Common Market was one of the major factors accounting for the rapid growth of world trade, increasing economic interdependence, and the success of the Bretton Woods System. Now, as the European economies continue to stagnate, fall behind technologically, and become more and more protectionist, the effects of EEC trade policies are changing.

Undoubtedly the most significant structural change is that the center of gravity of the world economy is shifting toward the Pacific basin. Although the United States still has a trade surplus with Western Europe, America's Pacific trade surpassed Atlantic trade for the first time in the mid-1970s.[10] Americans see their economic future in the Pacific area and in Latin America. In the Sunbelt, the emergent center of political power and economic growth in the United States, this is particularly true. As one American economist has put it, the United States is rapidly developing a complementary set of economic relations with the economies to its west and south.[11] Because the Pacific basin, including Japan and the Asian NICs, now surpasses the rest of the world in rates of economic growth, this ongoing shift in American trading patterns will most surely continue and have a profound impact on America's future determination of the location of its national interests.

In summary, the world economy is undergoing a profound transformation.[12] The contemporary shift in the nature and location of global economic activities is comparable in scale and importance to the tranformation that took place in the first half of this century when the United States displaced Western Europe as the center of the world economy.

These political, security, and economic developments raise a fundamental question: Can the American System continue to survive intact or will it disintegrate under the impact of these new sets of forces? As previously detailed, the foundations of the system have greatly eroded over the past decade. Political recriminations, strategic differences, and economic conflicts have damaged relations among the industrial democracies. These challenges to the American System raise major policy issues for the United States.

The first issue is whether the United States can maintain its present set of international commitments and, if not, where it should cut back on its overseas commitments. This issue must be faced because American power and its global commitments are no longer in a state of equilibrium. The growth of Soviet power and the relative decline of the American economy have made it more costly and difficult for the United States to maintain its military commitments in Western Europe, the Pacific region, and the Middle East. Although this imbalance has been developing over the better part of the past decade, President Ronald Reagan's massive expansion of the American military budget, the new emphasis on a nuclear war-fighting strategy, and the intense debate over intermediate range missiles have placed strategic issues once again on the national political agenda.

The second policy issue is the challenge posed for the United States and other industrial countries by the continuing growth of Japanese and, increasingly, of NIC trading competitiveness. Under the best of circumstances, the adjustment to this trade expansionism would be difficult. Until recently, the incorporation into the world economy of Japan with its export-led growth strategy was eased by the rapid rates of economic growth enjoyed by most other industrial economies; with growing economies there was room for all to expand their exports. In an era of reduced growth rates and increased protectionism, however, Japan's rapidly increasing competitiveness, now joined by that of the export platforms of South Korea and Taiwan, among others, raises the crucial issue of where these Pacific basin economies will fit into a slower growing and more protectionist world economy. Similarly, the rapidity with which comparative advantage has shifted in the direction of these economies places inordinate adjustment costs on the United States and other economies. The result has been the rise of powerful protectionist forces in the American economy and the increasing demand of American political leaders that Western Europe open its borders to these exports, thereby relieving competitive pressures on the American economy.

The issue of where Japan and the Asian NICs fit into an increasingly protectionist world is compounded by the knowledge that the international trading system is also becoming more and more a negotiated one. Because of the retardation of growth rates and the global overcapacity in a number of industrial sectors, the distribution of market shares among national producers is becoming to a considerable extent a function of international negotiations rather than letting the market decide who produces what and how much. The multifibre agreement, the "voluntary" restraint on Japanese automobile exports, and the cartelization of the steel industry are prime examples of this tendency. As these sectors are the traditional high-employment blue-collar industries, this subject is politically very sensitive as every government seeks to maximize its market share.

The question raised by this increasing politicization of the world economy is who gets left out. Because the United States and Western Europe have the most bargaining leverage, they have the greatest influence on the determination of national shares of the world market. Together they obviously seek to maintain their own relative positions and the status quo. Yet the sectors involved in the negotiations over market shares are frequently the ones in which Japan and the Asian NICs have, or are gaining, a comparative advantage. Thus, it is precisely those countries that, in terms of world economic efficiency, should have an increasing share of the market that tend to get left out in the negotiations.

The third issue facing the United States is an outgrowth of those already discussed. Will it be possible for the United States indefinitely to maintain its traditional and on the whole evenly balanced relations with both Western Europe and Japan? The political, security, and economic foundations upon which American foreign policy has rested are in a serious state of disrepair. Although the issues faced by the United States and Western Europe are divisive, the most vulnerable aspect of the American System, at least in the immediate future, may be the increasing economic tension between Western Europe and Japan.[13] As a consequence, the problem of holding together the interdependent world economy could become increasingly acute. As West European political and security concerns become more parochial and the West European economies become more fearful of foreign competition, the West European and Japanese poles of the American System threaten to move farther and farther apart and into opposition to one another. Also, one cannot discount the significance for the system of the recent growth of anti-Japanese sentiment in the United States and of Japanese resentments of American pressures.[14] In brief, the problem facing the United States and its allies in maintaining the American System has become immense.

In part, the problem is a transitional one, that is, the transition from a

declining global economic structure to its successor. Therefore, one may hope
that the problem will ease in the future. As the traditional industrial sectors
decline in the developed countries and are replaced by new, more competitive
industries, protectionist pressures may ease. Yet this hopeful view may be
much too sanguine. The solution to the global economic crisis ultimately
requires a major rejuvenation of the American and European economies.
Although there is evidence to suggest that this is beginning to happen in the
United States, there is little basis to believe the same of Western Europe.
Unless greater efforts are made to revitalize the economy of Western Europe,
it threatens to become a drag on world economic growth and an increasing
impediment to the further liberalization of international trade.

These centrifugal and divisive forces within the American System are
posing increasingly complicated choices for the United States. The interest
of the United States lies more and more in the economic development of the
Pacific basin. This requires that world markets be kept open to Japan, the
NICs, and an industrializing China. The American economy by itself would
find it very difficult, however, to provide an adequate market for their exports;
and for economic, political, and cultural reasons the United States still requires
ties to Western Europe. Yet unless Western Europe becomes once again what
it was in the 1950s and 1960s—that is, a positive factor in the growth of
international trade—the economic ambitions of Japan, China, and the Asian
NICs as well as the interests of the United States in the Pacific region and in
the world more generally are bound to be thwarted. Without exonerating the
United States for its protectionist policies or excusing Japan for its failure to
exercise economic leadership commensurate with its growing economic
power, the critical issue is the future course of Western Europe's foreign
economic policy. Unless this policy changes in a more liberal direction, the
United States may one day be forced to choose between its European and
pacific allies.

Throughout the postwar period, American policy has tended to be Euro-
centric. The United States has given primacy to its European interests in the
resolution of political, security, and economic matters. In the light of contemporary developments, however, one must ask whether this can continue.
As the world economy moves westward toward the Pacific and American
interests follow in the wake of this movement, should the United States give
higher priority to its relationship with Japan and the Pacific than it does to
its relationship with Western Europe? This is the question that will increasingly
face American economic and political leaders.

It would be foolhardy to suggest that the future course of American-Japanese relations will run smoothly. The political, security, and economic con-

flicts between the two countries are complex, and the issues that divide the two allies are profound indeed. Whether America and Japan will be partners or opponents in the economic development of the Pacific basin is a matter yet to be decided. With the exercise of prudence and restraint on both sides, there is no fundamental reason why a working partnership cannot continue to evolve. The costs of any other outcome would be exceptionally high for both countries.

I conclude with a hope and plea. The hope is that the United States and its two sets of allies can resolve the pressing issues that threaten to rend the American System. For over three decades this system, despite its many and serious imperfections, has provided these allies security and prosperity. It is highly doubtful that any conceivable substitute would do as well. Fortunately, despite the relative decline in its power, the United States still has the resources to provide international leadership and, in cooperation with its allies, find a substitute for the American System. The American market remains the world's largest; its engine of growth, the dollar, is still the basis of the monetary system, and the American nuclear umbrella retains its credibility. The plea is that the United States assume this leadership task but in so doing give greater attention to the interests and deep concerns of its allies. Unless present trends are overcome, however, it will be too late either to turn back the forces undermining the American System or to find a satisfactory alternative.

1. Robert Gilpin, *U.S. Power and the Multinational Corporation—The Political Economy of Foreign Direct Investment* (New York, 1975): 109-11; and Gardner Patterson, *Discrimination in International Trade; The Policy Issues, 1945-1965* (Princeton, NJ, 1966), 271-305.

2. Jacob Viner, *The Customs Union Issue*, Studies in the Administration of International Law and Organization, no. 10 (New York, 1950).

3. The problems posed by increasing West European protectionism for the future of world trade are treated by Miles Kahler, "European Protectionism in Theory and Practice," a paper prepared for the Council for European Studies, Conference of Europeanists, Washington, DC, October 14, 1983; and Gardner Patterson, "The European Economic Community as a Threat to the System," (unpublished paper, May 1982).

4. Gordon A. Craig and Alexander L. George, *Force and Diplomacy—Diplomatic Problems of Our Time* (New York, 1983), 147.

5. An excellent discussion of the evolution of American-Japanese security relations and the evolution of Japanese security thinking is Masashi Nishihara and Richard Betts, "U.S.-Japan Security Relations," Paper presented at the Shimoda Conference, 1983.

6. See Loukas Tsoukalis and Maureen White, eds., *Japan and Western Europe* (London: 1982).

7. *The Economist* (October 29, 1983):72.

8. Nishihara and Betts, 18.

9. Richard L. Sneider, "U.S. Interests and policies in Asia and the Western Pacific in the

1980s," in *The Common Security Interests of Japan, the United States and NATO* (New York, 1981).

10. Roy Hofheinz, Jr. and Kent Calder, *The Eastasian Edge* (New York, 1982).

11. William Branson, "Trade and Structural Adjustments in the U.S. Economy: Response to International Competition," (unpublished paper, September 22-23, 1983).

12. Michael Beenstock, *The World Economy in Transition* (London, 1983).

13. Robert Immerman, "European Attitudes Towards Japan: Trilateralism's Weakest Link," U.S. Department of State, Executive Seminar on National and International Affairs, 1979-80.

14. The following are examples of the new genre of anti-Japanese books: Russell Braddon, *Japan Against the World, 1941-2041—The 100-year War for Supremacy* (New York, 1983); Steven Schlossstein, *Kensei—A Novel of Computer-Chip Rivalry and the Trade War on America* (New York, 1983); and Marvin J. Wolf, *The Japanese Conspiracy—The Plot to Dominate Industry World Wide—and How to Deal with It* (New York, 1983).

2

From the Yoshida Letter
to the Nixon Shock

CHIHIRO HOSOYA

Soon after the signing of the San Francisco Peace Treaty in September 1951, Japan recognized the Nationalist government in Taiwan as the legitimate government of China and opened diplomatic relations with that government. But almost two decades later, Japan drastically changed her China policy and normalized relations with the government in Beijing, the People's Republic of China (PRC). This essay will examine the development of Japan's China policy between 1951 and 1972, focusing particularly on its relation to the East Asia policy of the United States.

Through the "Yoshida Letter," written only three months after the signing of the San Francisco Peace Treaty, Japan professed her intention to conclude a peace treaty with the Nationalist government in Taiwan. Subsequently, the Sino-Japanese Peace Treaty was signed on April 28, 1952, establishing diplomatic relations between Japan and the Nationalist government of Taiwan.

From the time of the conclusion of the San Francisco Peace Treaty the issuance of the Yoshida Letter, Prime Minister Yoshida Shigeru, partly influenced by the British, pursued an equidistant diplomacy vis-à-vis both Beijing and Taibei.[1] He originally thought that the Beijing government would become a Titoist regime. In this respect his reading of mainland China's political future was closer to that of the British than of the American government. Furthermore, Yoshida, a diplomat pursuing a British-type merchant diplomacy, anticipated sizable growth in Japan's trade with mainland China. For this reason, we may conclude that the Yoshida Letter did not represent his real intentions but instead a sacrificial offering that Japan had to give for the prompt restoration of national sovereignty, a sovereignty that would be possible only when the Peace Treaty took effect. He also presumably anticipated an early fulfillment of Japan's role in democratizing China. But Yoshida, bearing in mind Japan's total dependence on the United States for economic recovery and military security, found no alternative but to align his country with the United States' containment policy toward China.

The National Security Council defined the basic U.S. policy toward Japan after independence. It stipulated that it was the U.S. objective "to assist Japan rapidly to develop (1) the means for its defense, and (2) the capability to contribute to the defense of other free nations of the Pacific area." NSC 2/ 125 further stated that the United States "should encourage collective security arrangements in the Pacific area which would include Japan." At the same time, the document maintained that the United States should "seek to prevent Japan from becoming dependent on China and other communist-dominated areas for essential food and raw material supplies [and to] encourage Japanese contribution to the economic development of countries of South and Southeast Asia.[2]

In July 1952, Japan joined the Coordinating Committee for Export to Communist Areas (COCOM), which in the same year established the China Committee (CHINCOM) as its subsidiary to control export to China. The CHINCOM was designed to prohibit the exportation of strategic commodities to China by applying more strict criteria than the simple trade restrictions of strategic materials regarding other communist countries.

This kind of American containment policy toward China was not well received by the Japanese business community and the Japanese Ministry of International Trade and Industry (MITI), both of which hoped to promote trade with mainland China. Reflecting their desire to open such trade, the first nongovernmental barter trade agreement was signed between Japan and the PRC one month earlier. Although this move was not welcomed by the American government, the Japanese government tried to ameliorate the situation by introducing a policy of separating economy from politics (*seikei bunri*).

The Eisenhower administration however, began to show some signs of loosening the rigid American policy toward trade restrictions between Japan and the PRC. This relaxation of American policy stemmed partly from several auspicious phenomena in international relations, such as the death of Josef Stalin in March 1953 and the bright prospects of an armistice in Korea. The adminstation also hoped that the China market could soften the economic impact of Japan's loss of the special procurements which would disappear with peace in Korea.

On April 8, 1953, the National Security Council reevaluated the NSC 4/ 125 document on U.S. policy toward Japan. The council's discussion revealed President Eisenhower's favorable attitude toward Japan's trade with China. The president believed that "there was no future for Japan unless access were provided for it to the markets and raw materials of Manchuria and North China." According to NSC 4/125, the president also believed that "even on the short hand a certain amount of Japanese trade with Communist China should be permitted in place of the complete embargo and blockade which now exists."[3] Eisenhower's attitude toward Japan's trade with communist countries became more favorable in the following year. He not only used the word "permit" but also used the word "encourage."[4]

In contrast to Eisenhower's positive attitude, Secretary of State John Foster Dulles's posture continued to be stiff and resolute. For example, at the April 1953 NSC meeting, Dulles said, "It was not practicable to envisage any revival of Japanese sovereignty and physical control over Manchuria, but we could do a lot to assist Japan by encouraging Japanese trade with the Philippines and Malaya."[5] He believed that the United States should limit Japan's trade with mainland China as much as possible and strengthen Japan's economic ties with Southeast Asia.

As the Korean armistice was being signed on July 27, 1953, the Japanese Diet passed a resolution for the "promotion of Sino-Japanese trade." This Diet resolution demanded that the Japanese government temporarily bring down the trade restrictions to a level "as low as the Western European countries'." The truce in Korea no doubt heightened the expectations of Sino-Japanese trade in Japanese economic circles, and the Sino-Japanese trade question increasingly became one of the important issues in Japanese domestic politics. Just two months later, Diet members and businessmen formed the first Dietmen's group to inspect Japan's trade with China (Chūgoku tsūshō shisatsu giin-dan) and announced their plans to visit mainland China.

The overall thawing of the international situation, coupled with the above-mentioned domestic developments in Japan, necessarily had a subtle influence on Dulles's containment policy toward China. During a press conference on September 3, 1953, he revealed his intention to relax control over Japan's export trade with the PRC, stating, "It is quite possible that the Japanese might want to put their relationship on a basis more nearly that of other countries such as Britain, France and so forth."[6]

Although Japan had increased her interest in promoting trade with the PRC, the Japanese government's official negotiations with the United States about restrictions on trade with the PRC did not begin until October 1953, when Finance Minister Ikeda Hayato conducted a series of talks with Walter Robertson, assistant secretary of state for Far Eastern affairs. During the talks, Ikeda and his delegation asked the United States to bring the COCOM and CHINCOM lists of prohibited commodities down to the level applied to European countries. The United States approved this request on October 21, 1953.[7] Following the American approval, MITI took measures, on thirteen different occasions by September 1954, to remove a number of commodities from the COCOM-CHINCOM lists, thus bringing the number of items on the lists closer to those applied to Western European countries.

While these talks were being held between Ikeda and Robertson in Washington, a nongovernmental trade agreement was being negotiated in Beijing. This resulted in an agreement on October 29 for an exchange of trade representatives between the two countries. This arrangement was strongly opposed by Dulles.

The American amabassador to Japan, John M. Allison, wrote to Washington on September 3, 1954: "Tokyo with visible reluctance followed the American lead in maintaining its relations with the Nationalist Government, although it was originally inclined to the British approach and still basically holds to the theories of the durability of the Communist capture of China and of the possibility of facilitating the alienation of Peking from Moscow. Recently the Japanese have seemed increasingly disposed to a theory of 'Two Chinas.'"[8] Allison's observation indicates his sharp insight into Prime Minister Yoshida's China policy, which had not changed fundamentally since 1951.

In contrast to Yoshida's policy toward the PRC, Dulles's basic diplomatic strategy was to strengthen the Japanese defense capability against Communist threats in East Asia and to draw Japan into regional collective security arrangements. When the United States, during the Ikeda-Robertson talks, asked Japan to increase its ground forces to between 325,000 and 350,000 men, Japan responded by enlarging its current forces of 110,000 to only 180,000 in five years. Yoshida continued to dodge the issue by making minimum concessions to Dulles in the buildup of Japan's defense capability.

At the time of the first Dulles-Yoshida talks, Dulles had a "Pacific Pact" idea. This pact aimed at the establishment of a regional collective security system by island chain countries located in the periphery of China. Dulles's idea eventually materialized in three separate mutual security treaties (ANZUS, U.S.-Philippines, and U.S.-Japan security treaties) rather than in a single security treaty organization by those countries. But the original American plan to incorporate Japan into a more comprehensive collective security system would remain alive.

Because Yoshida wished to pursue an equidistant diplomacy toward Beijing and Taibei from the outset, he tried not to follow the U.S. military containment policy toward the PRC. Yoshida was willing to go along with Dulles's containment policy toward the PRC in terms of an economic embargo. But even this relatively mild policy met with vehement criticism from Japanese who held that Yoshida was subserviently following American policy.

Despite Japanese domestic opposition to Yoshida's China policy, the United States held fast to the idea of making Japan cooperate with the American military containment policy toward China. This American intention is seen in NSC 125/6, which indicated that the United States would "continue to explore the possibilities of collective security arrangements in the Pacific area which would include Japan."[9] It is also evidenced in one of the conclusions of the U.S. House Special Study Mission to Southeast Asia and the

Pacific. The report stated that it was desirable for the United States to "broaden these bilateral arrangements [a network of mutual security treaties that the United States concluded with the countries in East Asia and the Pacific area] into a regional pact [Pacific Pact]."[10]

Dulles took the initiative in forming the Southeast Asia Treaty Organization (SEATO) to fill the power vacuum likely to be created by the French military withdrawal from Indochina. Furthermore, when Communist Chinese forces began shelling Quemoy and Matsu islands, precipitating a crisis in the Taiwan Strait, Dulles resolutely signed a U.S.-Taiwan Mutual Security Treaty on December 2, 1954.

With events unfolding rapidly, Dulles presumably thought that his urgent task was to commit Japan to some kind of regional security arrangement. On his return from signing the SEATO treaty in September 1954, Dulles may have elicited Yoshida's opinion on Japan's commitment to some regional security treaty organization; or he may have made such a proposal during the Dulles-Yoshida talks on September 10. The Department of State, for instance, optimistically hoped that Japan would go along with the American plan. On October 12, acting Secretary of State Herbert Hoover, Jr. reported to the American Embassy in Tokyo that he believed Yoshida would be "eventually willing [to] lead Japan into Pacific defense arrangements despite constitutional muddle."[11]

In spite of American expectations, however, Yoshida had no intention of committing Japan to the kind of regional security arrangements the United States envisioned. In Yoshida's judgment, the Japanese Constitution and domestic political situation would not allow him to pursue such a course of action. Moreover, it was against his political philosophy to pursue a containment policy that was chiefly military in nature.

On September 26, 1954, Yoshida began his trip to Western Europe and the United States. He used this opportunity to try to forestall cooperation in the military collective security arrangements by proposing a "Yoshida Plan," which aimed at nonmilitary cooperation with the United Kingdom and, especially, with the United States. The Yoshida Plan, which he proposed to Foreign Minister Anthony Eden in London and subsequently to President Eisenhower and Secretary of State Dulles in Washington on November 9, 1954, had two salient points: (1) In order to cope with the Communist "peace offensive" in East Asia, Japan, Great Britain, and the United States should establish a joint organization in Singapore, to be headed by British High Commissioner Malcolm MacDonald. Further, the three countries should launch a "peace counteroffensive" and share information on Communist activies;[12] (2) There should be a $4-billion "Marshall Plan" for Asia in order to develop the countries of Southeast Asia.

This Yoshida Plan represents another instance of Yoshida's characteristically spontaneous diplomatic style. But it can also be viewed as his counter-offensive against or resistance to Dulles's militaristic diplomacy.

Although Dulles regarded Yoshida's political initiative as "a very interesting suggestion," he maintained that it would be better for Japan to cooperate with the SEATO nations, and he refused to give serious consideration to the Yoshida Plan. Dulles observed that "this kind of thing is something which should be handled within the framework of that Pact [Manila Pact]," and he maintained that "we want Japan drawn into collective activities in that area."[13]

During his stay in Washington, Yoshida tried to persuade Dulles by offering the wisdom and experience of the Japanese with regard to the China question. But Yoshida's political career was about to end: his cabinet resigned en masse soon after his return to Japan. When Hatoyama Ichirō replaced Yoshida as prime minister on December 10, 1954, Japan began a new era in its diplomacy.

The Japanese government headed by Hatoyama Ichirō and Ishibashi Tanzan was somewhat different from other cabinets of the postwar period. For one thing, both political leaders made diplomatic efforts to restore friendly relations with the Soviet Union and the People's Republic of China, while simultaneously maintaining friendship with the United States. Their attempt at this so-called multidirectional diplomacy (*zen-hōi gaikō*) stands out in the political history of postwar Japan. Prime Minister Hatoyama, in particular, tried his best to distinguish himself from Yoshida, who had been criticized for his "follow-the-United States" diplomacy. For this reason, Hatoyama had a strong desire to normalize Japan's relations with the two major communist countries.

While Prime Minister Hatoyama wanted to improve Japan's relations with these Communist neighbors, both the Soviet Union and the People's Republic of China had their own reasons for exploiting the situation to their advantage. Both searched for opportunities to mount an active peace offensive toward Japan to drive a wedge between Japan and the United States. Such opportunities seemed to have arrived when Japanese conservatives became involved in intra-and interparty rivalries over the issue of foreign policy and when various peace movements were gaining momentum. On October 12, 1954, the Soviet Union and the PRC announced a joint declaration proposing the promotion of extensive trade with Japan, the establishment of close cultural ties, and the normalization of diplomatic relations".[14] The two powers sent one message after another to the newly formed Hatoyama cabinet, expressing their hope for the normalization of relations with Japan (e.g., the Molotov statement of December 16; an editorial in *Izvestia* of December 22; and an editorial in *People's Daily* of December 30, 1954).

Japanese-Soviet negotiations for the normalization of relations began in London on June 3, 1955. Although the talks stalled many times, particularly over the question of the Northern Territories, and the original objective of concluding a peace treaty was not achieved, Japan and the Soviet Union did agree on October 19, 1956, to reopen diplomatic relations between the two countries.

Although Prime Minister Hatoyama achieved one of the diplomatic objectives he had set forth, the process unfortunately aroused domestic political problems, such as interparty and interfactional struggles and feuds among major political leaders. Conservative parties reorganized themselves, and this major political reorganization culminated in the establishment of the Liberal Democratic party (LDP) in the fall of 1955. Moreover, American Secretary of State John Foster Dulles did not welcome Japanese diplomatic attempts to normalize relations with the Soviet Union, and he often tried to restrain such efforts. From the beginning, the Japanese Foreign Ministry had not been enthusiastic about the negotiations, partly because Prime Minister Hatoyama dealt directly with the Soviet Union, bypassing the Japanese Foreign Ministry,[15] and partly because Foreign Ministry officials did not wish to initiate negotiations against the wishes of the U.S. government and former Prime Minister Yoshida.

Nevertheless, two events contributed to the creation of a climate favorable to improving relations between Japan and the Soviet Union—the four-power summit conference at Geneva in July 1955, and the establishment of diplomatic relations between the Soviet Union and West Germany in September. These events necessarily helped lessen the intensity of the Cold War on a global scale. In contrast, the situation in East Asia remained tense, particularly in the Taiwan Strait. In addition, the Japan-Taiwan peace treaty hampered attempts for better relations between Japan and the People's Republic of China. Consequently, Japan had fewer diplomatic options in dealing with the PRC than with the Soviet Union.

In this environment, it was uncertain whether the Hatoyama regime could pursue a China policy different from that of the preceding cabinet. One of the first tests came in March 1955, when Japan had to negotiate a third nongovernmental trade agreement. Late in the month, the PRC was about to send its delegation to Japan for the negotiations, but the Japanese Foreign Ministry expressed strong disapproval of the invitation extended to the Chinese delegation. Furthermore, the Japanese Federation of Economic Organizations (*Keidanren*) announced that they had to take part in the invitation and in trade negotiations with this group. At just this time, Secretary of State Dulles reportedly sent a message to Japan, warning that if Japan's major corporations were considering making positive moves to expand trade with the PRC, the United States would have to reconsider its economic relations with Japan.[16]

The agenda for Japan-PRC trade negotiations, scheduled to begin on April 1, 1955, included the establishment of trade representative offices and the arrangements for direct settlement of accounts in the respective currencies. But the most important thing was that both parties hoped eventually to raise this nongovernmental agreement to the level of an intergovernmental agreement. Premier Hatoyama shared this hope. If the scenario had been realized as he wished, Japan would have extended de facto recognition of the PRC, thus entering an entirely new stage of Sino-Japanese relations. It is said that Hatoyama had to give up his diplomatic efforts to achieve this objective because of vehement opposition from the United States.[17] (Minister of International Trade and Industry Ishibashi reportedly advised Hatoyama to ignore the American opposition.)

While the Sino-Japanese trade negotiations continued in Tokyo, Takasaki Tatsunosuke, director of the Economic Deliberation Agency forerunner of the present Economic planning Agency, held a secret meeting on April 22 with the PRC's Prime Minister Chou En-lai, who was then attending the Bandung conference. It was the first meeting of high governmental officials from Japan and the PRC. The meeting centered on the normalization of relations between the two countries. Chou En-lai emphasized the necessity for both countries to solve one problem after another through the establishment of a semi-governmental agency.

What is worth noting here is a statement made by Takasaki during this meeting: "Japan at present is under the 'supervision' of the United States, and the Japanese Government may not be able to comply with the proposal of your Government. But for the purpose of improving relations between our two countries even a little bit further, the Japanese Government wishes to begin with trade as a first step."[18] Takasaki's statement revealed the forbidding constraints on Japan's relations with the PRC.

Despite these constraints, Prime Minister Hatoyama on April 27 expressed his intention to extend the "support and cooperation of the Japanese government" to the agreement under negotiation, hoping to expedite the trade negotiations. It was only after both delegations exchanged letters confirming Hatoyama's statement that a third Sino-Japanese nongovernmental trade agreement was signed on May 4, 1955. As a result, the total trade volume between Japan and the PRC increased from $35 million in fiscal year 1953 to $150 million in fiscal year 1956. In accordance with the terms of the third trade agreement, both countries held trade fairs in 1955-56. Moreover, the two countries actively engaged in cultural exchanges. On the governmental level, the consuls general of the two countries residing in Geneva opened official channels on July 15, and discussed the problem of Japanese repatriates in mainland China.

American relations with Communist China were quite different. Secretary of State Dulles obstinately refused to relax the embargo on the PRC begun during the Korean War. The Department of State did not allow even a single panda to be imported to the United States. Moreover when Chou En-lai proposed exchange of journalists in August 1956, the Department of State refused to grant exceptions to the rule prohibiting all travel to mainland China.

Japan's policy of separating economy from politics had obvious limitations. Substantial expansion of trade with the PRC would eventually come into conflict with the trade restrictions imposed by the COCOM and CHINCOM, and the establishment of trade representative offices would turn an economic issue into a political one. Consequently, in spite of the support and cooperation that the Japanese government had provided the third Sino-Japanese nongovernmental trade agreement, Japan had to postpone implementation of the agreement. And this was the atmosphere in which Hatoyama resigned from his premiership.

Ishibashi Tanzan, who took over on December 23, 1956, felt it his mission to break the stalemate over the China policy. Ishibashi was a liberal with a special concern with Chinese affairs. It is conceivable that, if the Ishibashi cabinet had remained in power, Sino-Japanese relations would have taken a somewhat different course. But illness forced Ishibashi to resign after only two months in office. On February 25, 1956, he was succeeded by Kishi Nobusuke.

Japanese relations with the People's Republic of China during the Kishi cabinet were the worst since the Yoshida cabinet. Provoked by the May 2, 1958, national flag incident at Nagasaki, involving the hauling down of a Chinese flag by Japanese right-wingers the Beijing government announced that it would terminate all economic and cultural exchanges with Japan. It seemed that all the efforts made for normalization of relations under the "piling up system" would come to nothing and that they would have to start all over again.

Prime Minister Kishi delineated his foreign policy objectives as follows: to repair strained relations with the United States which had been caused by Japan's rapprochement with the Soviet Union and the PRC; and to satisfy the demands of Japanese nationalism by turning the U.S.-Japan security treaty into a more equal arrangement. Furthermore, the Kishi cabinet sought American capital for Japanese advancement into Southeast Asian markets. For Kishi the Chinese market had only secondary importance. In short, his foreign policy was much closer to that of Dulles. It is ironic that, although Kishi had criticized Yoshida for his servility to American policy, as prime minister he found himself more pro-American than Yoshida had ever been.

Prime Minister Kishi's statements and actions elicited disappointment and suspicion from the PRC. When Kishi visited Taiwan and publicly supported Chiang Kai-shek's declared determination to recapture the Chinese mainland, the Beijing government was issued a statement in July 1957 bitterly censuring the Kishi government.

Thus, Sino-Japanese political relations deteriorated, and an abortive attempt in September 1957 to negotiate a fourth Sino-Japanese nongovernmental trade agreement was an important factor in terminating various nongovernmental exchanges between the two countries. The most difficult issue was again the question of establishing offices of trade representatives. Although the Chinese proposed to make the trade representative offices quasi-governmental agencies, the Japanese wished to preserve their nongovernmental character. One of the most important questions in this connection was whether the trade offices had the right to fly their national flags. The Japanese government ultimately decided to deny this right on April 9, 1958. The Beijing government rebuked the Japanese for not providing definite assurances to carry out the terms of the agreement under negotiation. The proposed fourth trade agreement never materialized.

One of the dominant factors that hurt Sino-Japanese relations was the domestic situation in the PRC. China was about to make major policy changes, launching into its Great Leap Forward and establishing people's communes. These changes in domestic policy made Chinese policy toward Japan less flexible and more aggressive. In addition, the PRC's exchanges with the United States assumed an increasingly militaristic character; the large-scale Chinese shelling of Quemoy and Matsu islands in late August 1958 eloquently revealed the extent to which the relations between the United States and the PRC had deteriorated. On the other hand, the reemergence of the PRC as a military threat further facilitated cooperation between Japan and the United States.

Sino-Japanese relations in the 1950s went forward and backward in repeated movements, reflecting the character of each cabinet of the postwar period. When Sino-Japanese relations improved, Japanese-American relations deteriorated. Conversely, when Japan sought to strengthen its ties with the United States, Japan's relations with the PRC became strained. This basic pattern of trilateral relations during the 1950s remained essentially intact through the 1960s.

In the 1960s, Ikeda Hayato and Satō Eisaku assumed the leadership of the Japanese government after the fall of Kishi Nobusuke. Ikeda's China policy resembled Yoshida's equidistant diplomacy vis-à-vis both Beijing and Taibei. In contrast, Satō regarded the PRC as a threat and was instrumental in worsening Japan's relations with Beijing. In short, Satō was a successor to Kishi.

The most urgent task in foreign policy for Ikeda, who became prime minister in July 1960, was to mend Japanese-American relations, which had deteriorated because of the political turmoil caused by the revision of the

U.S.-Japan security treaty. (See Tadashi Aruga's essay, chapter 4.) Therefore, for the Ikeda cabinet, the improvement of relations with the PRC had to come after restoration of friendship with the United States. Although the international political situation became increasingly multipolar, and France made diplomatic moves that eventually led to recognition of the Beijing government in January 1964, Prime Minister Ikeda had no intention of exploiting the situation to improve political relations with the PRC. Instead, he held to his basic position of seeking political cooperation with the United States with regard to China policy. This is evidenced by Japan's attitude toward the question of Chinese representation in the United Nations. In the General Assembly of the United Nations in the fall of 1961, Japan and the United States jointly proposed a resolution designating the Chinese representation question as a substantial question. Ikeda maintained his commitment to co-operate with the United States.

So far as Japan's diplomatic efforts to normalize relations with the PRC were concerned, Prime Minister Ikeda's basic principles were: Japan would not recognize the Beijing government before the United States did so; and Japan would mediate between the United States and the PRC with a view to persuading Washington to improve relations with the PRC. Ikeda hoped to create a situation that would enable Japan to recognize the Beijing government.[19] But during his June 1961 meeting with President John F. Kennedy in Washington, Ikeda was surprised to find that President Kennedy and Secretary of State Dean Rusk shared the view that Beijing was more dangerous than Moscow.[20] Given Washington's animosity against Beijing, Ikeda thought it out of the question for Japan to seek normalization of Japan's relations with the PRC.

Ikeda, however, made an exception in Japan's trade with the PRC, something that had been promoted on the principle of separation of economics from politics. As Ikeda told Kennedy, "Japan historically and traditionally has had special relations with the Chinese Continent. I think it would be reasonable for Japan to engage in at least as much trade as the Western European countries are currently doing."[21] Ikeda hoped to adopt a deferred payment system, as West European countries had, in order to expand Japan's trade with the PRC, and by May 1962, there was a consensus on this point within the Japanese government. But William Averill Harriman, assistant secretary of state for Far Eastern affairs, replied, "I am opposed to the expansion of Japan's trade with Beijing. It is desirable for Japan to take a wait-and-see attitude toward Communist China, which is experiencing economic difficulties." The Japanese Foreign Ministry, however, ignored Harriman's warning, arguing that "there would be no problem for Japan to promote trade with China under the same conditions as the Western European countries."[22]

In September 1962, Japan began negotiations for a new nongovernmental trade agreement in Beijing. Matsumura Kenzō a senior member of the Liberal Democratic Party, engaged in preliminary discussions with Chou En-lai. The series of talks between Matsumura and Chou resulted in a basic agreement on the "promotion of trade" and the "normalization of relations, including political and economic relations, under the gradual and piling-up system." This agreement was instrumental in producing a "memorandum concerning Sino-Japanese trade," which was signed by Takasaki Tatsunosuke and Liao Ch'eng-chih on November 9, 1962. The Sino-Japanese trade, which came to be known as "L-T trade," continued to increase. Because of the major figures involved in the making of the agreement, the memorandum was regarded as a quasi-governmental agreement. In addition, the memorandum stipulated that deferred payments could be made for part of the commodities traded. The Chinese responded to the establishment of trade offices more flexibly than in the past, and a memorandum of agreement, including the exchange of news-paper reporters, was agreed upon in April 1964.

Although the Chinese adhered to the principle that economics cannot be separated from politics, they began to take a more flexible attitude. One contributing factor was Beijing's deteriorating relations with Moscow. In the 1950s, China depended on the Soviet Union for 60-80 percent of its foreign trade. As relations between the two countries became increasingly strained, China, while emphasizing the policy of self-reliance, sought to import needed industrial goods and technology from other advanced countries. Western Eu-ropean countries and Japan as exporters were precisely the countries to meet such needs. Moreover, observing a certain trend for U.S.-Soviet détente grow-ing since the late 1950s, Beijing began to suspect that the United States and the Soviet Union were conspiring together against China. In order to cope with the two superpowers and also to frustrate the United States' containment policy, the Chinese saw that it would be to their advantage to seek a rap-prochement with Japan and Western Europe.

Under the agreement on the "L-T trade," Japan adopted a deferred payment system. Japan went as far as to allow the Export-Import Bank to finance the export of a vinylon plant. But the United States expressed strong opposition to this scheme. During the meeting of the U.S.-Japan joint trade and economic committee on December 3, 1962, President Kennedy warned Japan: "The major question facing us today is the growth of Communist forces in China, and how to contain Communist expansion in Asia. I hope [this committee] will consider what the United States and Japan as allies can do, and what roles they can play in order to prevent Communist domination of Asia." Several days later, Assistant Secretary of State Harriman also addressed a note to Japan, saying that the United States did not favor Japan's decision to extend deferred payment arrangements to Communist China.[23]

Despite American opposition, in August 1963 the Japanese government decided to grant deferred payments, using the Export-Import Bank loans to finance Kurashiki Rayon's export of a vinylon plant to the PRC. This bold move distinguished the Ikeda government from its successor, the Satō government. But the decision of the Japanese government worsened relations with the Nationalist government in Taiwan, and the Ikeda cabinet had to repair relations with Taibei by sending another "Yoshida Letter" (addressed to Chang Ch'ün) in May 1964.

After Prime Minister Ikeda resigned because of illness, Satō Eisaku a younger brother of Kishi Nobusuke, organized his cabinet on Novenber 9, 1964. Shortly before Satō's assumption of the premiership, however, the PRC, successfully exploded its first nuclear bomb. By beginning the bombing of North Vietnam in February 1965, the United States on its part escalated its military intervention in the Vietnam War. To counter this, the PRC increased its aid to North Vietnam. Thus, the confrontation between the United States and the PRC in the Indochinese peninsula was taking an increasingly ominous form.

Furthermore, parallel to the Great Cultural Revolution that began in late 1965, the PRC launched a "revolutionary diplomacy," advocating radical revolutionary slogans. Although China opted for a foreign policy to isolate itself, the United States and the Soviet Union signed the partial nuclear test ban treaty in August 1963, and the U.S.-Soviet détente gathered momentum. Moreover, during the latter half of the 1960s, Japan also promoted friendship with the Soviet Union through various administrative agreements (consular affairs, aviation, etc.) and discussions on Siberian development (especially the Tyumen oil field).

China viewed this situation as dangerous, possibly leading to a political situation in which Japan, the United States, and the Soviet Union would together confront the People's Republic of China. An editorial appeared in the *People's Daily*, as early as 1966, saying that Japan was a party to the "U.S.-Soviet Holy Alliance," and some Chinese leaders also made similar remarks in February 1969.

In November 1967, Prime Minister Satō and President Lyndon B. Johnson announced in Washington that "it is important to create a situation in which countries in Asia may not be influenced by the threats from Communist China."[25] During the latter half of the 1960s, Japan's China policy thus came closer to the American policy, and Japan's relations with China deteriorated. Whereas the Satō cabinet prohibited the use of the Export-Import Bank financing and deferred payments for Japanese trade with the PRC, the latter cast an ominous shadow over cultural exchange when it expelled Japanese journalists.

Despite the apparently intensifying conflict between the United States and

China during the latter half of the 1960s, however, there was an undercurrent searching for a way out of the Chinese isolation. For instance, at a hearing of the U.S. Senate Foreign Relations Committee in March 1966, A. Doak Barnett proposed a "containment policy without isolation." On the governmental level also, the United States in mid-1968 took measures to moderate restrictions on travel and trade with China. With Richard Nixon's election to the presidency in January 1969, the United States made more serious moves to improve relations with China. The first indication of such moves was the American suspension of the Seventh Fleet patrol of the Taiwan Strait. Soon after this, China and the United States resumed the ambassadorial-level conferences in Warsaw on January 20, 1970, after an interruption of two years.

Trapped by the rhetoric of a "shared recognition of Communist threats," the Japanese government overlooked the subtle but important signals exchanged between the United States and China, and President Nixon's announcement in July 1971 of his scheduled visit to Beijing came as a total surprise. Hence the "Nixon Shock." And the trilateral relations among Japan, the United States, and China that defined the political environment in postwar East Asia assumed a completely new aspect.

1. Chihiro Hosoya, "Japan, China, the United States and the United Kingdom 1941-52: the Case of the Yoshida Letter," *International Affairs* 60 (spring 1984): 247-59.

2. U.S. Department of State, *Foreign Relations of the United States* (hereafter cited as *FRUS*), *1952-1954*, vol. 14, *China and Japan*, part 2 (Washington, D.C., 1985), 1300-1308.

3. Ibid., 1406-08.

4. John Dower, *Empire and Aftermath: Yoshida Shigeru and the Japanese Experience, 1878-1954* (New York, 1979), 581.

5. *FRUS 1952-1954*, 14(2): 1406-08.

6. Ibid., 1490-91.

7. Miyazawa Kiichi, *Tokyo-Washington no mitsudan* (Secret talks between Tokyo and Washington) (Tokyo, 1975), 206-09, 259-63.

8. *FRUS 1952-1954*, 14(2): 1491-96.

9. NC 125/6, June 25, 1953, Papers of the National Security Council, National Archives.

10. Hosoya Chihiro and Aruga Tadashi, eds., *Kokusai kankei no hen'yō to Nichi-Bei kankei* (Changing international affairs and Japanese-American relations) (Tokyo, 1987), 60.

11. *FRUS 1952-1954*, 14(2): 1743-45.

12. Ibid., 1775-77.

13. Ibid., 1779-80.

14. *Izvestia*, 22 Dec. 1954; *People's Daily*, Dec. 30, 1954.

15. A. Domnitsky was former acting head of the Soviet delegation on the Far Eastern Commission. On the Domnitsky letter and subsequent developments, see Foreign Ministry, ed., *Gaimushō no hyakunen* (One hundred years of the foreign ministry), vol. 2 (Tokyo, 1969), 841.

16. Furukawa Jōtarō, *Nit-Chū sengo kankei-shi* (Postwar Sino-Japanese relations) (Tokyo, 1981), 114-15.

17. Ibid., 116-18.

18. Okada Akira, *Mizutori gaikō hiwa* (Hidden history of underwater diplomacy) (Tokyo, 1983), 48-57.

19. Itō Masaya, *Ikeda Hayato, so no sei to shi* (lkeda Hayato, his life and death) (Tokyo, 1966), 175-78.

20. Furukawa, *Nit-Chū sengo* 201.

21. Itō *Ikeda Hayato*, 175.

22. Furukawa, *Nit-Chū sengo*, 202.

23. Ibid., 215.

24. Hosoya and Aruga, *Kokusai Kankei* 71.

3

China in Japanese-American Relations

WARREN I. COHEN

The way in which Japan and the United States worked with differences in perception of and policy toward China from 1950 to 1972 provides a useful case study of how friendly nations of unequal power cope with disagreement. Assuming the persistence of a shared estimate of the threat posed by the Soviet Union over the next decade, the manner in which they dealt with their disparate views of China allows for considerable optimism as Americans and Japanese struggle with a host of conflicts over economic policy.

In the course of negotiations for a treaty of peace that would end the American occupation of Japan, Japanese leaders yielded on a secondary issue, policy toward China. They yielded in order to ensure ratification of the treaty by the U.S. Senate and to enhance friendship with the nation upon which Japan depended for economic aid and military protection. In the years that followed, an increasingly independent, stronger Japan chipped away at the American position on China and, with the support of other friends of the United States, most obviously Great Britain, undermined American policy— without alienating the United States. In the 1970s, the United States moved rapidly to adopt policies similar to those of Japan, and the issue disappeared. Although Ambassador Edwin Reischauer argued to the contrary in 1966, at no time did the differences over China constitute a danger to the alliance. There is ample evidence to indicate that some Americans and some Japanese were intensely unhappy at various points, but the issue was only one of a host of commonplace irritants of the sort that have provided employment for diplomats for centuries.

From the end of World War II until June 1950, China was not an issue between the United States and Japan. Early in the year the United States was encouraging Japanese trade with the newly proclaimed People's Republic of China. Dean Acheson was still thinking of trade as a means of weaning a Communist China away from the Soviet Union, still assuming the United

States would recognize Mao's regime eventually. American trading policy was more liberal toward China than toward the Soviet Union.[1] Japanese leaders and American leaders seemed alike in their ability to conceive of a Communist China independent of the Soviet Union and constituting little threat to the vital interests of their country.

In March 1951, after the People's Republic allied itself with the Soviet Union, trade policy distinctions in its favor ceased, and Beijing was thereafter treated like Moscow and its East European satellites. Acheson, however, had not yet surrendered his fundamental policy of seeking to prevent China from becoming an adjunct of Soviet power. Even after war broke out in Korea, he was still looking for a way to develop a differential trade policy more favorable to China than to other Soviet bloc nations.[2]

China's intervention in Korea undermined Acheson's policy of moving toward accommodation with China. By December 1950, the United States had chosen to pursue economic warfare against China and was urging its allies to do the same. Of its friends and allies, Japan, occupied by American troops, was the most responsive. Japanese traders, in the Osaka region in particular, were eager to maintain and expand trade with China. The Japanese government, however, assessing its interests in light of existing internal and external pressures and those that might be brought to bear, followed the American lead.

Speculation about Japanese decision making in the winter 1950-51 is unnecessary, given the ease with which we can study the evolution of China as an issue in the course of 1951. Center stage was occupied by John Foster Dulles, special advisor to the secretary of state, and Prime Minister Yoshida Shigeru. Dulles, Republican party spokesman on foreign policy, had been brought into the department in hope of containing Republican harassment of the administration. As his specific assignment, he undertook the drafting and negotiation of the Japanese peace treaty.

The principal issue confronting Dulles and Yoshida was that of future arrangements for Japanese security. Questions about China intruded in the process of developing a peace treaty largely because of differences between the United States and Great Britain. The United States and five other members of the Far Eastern Commision (FEC), nominal overseers of occupied Japan, continued to recognize the Guomindong regime on Taiwan as the government of all of China. Great Britain and five other members of the commission had chosen to recognize the Communist regime on the mainland. The American government chose to bypass the FEC, draft a treaty acceptable in Washington and Japan, and negotiate bilaterally with the nations represented on the commission. At least in the drafting of the treaty, the United States intended to circumvent the question of choosing between the two Chinas. The British government, however, persisted in forcing the issue.

The focal point of the Anglo-American dispute in the early months of 1951 was the British demand that the People's Republic of China be invited to the peace conference. A related issue was the matter of Japanese trade with China. Sir Oliver Franks, British ambassador to the United States, argued that, for Japan to function on a self-sustaining basis, it would have to have good relations with Beijing. He insisted its trade with China was most important.[3] Dulles, however, was looking for alternative markets and sources of raw materials for Japan, apparently thinking about Southeast Asia. The British government, however, indicated its unwillingness to see Japan move in any direction but toward China.[4] The British government refused to commit itself to granting most-favored-nation treatment to Japan and opposed Japanese participation in the General Agreement on Tariffs and Trade (GATT), even as a nonvoting observer. Fearing Japanese competition in traditional British markets and unwilling to open its home markets to Japan, London candidly sought to channel Japanese trade toward China. Japanese recognition of Mao's regime would facilitate that trade as well as provide endorsement of the earlier British decision to break ranks with the United States and abandon Guomindong China.

Yoshida raised the issue in January 1951.[5] He spoke of the long-term necessity for Japan to trade with China and his belief that before long the Communist government would minimize political obstacles to trade. He also advanced an idea with which many Japanese remained enamored throughout the 1950s and 1960s: that Japanese, because of their long experience with China, were best suited to spread democracy there. The views Yoshida expressed in January 1951 never changed and reflected the view that prevailed among Japanese leaders for the next two decades. Japan was willing to come to terms with the rump regime of Jiang Jieshi (Chiang Kai-shek)—most Japanese leaders were intensely anticommunist. The fact that the United States, the nation upon which Japan would be dependent for some time after the occupation, wanted Japan to recognize the Republic of China made that decision relatively easy. But neither Yoshida nor many of his colleagues were willing to abandon the right to trade with the People's Republic. Few Japanese feared that contact with the Chinese Communists would subvert Japan; on the contrary they were confident, as Yoshida indicated, that the contact would change China. Pushed in different directions by the United States and Great Britain, Japan sought to antagonize neither, while exploiting Anglo-American differences to maximize Japan's freedom to pursue a two-Chinas policy. It was not an easy task, but Yoshida and his successors managed well.

For Dulles the task was complicated by a domestic political context bordering on national hysteria after the recall of General Douglas MacArthur and by his own mistrust of Acheson's steadfastness on the China issue. Dulles had to draft a treaty, satisfactory to the Japanese and the British, which would also be acceptable to a U.S. Senate ridden with hostility to the administration and a people intensely hostile to a Communist China that was killing Americans in Korea.

To keep British support, the Americans were forced to devise a compromise by means of which neither claimant to legitimacy in China would participate in the peace conference or sign the treaty. Instead provision was made for Japan to negotiate a bilateral peace treaty along the lines of the original treaty with the China of its choice. The British were not happy with the compromise. Jiang was outraged, but Dulles succeeded in pacifying Jiang's friends in Washington—demonstrating the wisdom of the decision to bring him into the government.[6]

Before working out the agreement with British Foreign Secretary Herbert Morrison, Dulles was determined to learn where Yoshida stood. He asked Ambassador William J. Sebald to confront Yoshida with various alternative means of arranging a peace settlement with China, including the possibility that Japan might sign a treaty with the People's Republic. What were Japan's preferences?[7]

Yoshida's reply, presented by Vice Foreign Minister Iguchi Sadao, was everything for which Dulles might have hoped. Iguchi stated categorically that Japan intended to seek peace with the Republic of China (ROC) and did not desire the signature of the People's Republic (PRC). Japan preferred to have the ROC sign at the ceremony during which the multilateral treaty would be signed but was agreeable to a separate concurrent ceremony or, if that proved impractical, to a later ceremony. Iguchi also indicated his awareness that postponement of a treaty with the ROC "might unduly delay ratification [by the] US Senate."[8]

Armed with this assurance, which he did not share with his British colleague, Dulles offered and Morrison accepted a proposal that no Chinese government would sign the multilateral treaty but that Japan would be free afterward to do business with the China of its choice. The British cabinet, wanting assurance that the Japanese would never sign with the ROC, balked briefly. Dulles informed Acheson that Clement Attlee opposed giving Japan the right to conduct its foreign relations with China and wished to reserve that power for the FEC. The British position was untenable, and they quickly yielded the point in return for minor concessions on other points in the draft treaty. The Japanese would be free, after the treaty was signed, to sign a bilateral treaty with either Chinese regime. In the months that followed, Dulles struggled to hold Yoshida in line while the British worked frenetically to steer Japan toward the PRC.[9]

For Yoshida, the ideal situation would have been one in which the Americans and British, agreeing on a two-Chinas policy, would urge him to trade with both. Then he could have done as he pleased and disarmed his critics among ROC or PRC enthusiasts in Japan by alleging that he had yielded to force majeure. Instead he had a delicate situation in which a misstep might jeopardize the peace treaty—or at minimum, its ratification by one or more important powers.

Acheson and Yoshida met shortly after Yoshida landed in San Francisco to attend the peace conference. Yoshida asked how he might respond best to questions about China, and Acheson suggested that he reply that the matter was being studied—that no decision had been reached. Dulles, eager to assure the ROC and its friends in the Senate, pressed for Japanese establishment of an overseas agency in Taibei as soon as possible. Acheson seemed less concerned.[14]

Dulles was not happy with Acheson's handling of the China question in the meeting with Yoshida and quickly reported the tone to Senator H. Alexander Smith (R-NJ), one of the more respected friends of the ROC. Dulles led Smith to believe that "Acheson left the door open for Japs to recognize and make a treaty with Communist China and not Nationalists."[11] Dulles was so disturbed that a meeting was arranged between Smith and Yoshida at which the Japanese prime minister assured Smith he had no intention of signing a treaty with the PRC. He might postpone signing with either the ROC or the PRC, but he implied his intent to sign with Jiang's government.[12]

British efforts failed to persuade Dulles of the undesirability of a Japanese treaty with the ROC. Morrison spoke of problems he would face in Parliament if Japan recognized the ROC. His successor, Anthony Eden, reiterated British opposition to Japanese recognition of Jiang's regime—especially before the multilateral treaty came into force.[13] From Dean Rusk, in Tokyo, Dulles received indications that the British were urging Yoshida to reassess his policy toward China. Ambassador Sebald believed British efforts were bearing fruit, that Yoshida was reluctant to offend either power before Japan regained its sovereignty, and that he was unwilling in any event to accept an agreement with the ROC that would jeopardize trade possibilities with the mainland.[14] Churchill and Eden were coming to Washington after Christmas, and Dulles was not confident of Acheson's steadfastness on the issue. Having spent over a year manipulating Acheson, the British, the ROC, the Japanese, and the U.S. Senate, Dulles was not going to lose the game at this juncture. He flew to Tokyo to force a commitment from Yoshida.

Yoshida and Dulles met on December 13, and a record of that meeting alleges that, before Dulles addressed the issue, Yoshida handed him a draft of an agreement to establish relations with the ROC.[15] Then Dulles read him a memorandum stating that the American people would want to know prior to ratification if Japanese foreign policy would be compatible with American foreign policy, especially toward China. He suggested that Japenese interests would be served best by negotiating a treaty with the ROC that would come into force after the multilateral treaty. The treaty with the ROC would be applicable only to territory under actual control, leaving Japan free to do as it pleased later about the rest of China.

Yoshida replied on the following day.[16] He had no objection in principle but was reluctant to act as Dulles wished if the British were strongly opposed. Dulles suspected Yoshida was fearful that British dissatisfaction would result in obstacles to Japanese trade in sterling bloc areas of Southeast Asia and Africa. Yoshida also resumed his theme on the role Japan might play in weaning China away from the Soviet Union.

Dulles decided to force the issue. The Senate, a majority of whose members were on record as disapproving ties between Japan and the PRC, was his principal instrument, including Senator Smith and Senator John Sparkman (D-Alabama), who were in Tokyo to assist in his efforts. On December 18, he presented Yoshida with a draft of a letter, "essentially embodying the present Japanese position," which Dulles wanted Yoshida to send to him.[17] He told Yoshida that Smith and Sparkman "felt that such a letter from Mr. Yoshida would be the minimum without which it would probably be impossible to obtain ratification of the treaty." Forced to yield, Yoshida tried to gain something in exchange, stressing the importance of a loan to Japan from the American government, a matter to which he returned several days later.

Also on December 18, Acheson met with Franks who expressed British objections to Dulles's memo to Yoshida. Cabling Dulles, Acheson professed to having argued the American case but stressed the desirability of maintaining agreement with the British. Clearly, Anglo-American amity had a higher priority on Acheson's agenda than it did on Dulles's. Dulles professed that his draft letter for Yoshida, now known as "the Christmas present," was consistent with Acheson's desires and asked Sebald to let Yoshida know he wanted it on December 23 and would then hold it "subject to future determination."[18]

Fending off ROC demands for a bilateral treaty prior to Senate ratification, Dulles then cornered Acheson. Advising the secretary of state that he had learned on 26 December that Yoshida was sending him a letter, the text of which he had not yet seen, he reported that Senators Smith and Sparkman knew of Yoshida's position. In a scarcely veiled threat, Dulles wrote: "It would therefore be extremely awkward, from the standpoint of Senate ratification, if the Executive as a result of the Churchill talks, were to agree to seek to get Yoshida to retreat from the position toward China which he expressed to the two Senators and which no doubt they will report to their colleagues."[19]

Whether his letter to Dulles expressed views that Yoshida held freely can never be determined absolutely. What is clear, without a shadow of a doubt, is that the letter was drafted by Dulles and that Yoshida was forced to send it, under threat that the U.S. Senate could withhold ratification of the peace treaty. Yoshida might have called Dulles's bluff but chose instead to request a loan as a quid pro quo.

It will be no surprise to the student of American-East Asian relation that in 1951 Japan defined its policy toward China under pressure from the United States. What is most interesting is that the Yoshida letter was designed primarily to box in Acheson and Truman so that they would not be tempted to yield to Churchill and Eden. Dulles accepted Iguchi's and Yoshida's assurances of their intentions to recognize the ROC and saw British pressures to the contrary as the only obstacle to that outcome. He was prepared to use the power and influence of the United States to insist on the outcome he wanted, to ride roughshod over the sensibilities of a British government he did not trust and whose interests in East Asia he did not see as congruent with those of the United States.

From the perspective of Dulles and many of his Republican colleagues, the weakness in the American posture was Acheson, a man known to be intensely hostile to Jiang and the ROC, a man who certainly was more interested in propitiating the British than in appeasing the Nationalist Chinese. The specific purpose of the Yoshida letter was to commit the Japanese to a treaty with the ROC before Acheson could compromise with the British. The threat of the Senate withholding ratification, or at the very least of another ugly fight between Senate and Executive, closed the circle on the Truman administration.

In 1951, the Japanese government yielded to American pressures and committed itself to a bilateral treaty with the Republic of China. In so doing, it retained American goodwill at minimal cost, given all indications that Yoshida had intended to do so of his own free will. At the same time, Japan retained the freedom it desired to work out its economic relations with China, especially those territories not under ROC control subject of course to the overwhelming exception of the price it might have to pay in its relations with the United States and other friends hostile to the PRC. Moreover, by playing the British against the Americans and stressing his own domestic political problems, Yoshida could suggest, as he did, that the Americans owed him something. Even the British won a little, thanks to Acheson and Yoshida, including delays in the signing of the bilateral treaty and limitations on its scope. If it had not been for Dulles's efforts, they might have accomplished much more. Although Jiang clearly thought otherwise, the ROC also fared reasonably well. In short, the diplomacy of 1951 demonstrates how nations sharing similar fundamental security interests can work out a reasonable compromise on discordant issues, despite extreme disparities in power. Both Dulles and Yoshida had reason to be proud of their efforts.

After the peace treaty was ratified and the Japanese had signed a bilateral treaty with the ROC, trade with the PRC became the issue. For those American allies and friends who had not recognized the PRC before the Korean War, recognition was inconceivable in the 1950s: the political climate in the United States was too explosive, especially during the frenzied days when Senator Joseph McCarthy held sway.

The United States maintained a total embargo on trade with the People's Republic. The Truman administration had begun economic pressure as a way of calling Beijing's attention to the importance of trade with the West—part of Acheson's effort to prevent the Chinese Communists from allying with the Soviet Union. During the Korean War, that pressure was intensified, and then all trade halted as punishment for Chinese intervention. The embargo was maintained by the Eisenhower administration initially as a bargaining chip during negotiations for a settlement in Korea. After the war, the administration continued the embargo as a means of delaying the modernization of the PRC and of increasing the burden on the Soviet Union. It was continued long after evidence indicated its ineffectiveness and after impressive arguments that the policy was counterproductive, forcing greater PRC dependence on Moscow. Despite a growing demand from American businessmen and changing public attitudes toward the PRC in the mid-1950s, the Eisenhower administration held fast because of military insistence, pressures from Assistant Secretary of State Walter S. Robertson and the Republican right, and the low priority the issue had for the president.

At no time was Washington able to get its major allies to agree to a complete embargo. American diplomats wheedled and cajoled, but neither the Truman nor the Eisenhower administration was willing to exert the pressure necessary for compliance. Despite military demands for maximum pressure, Truman and Acheson and Eisenhower and Dulles placed a higher premium on good relations with their allies than on compliance.

The impossibility of a complete embargo even by NATO countries meant the next step was to work out lists of strategic items that would be denied to the Soviet bloc. Ultimately two lists emerged, one directed at the Soviet Union and its East European satellites and a second, markedly more restrictive list, aimed at the PRC. The difference between the two was known as the China differential. In the years that followed initial agreement on the two lists, there was constant tension between the United States and its allies, with the latter arguing for a less restrictive list of items to be sold to the Soviet Union and for elimination of the China differential. In 1951, Congress passed the Mutual Defense Assistance Control Act—or the Battle Act—which, in effect, denied

American aid to any nation trading in strategic materials with the Soviet bloc. For those dependent on American largesse, the message was clear.

The Japanese government, under Yoshida and his successors, persisted in the desire for a two-Chinas policy. Japan was eager for more trade opportunities with the PRC. Some businessmen with ties to the ruling party pressed within its councils for trade expansion, and the Japanese Socialist party used the government's reluctance to offend the United States as an issue with which to embarrass it. Within the bureaucracy, especially within the Ministry of International Trade and Industry (MITI), there was a demand for more trade to bolster a very frail economy. For some Japanese, policy toward China became a nationalist issue, a way of asserting independence from the United States.

One striking feature of the debate within the American government was President Eisenhower's persistent and open expression of sympathy for Japan's position and his disdain for both the China differential imposed on allied exports and the United States total embargo against China. In private interviews, cabinet meetings, and press conferences, the president expressed concern for the Japanese economy and the thought that trade with China might be more helpful than not. In the critical period of 1956-57, the president deliberately undermined efforts to force the allies into line on the China differential but acquiesced in the continuation of the American trade embargo.

Once again, as the issue of policy toward China reemerged between the United States and its allies, it was Great Britain and not Japan that took the lead. Japanese leaders were content to sail in Britain's wake. Like Eisenhower, they were probably confident that, when trade restrictions were eased, Japan rather than Great Britain would be the primary beneficiary.

In December 1955, however, the British warned that if the China differential was not eliminated by agreement, they would remove it unilaterally. Admiral Edwin T. Layton, deputy director for intelligence of the Joint Chiefs of Staff (JCS) reacted strongly in a memorandum for Admiral Arthur W. Radford, chairman of the JCS. Layton warned that the proposed British action was the "equivalent of directly supporting an expansion of Communist China's military forces." It would lead to economic and then political recognition and elimination of the differential by nearly all the other countries involved, and then the British would seek to emasculate COCOM controls, allowing unrestricted trade with all communist countries. For Japan in particular, Layton prophesied doom. Noting rising trade between China and Japan, he feared it was "problematical if the two mutually compatible economies can be kept separate in absence of restrictions. Once joined, the Japanese economy would become dependent upon Chinese supplies, vulnerable to Communist withholding of raw materials, and thereby susceptible to induced industrial and labor unrest."[20]

pan were not far behind—induced the Eisenhower administration to agree to negotiations. Defense intelligence denounced the British as the most persistent and unreasonable of those countries generating pressure but noted that even strong supporters of the American position such as Italy and Turkey were having trouble with their business communities. The Joint Chiefs were given little reason to hope for a successful outcome, but with the Suez crisis intervening, the United States induced the British to wait a year, until May 1957, before all the concerned parties met to discuss the reduction or elimination of the China differential.[27]

In the interim, the American government carried out a careful assessment of its relations with Japan, "The Present and Projected Foreign Relations of Japan (1956-1961)." Japan was expected to become increasingly nationalistic and assertive. The Department of State Office of Intelligence Research (OIR) contribution to the assessment warned that Japan's association with the West would become peripheral unless changes toward greater equality in the relationship were accepted by the United States. Reference was made to the Ryukyus and Bonins, the security treaty, and trade restrictions as areas in which the United States would have to make concessions. In addition, OIR noted that "the one major area in which U.S. policy is firmly opposed by virtually all segments of Japanese opinion . . . is in Japan's desire for closer trade and eventual diplomatic relations with Communist China." OIR reported that "Prime Minister Hatoyama was testing the limits of American patience on the trade issue" and warned that the issue of policy toward China threatened to become "a serious irritant" in Japanese-American affairs.[28]

From Tokyo, Allison, now ambassador, sent a report similar to the OIR paper, stressing the need for more consultation with Japan. Although trade and general relations with the PRC were not the most important issues in the eyes of the embassy staff, Japanese resentment was detailed. It was clear that Allison and his staff viewed Washington's behavior on the China differential issue as damaging. They urged their government not to ask more of Japan than other countries were willing to do, not to allow other countries to seize trade opportunities the Japanese needed and saw as their own. The Japanese were reported to be upset by the failure of the United States to respond to an urgent Japanese request to sell certain items to the PRC under the exceptions procedure, despite the knowledge that several European nations were using the exceptions procedure without prior notification.[29]

To the limits of its power, the Department of State did respond to Japanese pressures. Defense intelligence sources informed Admiral Radford that State had already taken an interim policy and informed the Department of Defense and the NSC "post facto." The State Department had offered to agree to specific items the Japanese had listed in return for Japanese support in holding the line on other items. Japan did not agree, and the American negotiators settled for a promise of more discriminating use of the exceptions procedure. Radford was warned of a strong element within State eager to abolish the China differential. But Secretary Dulles was not interested in doing anything to strengthen Hatoyama ("We don't think much of him."), and Japanese concerns about trade imbalance with the PRC did not move him.[30]

In December 1956, the American government's hopes for a Japanese premier more sympathetic to American policy toward the PRC were dashed when the Liberal Democratic party (LDP) selected Ishibashi Tanzan—the candidate least favored in Washington. Ishibashi, former MITI minister, had been an outspoken proponent of increased trade with the PRC. Robertson met with Ishibashi to remind him of American policy and to ask for his cooperation. Ishibashi said all the right things, promising to abide by Japan's international agreements, but there was every reason to assume that his government would attempt to modify those agreements to eliminate the China differential.[31]

Simultaneously, the American government worked to defend Japan's share of the American textile market. At a cabinet meeting in January, Secretary of Commerce Sinclair Weeks reported on his successful efforts and his warnings to the American Cotton Manufacturers Institute.[32] The president indicated his pleasure, and Dulles remarked that, if negotiations had broken down, "the Japanese would almost assuredly have begun to develop closer relations with Communist China." As a weapon against American protectionists, Japan's desire for trade with the PRC proved most effective.

A few days later, at another cabinet meeting, Eisenhower asked again for a study and review of policy on control of exports to communist countries. He was reminded that such a study was under way. Still the bureaucracy stalled. In March, Japan's new prime minister, Kishi Nobusuke, preferred by the American government to his two predecessors, pushed. He publicly announced his desire to go to Washington to discuss his "long cherished idea" of expanding trade with the PRC. Before the month was over, Eisenhower was in London, where talks with British leaders reinforced his determination to get action on the issue. Leading American businessmen, such as Henry Ford II, indicated an interest in trade with the PRC. At a news conference on April 10, Eisenhower "presented a strong argument for increased trade with Communist China by friendly nations, particularly the economically hard pressed Japanese and the British." He delivered a lecture on Japan's economic dilemma and offered one of his favorite arguments, that a nation's economic well-being is as important to its security as is its military power.[33]

British and Japanese pressure on the United States mounted and the administration defended itself against sniping from within by indicating that it was yielding reluctantly under pressure. America's embargo against trade with the PRC would not be compromised. The *New York Times* offered editorial support, favoring relaxation of the American position on allied trade to avoid forcing the British to act unilaterally and to set a favorable tone for Eisenhower's first meeting with Kishi.[34]

The allied control committee met in Paris in May, and quickly "the British and several other allies were reliably reported to be extremely unhappy with the United States proposals." The United States was prepared to relax controls but fought to retain a significant China differential. The British, French, Japanese, and Belgians were reported to be pushing hard. On May 23, a deadlock was announced, and a week later the British acted unilaterally to eliminate the differential. The majority of America's allies, including Italy, Norway, and West Germany, soon followed suit, but not Japan. The Japanese chose to wait at least until Kishi travelled to Washington to take Eisenhower's measure.[35]

In the United States, the response to British action was fascinating. Senator Lyndon Johnson (D-Texas), majority leader, called for a new look at American policy toward China. There were reports of various moves in the Senate to neutralize Senator William Knowland and other friends of Jiang and the ROC. Powerful southerners voiced the view that it would be useful to redirect Japan's textile exports toward China. Others spoke of the value of Japanese trade with China in terms of relieving the United States of the burden of sustaining the Japanese economy. Finally, the president spoke in support of Britain's decision to act unilaterally and stepped up his efforts within the government to ease pressures on Japan. James Reston of the *New York Times* criticized Eisenhower for allowing his administration to perpetuate policies rejected by the allies and in which he did not himself believe.[36]

Dulles called Eisenhower and referred to talk that the secretary and the president had split on the question of trade with China.[37] He received no comfort, Eisenhower reiterated his arguments against antagonizing allies and attempting to obstruct trade. Dulles noted that the president was unaware that it was an executive order, not a legislative act, that prohibited American trade with the PRC. Reston's point was underscored: the president's views were clear, publicly and privately stated, but he was unwilling to use any more of his political capital to force a policy change on the rest of his administration.

Kishi moved well in this context. Dulles had provided Eisenhower with a favorable assessment of the new Japanese premier, indicating that trade with China was one of seven items he wished to discuss. Curiously, Dulles's memo ignored the trade question, although arguing in unyielding terms on most of the other points. Publicly, Kishi promised to abide by the American-dictated controls on trade with China, asking that the controls be reasonable. At the same time he asked for fair access to American markets and for a long-term low interest loan. He would not go home empty-handed.[38]

Dulles, with Assistant Secretary Robertson pushing hard behind him, tried to indicate that the administration was holding the line. In San Francisco he discussed the type of communism practiced in China, calling it a "passing phase" in Chinese history—an obvious attempt to put aside the argument that the regime had established itself beyond doubt and that the logic of the situation required accommodation with it. In hearings generated by Senate interest in a more flexible American policy toward the PRC, Secretary Weeks argued against the relaxation of the trade embargo. If Eisenhower had intended to shift policy, it seemed that his cabinet was neither ready nor willing. On the other hand, it is likely that Dulles and Weeks were covering the president's right flank as the administration prepared to acquiesce, despite strong Pentagon opposition, in the total elimination of the China differential by its allies.[39]

In July 1957, allied negotiations on trade controls resumed. A report from Tokyo indicated that the Japanese negotiator hoped to win agreement on relaxation and that Japan hoped to "win a fair share of mainland market." However, the Japanese did not want to alienate Americans by acting unilaterally, as the British had done. A subsequent article on the effects of inflation on Japanese exports also indicated that MITI would propose to the cabinet a solution in the form of elimination of the China differential—a posture approximating that of Great Britain. Again, MITI officials declared that Japan would not act unilaterally. Two days later came the announcement that "the Japanese Government today lifted certain restrictions on trade with Communist China." Japan was now "in line with Britain and other European countries already trading with the Peiping Government." The cabinet had approved a list identical to that of the British. A probably inspired story declared that Kishi had planned to move slowly, in deference to the United States but that the pressure had become too great as Japan's trade imbalance grew. Two weeks later a report from Paris revealed that the fifteen nations negotiating on trade controls had reached almost complete agreement. Finally on August 6, word came that the United States had yielded to pressure from its allies to ease still further controls on trade with the PRC. The American delegates in Paris had surrendered "under instruction from Washington."[40]

As Knowland, Robertson, and others of their ilk had feared, eliminating the China differential was only the beginning. A few months later, the Gaimushō informed the Department of State that the Japanese government had agreed to the exchange of trade offices or missions between private Japanese trade organizations and the official trading corporation of the PRC. The Gaimushō assured the United States that Japan's action was not a step toward recognition. The State Department warned that the Chinese would exploit the opportunity for political purposes, but the United States was unwilling to exert serious pressure. A National Intelligence Estimate in December 1957 indicated American uneasiness over Japanese links with the PRC but concluded that, despite the attractions of China, "the Japanese generally recognize the primary importance of their defense and economic ties with the United States and the West; fears that these ties may be jeopardized inhibits them from seeking too close a relationship with the Chinese Communist regime.[41]

In sum, American pressure on its allies, including Japan, to restrict trade with the PRC significantly more than trade with the Soviet Union, failed in 1957. Subjected to countervailing pressures by the British, with whom the Japanese were in discreet collusion, the Eisenhower administration yielded. Keeping friends happy was more important than maintaining a policy that was only marginally effective. Moreover, in 1957 the president, having been reelected, was willing to take the political risks necessary to end efforts to isolate the PRC—efforts he deemed unrealistic and unwise. He surrendered to internal opposition on the more emotion-laden issue of American contacts with the PRC, despite indications of support in the Senate and the American business community. The Japanese played the game with considerable skill, allowing the British to bear the brunt of American irritation, basing their own case on the desperate conditions of their economy. Although Eisenhower demonstrated his sympathy for the Japanese position throughout the mid-1950s, it was clearly easier for the Americans to yield to the trusted Kishi in 1957 than earlier to Hatoyama or Ishibashi.

From 1957 to 1971, China declined in importance as an issue in Japanese-American relations. There is no doubt that there were differences, deceptions, and misunderstandings in these years, but they were never very serious, nor was great pressure brought to bear by either side upon the other. The Japanese aggressively pursued a two-Chinas policy and commercial opportunities on the mainland. Some Japanese actions displeased some American officials, but American leaders outside the Pentagon were moving toward what was later called a policy of "containment without isolation" toward the PRC. President Kennedy's obsessions about China, fear of domestic repercussions, fear of sending the wrong message to China, distractions with other issues, and the war in Vietnam all delayed changes in American policy, but Washington generally found it easier to acquiesce in allied contacts with the PRC.

The subsiding of American pressures, however, was only part of the story for Japan. Neither ROC nor PRC leaders were pleased with Japan's blatant two-Chinas policy, and they used every means available to them to force the Japanese to choose. Within Japan, businessmen, politicians, and diplomats lined up in support of the demands of one or the other Chinese claimant. In the late 1950s and early 1960s, the United States found itself in the curious role of putting pressure on the ROC to accept Japan's growing ties with the PRC.

Jiang and his aides in Taibei were shaken in the mid-1950s by Japan's unofficial agreements with the PRC on trade, fisheries, cultural exchanges, and the repatriation by China of Japanese war criminals held by the Beijing regime. Tensions rose after the Kishi government renounced the China differential. A visit to Taibei by Kishi soothed Jiang a little, but in March 1958 Japan signed its fourth unofficial trade agreement with the PRC. After long and difficult negotiations, each side agreed to allow the other to fly its national flag over its trade mission office. Jiang was outraged by the symbolism of the PRC flag flying in Tokyo and threatened the total cessation of ROC trade with Japan. Although American analysts thought such a step would have disastrous results for Taiwan, they also knew that the issue was one on which he might not yield.[42] For the Japanese, trade with Taiwan exceeded their immediate hopes for trade with the PRC. American good offices were used to devise a face-saving arrangement. The Japanese government declared that the flags had no legal significance. Neither trade mission had diplomatic or official status. The American government persuaded Jiang to settle for this gesture. In fact the trade missions contained government officials on both sides, with Gaimushō and MITI personnel serving in Beijing, as their counterparts did in Tokyo.

In March 1959, an American assessment of relations with Japan found them "relatively close." Major problem areas listed were the need for revision of the security treaty, settlement of the Ryukyus issue, bilateral trade relations (especially "adequate and expanding export opportunities" for Japan in the United States), Japan's defense effort, and Korean-Japanese relations. Even among the lesser problems mentioned, relations with China were not included. A few days later, the NSC was offered an operations plan for Japan which, while stressing other issues, did mention the Japanese expectation of American acceptance of a PRC-Japan modus vivendi short of political recognition. The American government was advised to continue to use its good offices to hold the ROC and Japan together and to "foster a Japanese awareness" of the dangers of expanding trade with the PRC.[43]

By 1960, Beijing was showing considerable flexibility. The growing rift with the Soviet Union required the PRC to find alternative sources of needed technology and alternative markets for its goods. Although political goals were never far from the surface in Maoist China, economic needs for trade with Japan were more pressing than they had been in the 1950s. At the same time, Japan's spectacular economic recovery was becoming apparent to the world. In May 1960, NSC papers on Japan shifted from fretting about the frailties of the Japanese economy to expressions of wonder at its rate of growth.[44] PRC efforts to block the renewal of the Japanese-American security treaty and support of opposition parties in the Japanese elections heightened tensions briefly. After the fall of Kishi, however, overtures by Zhou Enlai (Chou En-lai) to sympathetic LDP faction leaders brought results.

In 1962, Matsumura Kenzō, an LDP leader, and Zhou negotiated an agreement to facilitate long-term trade arrangements. Out of this agreement came the establishment of liaison offices in Tokyo and Beijing. Trade between the countries began to grow again, surpassing the previous high in 1958. Japan's two-Chinas policy seemed to be paying off. However displeased, the Americans went along. Jiang, on the other hand, was intensely unhappy. A series of incidents in late 1963 led to a new crisis in Japanese-ROC relations and American good offices were again necessary.

In August 1963, the Ikeda government approved Export-Import Bank funding, a five-year deferred payment plan, to allow the Kurashiki Rayon Company to sell a $22 million vinylon plant to the PRC—the kind of project Dean Rusk decried as "aid not trade." Vigorous protests from the ROC were rejected. In the months that followed, tension was raised by reports that Prime Minister Ikeda Hayato had declared that the ROC could never recover the mainland and by Jiang's public denunciation of Japan, blaming Japanese aggression for the loss of the mainland—his first such attack since the end of the war. The crisis was precipitated by Japan's handling of a PRC defector.

Jiang's government chose to focus on the defector issue—the one over which the Japanese government probably had least control. Japan could hardly force the man to go to Taibei if he wanted to go elsewhere. But in Taibei the Japanese ambassador was subjected to intense harassment, including the stoning of his residence. Recalled to Tokyo in November, he warned Ikeda that the ROC would not hesitate to break relations if the defector was allowed to return to the PRC. Admiral Jerauld Wright, American ambassador to the ROC, urged Chen Cheng, Jiang's vice president, not to take strong action against Japan.[45] Chen replied with a litany of ROC grievances against Japan. At the end of the year, the defector chose to go home and the Japanese allowed him to return. Jiang immediately recalled his ambassador from Tokyo, suspended all government procurement from Japan, and indicated his intention to break relations.

The American government sprang into action on December 31, 1963. In Washington, Roger Hilsman, assistant secretary of state, called in the Chinese minister (the ambassador was ill) to express serious concern. He advised him that Secretary Rusk wanted the ROC government informed that the action already taken would affect the Japanese public adversely and make it more difficult for Rusk to win Japanese support for the ROC, especially in the United Nations. On the same day, Ambassador Wright met with Jiang to warn that the United States would not like to see the ROC break relations with

Japan and that such an action would have a "serious if not disastrous effect" on the ROC's position among friendly nations and result in an increase of PRC-Japanese ties. Jiang, as was his wont, blamed the United States for the problem: the Americans coddled Japan, and the defector case was a direct result.[46]

Jiang restrained himself, and the Japanese did what they could to smooth things over. Yoshida flew to Taibei to discuss the issues with Jiang and his aides. Upon his return, with authorization from Ikeda, Yoshida wrote a private letter assuring Jiang that Export-Import Bank funds would not be used to provide credits to finance exports to the PRC. A subsequent mission to Taibei by the Japanese foreign minister helped, but probably not as much as the angry reaction from Beijing. In November 1964, when the new Japanese prime minister, Satō Eisaku, indicated that he would honor the assurances offered by Yoshida, the PRC cancelled a series of contracts with Japanese firms and withdrew from negotiations with others. Tokyo could not keep everybody happy, and now it was Jiang's turn to smile, however briefly.

By the time Satō became prime minister, Japan's recovery was well under way and a number of bilateral trade problems began to plague Japanese-American relations. Japanese tolerance of remnants of the American occupation, such as continued United States control of Okinawa, was ebbing. As the Japanese recovered their self-confidence, pressure mounted on successive Japanese governments to assert independence from the United States. Policy toward China was a relatively minor issue among many.

Satō was no less interested than most other Japanese leaders in increasing exports to the PRC. Trade was hardly an issue in Japan. The real question was the extent to which various advocates were willing to offend the ROC and the United States. Satō was more sympathetic to Jiang's regime than Ikeda and others among his predecessors had been. His position reflected the dominant position among LDP faction leaders and big business in Japan. Moreover, Satō's agenda gave priority to items that required concessions from the United States. As a result, he was quick to demonstrate his support for the United States, even on issues that were highly unpopular in Japan, such as policy toward Vietnam. His strategy was to have the American government view him as a loyal friend and to grant concessions to Japan to keep his government in power. For precisely these reasons, he was unpopular in Beijing. The PRC would do nothing that might strengthen him, hoping that after his fall, a leader more responsive to its interests would take power. Unhappily for the PRC, Satō managed to retain power for a long time, and PRC needs were too great in the absence of Soviet bloc support to refuse to trade with Satō's Japan. Indeed, it was during Satō's premiership that Japan became the principal trading partner of the PRC, with minimal carping from the United

States. Perhaps the greatest injustice, however, was perpetrated by the United States, when it betrayed Satō in 1971.

A CIA analysis of "The China Problem in Japanese Politics," prepared while Ikeda was still premier, indicated American awareness that Japanese moves were going beyond trade and pointed to the eventual establishment of diplomatic relations.[47] The only issues were "the manner and the timing" of Japan's "inevitable approach to Peiping." Satō's victory over Ikeda probably slowed the process and the Great Proletarian Cultural Revolution required postponement.

One example of how Satō could exploit American hopes and fears was indicated during negotiations over Japan Air Lines' landing rights in the United States. In a memorandum prepared for President Lyndon Johnson, Assistant Secretary of State Thomas Mann recommended American concessions to break the deadlock.[48] He informed the president that the issue had political importance in Japan where Satō was under fire for being subservient to the United States. Mann mentioned Satō's support on Vietnam, on relations with the PRC, the Chinese representation issue at the U.N., and respect for the ROC. Satō had put himself on the line for the United States. Here was something the United States could do for him.

Ambassador Reischauer played on the image of Satō as a supporter of American efforts toward China. In February 1966, he reported that Satō had created new machinery for examining Japanese shipments to the PRC in an effort to prevent materials of strategic value from slipping through.[49] He forwarded information indicating that Satō had denied the use of Export-Import Bank funds to facilitate trade with PRC and had stepped up intelligence collection as evidence of growing awareness of the PRC threat.

By 1966, however, American leaders had little time to think about Japan and any of the issues that existed on a bilateral level. Increasingly, they were consumed by the war in Vietnam. Within the United States, pressures mounted for changes in American policy toward China. In March a meeting of American chiefs of mission throughout East Asia called upon their government to "mitigate the impression of inflexibility and rigidity in our approach to China." They called for lifting the embargo on nonstrategic trade and for increased cultural contacts. A CIA report in June, "Economic Benefits to Communist China of a Removal of U.S. Trade Controls," confirmed that U.S. sales of machinery to the PRC would make little difference to the development of the Chinese economy: "the Chinese can usually satisfy their needs by buying in Western markets or Japan."[50]

In this atmosphere of intense concern over Vietnam-related issues and renewed consideration of American policy toward trade with China, Rusk went to Japan in July 1966. Talking to American correspondents in Kyoto ("a Deep Press Backgrounder—no attribution of American sources"), he indicated that Vietnam issues had dominated his agenda. Asked about Japan and the PRC, Rusk was characteristically vague on the U.N. question, but he did indicate that, despite some unhappiness with easy credit terms Japan was allowing the PRC, trade "wasn't a matter that was pressed very hard." The American government still went through the motions of complaining about allied trade with the PRC for fear that making it too easy would lead to demands for even fewer restrictions.[51]

Probably the loudest warning on the seriousness of policy toward China as an issue in Japanese-American relations was sounded by Reischauer in August 1966.[52] He argued that the danger areas in the relationship were not bilateral problems but Japanese apprehensions about Chinese-American tensions. The Japanese, he contended, believed that, as the stronger of the two adversaries, the United States could take the steps necessary to ease tensions with Beijing. The Satō government had given strong support to the United States, but the Japanese people were decidedly unhappy and a large part of the LDP was restive on the issue. The illogic of American insistence that Taibei alone represented China focused attention on the issue as one on which Japan should assert itself. Reischauer expressed his support for the containment of China, self-determination for Taiwan, and other tenets of American faith, but argued that the United States paid too high a price for its position on the issue. Clearly American policy toward China was a burden for its diplomats.

Hearings in the Senate underscored shifts in American elite opinion. The time had come for change, but Johnson and Rusk, who understood this, were trapped by the war in Vietnam and their rationalizations for it. When overtures to Beijing were made in May 1968, in the form of an invitation for Chinese journalists to cover the American elections and a conciliatory speech by Undersecretary of State Nicholas Katzenbach, it was too late. Little changed before Richard Nixon became president.

Nixon and his national security adviser, Henry Kissinger, understood both Satō's support for the United States and his needs. In addition, Nixon needed help from Satō on an unrelated issue—textiles. In November 1969, Satō met with the president in Washington and achieved the desired agreement on Okinawan reversion, to occur in 1972. In return Satō agreed to a communique that declared Japan's support for American policy toward Vietnam and China—as unprovocatively as Satō could get the Americans to state the point. He promised support on the textile question, but no progress was made in 1970.[53]

In December 1970, in his year-end report, Ambassador Armin Meyer in Tokyo warned Washington that, unless issues such as China were handled properly, the American-Japanese partnership might be damaged.[54] He recommended a coordinated Japan-American approach to the China issue in 1971. Satō, on his part, was confident of his longtime friendship with Nixon and of American intention to cooperate with Japan. He was unconcerned by the Japanese nightmare that the United States would steal a march on Japan by suddenly recognizing the PRC. But in March 1971, a major dispute over textiles broke out between Japan and the United States. Nixon and Kissinger were convinced that Satō had not kept his part of the bargain. The president sometimes seemed obsessed with demonstrating that he was not a man to be crossed, and anger over the inability of Satō to deliver the concessions Nixon needed to meet his campaign promise to American textile interests boded ill for the partnership.

Simultaneously, Nixon and Kissinger were moving toward extraordinary changes in American policy toward China. A series of signals had been exchanged with Zhou Enlai, and both sides were prepared to meet to bring about a rapprochement. Analysts in the Department of State stressed the importance of keeping Japan informed. A series of Japanese leaders had restrained their own desire for normalization of relations with the PRC and, at the urging of the United States, had taken unpopular stands on the question of China's representation at the U.N. Satō had probably risked more than any of his predecessors to support American policies. Nixon and Kissinger were aware of his vulnerability. On July 15, 1971, Nixon had his revenge, announcing Kissinger's visit to China and his own forthcoming trip—without prior consultation with Satō, without giving Satō warning sufficient to protect himself. The first of the Nixon "shokku" constituted the last instance in which China served as an irritant in Japanese-American relations. Hardly more than a year later, Satō's successor Tanaka Kakuei was in Beijing, announcing the normalization of Japanese-Chinese relations. Japan asserted itself with finality on the issue, and Americans and Japanese found other, probably more enduring, issues with which to irritate each other.

In a number of ways, China was unquestionably an issue in Japan-American relations from 1950 to 1972. Japan wanted unrestricted access to mainland markets and was usually willing to pay the price the PRC demanded. But as is often the case, relations between Japan and the PRC had to be worked out in a multilateral context. Japan could not advance its interests with the PRC without sacrificing interests on Taiwan or endangering advantages obtained from good relations with the United States. The object of Japan's diplomacy was, obviously, to maximize opportunities to expand trade with the PRC while minimizing the price to be paid on Taiwan and in the United States. This is the stuff of international politics, and Japan played the game well.

Chalmers Johnson has called Japan's strategy toward China prior to 1972 "one of the most skillfully executed foreign policies pursued by Japan in the postwar era—a clever, covert adaptation by Japan to the Cold War and a good example of Japan's essentially neo-mercantilist foreign policy."[55]

In the 1950s, when Japan appeared to have little leverage, Japanese diplomats won everything they needed. They succeeded in opening and expanding trade with the PRC while enlarging their trade and investments with the ROC—and maintaining excellent relations with the United States. In the 1960s, as Japan grew stronger, it continued to gain in all directions. To be sure, Jiang tried to punish the Japanese and caused some minor difficulties, and PRC authorities squeezed hard from time to time, but for every step backward there were at least two steps forward. Often ungraciously, sometimes with stern lectures, the United States steadily acquiesced in Japanese demands. Most striking is Eisenhower's strong sense that Japanese trade with the PRC was appropriate and good for the United States as well as for Japan. It is also obvious that American acquiescence in Japanese trade with the PRC was often a substitute for greater liberalization of the American home market. At no time was China per se a dangerous issue in Japanese-American relations.

American policy toward the PRC was tragic, especially for the Americans and Chinese, Koreans, Vietnamese, Laotians, and Cambodians killed along the way. There was no tragedy for Japan—only a nuisance that Japanese leaders managed to maneuver around quite well—until American policy, in what was otherwise its most sensible hour (Nixon's move toward accommodation with China), undermined Satō. Japanese leaders, like all national leaders and most people generally, would have preferred complete freedom of action. In practice, nations and friends are confronted by each other's needs and desires, rational or otherwise, and must compromise. Americans and Japanese did this well on the China issue from 1950 to 1972, and there is every reason to expect them to do as well on the issues that irritate these friends in the 1980s and 1990s.

1. Joint Chiefs of Staff 1721/43, 16 January 1950, *Declassified Documents Reference System* (hereafter DDRS) (79)33A; State Department Position Paper, 26 March 1951, U.S. Department of State, *Foreign Relations of the United States* (hereafter FRUS), 1951, vol. 7 *Korea and China*, part 2 (Washington, 1983), 1953-63. See Nancy Bernkopf Tucker, "American Policy toward Sino-Japanese Trade in the Postwar Years: Politics and Prosperity," *Diplomatic History* 8 (1984): 183-208.

2. *FRUS 1951*, 7(2): 1953-63.

3. Memorandum of conversation, 30 March 1951, *FRUS 1951*, 6: 953-54.

4. Lewis Douglas to Acheson, 26 February 1951, Ibid., 896-87.

5. Memorandum of conversation, 29 January 1951, Ibid., 827-30.

6. Memorandum of conversations 31 May, 2 June, 6 June, 15 June, 19 June 1951, Papers of Wellington Koo, Box 184, Columbia University.

7. Dulles to Sebald, 16 May 1951, *FRUS 1951*, 6: 1044-45.

8. Sebald to Dulles, 19 May 1951, Ibid., 1050. For the argument that Yoshida was determined *not* to sign a peace treaty with the ROC, see Michael M. Yoshitsu, *Japan and the San Francisco Peace Settlement* (New York, 1983), 67-83.

9. Dulles to Acheson, 6 June, 7 June, 8 June 1951 and John Allison to Rusk and Dulles, 11 June 1951, *FRUS 1951*, 6: 1107-10.

10. Memorandum of conversation 3 September 1951, Ibid., 1315-17.

11. Memorandum of meeting, undated, Ibid., 1326-28.

12. Ibid.

13. Memorandum of conversation 9 September 1951, Ibid., 1343-44; David Bruce to Secretary of State, 22 and 23 November 1951, Ibid., 1408-10.

14. Sebald to Acheson, 30 November 1951, Ibid., 1419-21.

15. Ibid., 1436-38.

16. Dulles to Allison, 14 December 1951, Ibid., 1438-39.

17. Memorandum of conversation, 18 December 1951, DDRS (75), 128F.

18. Acheson to Dulles and Sebald, 18 December 1951, *FRUS 1951*, 6: 1448-50.

19. Dulles memorandum of conversation with Koo, 27 December 1951, Ibid., 1473; Dulles memorandum for Acheson, 28 December 1951, DDRS (75), 129.

20. Memorandum for Chairman, JCS, 7 December 1955, DDRS (80), 358B.

21. "Discussion at the 271st Meeting of the National Security Council, Thursday, December 22, 1955" DDRS (81), 497B.

22. Robert J. Donovan, *Eisenhower: The Inside Story* (New York, 1956).

23. "Eden Talks, 31 January 56," Memorandum of Conversation, February 7, 1956, DDRS (81), 584B.

24. *New York Times*, February 1956, 1 and 6 February 1956, 8.

25. Joseph M. Dodge to Admiral W.S. Delany, 13 February 1956 DDRS (78), 233A; RADM Edwin T. Layton for Chairman, JCS, 16 February 1956 DDRS (80), 359A; *New York Times*, 21 February 1956, 7 and 8 March 1956, 1; CFEP-501, DDRS (81), 32A; "U.S. Position on China Trade Controls," 9 April 1956, DDRS (80), 366A.

26. Burton I. Kaufman, *Trade and Aid: Eisenhower's Foreign Economic Policy, 1953-1961* (Baltimore, MD and London, 1982), 63; *New York Times*, 17 May 1956, 1, 23 May 1956, 14, and 26 May 1956, 16.

27. Colonel Robert Totten for Chief, JCS, 22 May 1956, DDRS (80), 359B.

28. 12 September 1956, DDRS (70), 194C.

29. 21 September 1956, DDRS (82), 000203.

30. General Richard Colliers to Radford, 5 October 1956, DDRS (80), 360A; *Minutes of Telephone Conversations of John Foster Dulles 1953-60*, 22 October 1956, Eisenhower and Dulles.

31. *New York Times*, 16 December 1956, 42; 20 December 1956, 2; 21 December 1956, 8, and 26 December 1956, 3.

32. Cabinet minutes, 18 January 1957, *Minutes and Documents of the Cabinet Meetings of President Eisenhower*, Reel 5 (University Publications of America, 1980).

33. Record of action, 22 January 1957, *Minutes and Documents; New York Times*, 1 March 1957, 6, 25 March 1957, 4, 29 March 1957, 6, 11 April 1957, 1.

34. *New York Times*, 19 April 1957, 4, 20 April 1957, 3, 21 April 1957, 1, 22 April 1957, 24.

35. *New York Times*, 7 May 1957, 1; 22 May 1957, 3; 23 May 1957, 6; 31 May 1957, 1; 22 June 1957, 4.

36. *New York Times*, 4 June 1957, 1; 6 June 1957, 1, 17.

37. *Minutes of Telephone Conversations of John Foster Dulles 1953*, 11 June 57 (UPA).

38. Dulles memorandum for Eisenhower, 12 June 1957, DDRS (79) 195B; *New York Times*, 26 June 1957, 10.

39. *New York Times*, 3 July 1957, 4, 1; 10 July 1957, 10.

40. *New York Times*, 10 July 1957, 7; 14 July 1957, 32; 16 July 1957, 11; 17 July 1957, 3, 2 August 1957, 3; 6 August 1957, 3.

41. Briefing memorandum, undated [September or October 1957], DDRS (82), 00024; NIE 12-2-57, 3 December 1957, DDRS (77), 6A.

42. "Effects on Taiwan of a Cessation of Taiwan—Japan Trade," 26 March 1958, DDRS (75), 129D.

43. NSC 5516/1, 30 March 1959, DDRS (81), 175A; DDRS (81), 175B.

44. See, for example, "Report on Japan," 4 May 1960, DDRS (82), 000224; NSC 6008, 20 May 1960, DDRS (82), 000607.

45. *New York Times*, 8 November 1963, 3; Wright to Rusk, 1 December 1963, DDRS (77), 118C.

46. Rusk to Wright, 31 December 1963, DDRS (77), 118E; Wright to Rusk, 31 December 1963, DDRS (77), 118D.

47. 1 May 1964, DDRS (77), 22H.

48. 29 May 1965 DDRS (76), 89A.

49. Reischauer to Department of State, 14 February 1966, DDRS (78), 84B.

50. FE Chiefs of Mission to Rusk, 2 March 1966 DDRS (78), 179B; CIA memorandum DDRS (80), 126A.

51. American Embassy, Tokyo to Department of State 8 July 1966, DDRS (77), 334C.

52. Reischauer to Rusk, 13 August 1966, DDRS (78), 69C.

53. Armin H. Meyer, *Assignment: Tokyo* (Indianapolis, IN, 1974), 122.

54. Meyer, 123.

55. Chalmers Johnson, "The Patterns of Japanese Relations with China, 1952-1982," *Pacific Affairs* 59 (1986): 405.

4

The Security Treaty Revision of 1960

TADASHI ARUGA

In 1960, a new security treaty was concluded between Japan and the United States, and its ratification caused a political turmoil in Japan. The episode obviously belongs to the past era of U.S.-Japanese relations, during which the United States continued to play the role of the powerful, confident, and generous protector of the "Free World." Since then, great change has taken place in both countries, in their mutual relations, and in the international context of their relations. The security treaty of 1960, however, has survived despite these twenty-five years of drastic change. It may, therefore, be worth reviewing the episode of 1960 in historical perspective, reflecting on such questions as how the treaty was negotiated and why the treaty generated such strong opposition in Japan.

When Japan regained its sovereignty in 1952, it began a new national career without consensus on defense and security issues. The Socialist parties, representing the neutralist-antiarmament segment of the public, stood for a policy of unarmed neutrality. Because Article IX of the Constitution of 1947 seemed to many Japanese to be the embodiment of new national identity, the Socialists were able to claim legitimacy for their stand. For them, unarmed neutrality was not only a matter of better security but also a matter of principle. They were more critical of the security alliance than of the peace treaty itself. They were split into the right and left wings over the issue of approving the partial peace treaty, but both groups were opposed to the security treaty. Although the conservative parties accepted security ties with the Unites States, some conservatives were discontented with the unilateral character of the security treaty of 1951, considering it unbecoming for a sovereign nation. Many conservatives, especially Prime Minister Yoshida's rivals, desired to begin rearmament and to negotiate treaty revision with the United States as soon as possible.[1]

The security treaty of 1951 gave the United States the right to position its military forces in and around Japan without imposing any legal responsibility to defend Japan. The treaty provided merely that these forces "may be utilized to contribute" to the security of Japan. Furthermore, the United States, while assuming no definite defense responsibility, could use its forces in Japan for purposes not directly related to the defense of Japan. If the purpose was "to contribute to the maintenance of international peace and security in the Far East," the United States could freely use Japanese bases for offensive operations. This unilateral character was the major source of dissatisfaction for conservative nationalists. The treaty contained an article providing that U.S. forces could be utilized "at the express request of the Japanese government" to put down "large-scale internal riots and disturbances in Japan."[2] Although many Japanese conservatives were afraid of indirect aggression by their communist neighbors, they were not comfortable with this provision, which reminded them of the impotence of their nation. Premier Yoshida's conservative rivals, expressing conservative nationalism, advocated rearmament through constitutional revision, reexamination of reforms introduced under the occupation, and a quest for more independent diplomacy, which included revisions in the security arrangement with the United States.

Yoshida and his followers had ascended to power during the occupation and had brought forth the peace settlement of 1951. On the other hand, his rivals, mostly outsiders under the occupation regime, had been "purged" for several years, and some had been imprisoned as war criminals or suspects in Sugamo prison. Naturally, they were more critical of the legacy of the occupation, especially of its earlier phase, and took a more critical attitude toward the present security arrangement. They tended to represent conservative nationalism in their challenge to Yoshida's leadership. Hatoyama Ichirō was their central figure. His illness had delayed his challenge to Yoshida, but he finally succeeded in reaching the seat of power in December 1954.

The new premier emphasized a "spirit of friendship and love" as the spiritual basis of his domestic and international policies. He took a positive attitude toward improving Japan's relations with its communist neighbors, contending that ways should be sought for peaceful coexistence with communist nations. He enjoyed great popularity for a while; in February 1955, Hatoyama's Democratic party considerably increased its seats in the lower house at the expense of the Liberals. In spite of the increases, however, the governmental party still remained a minority in the lower house. This lack of majority support for the government, and the prospect of a Socialist power challenge, stimulated a merger movement among the Democrats and the Liberals. In the fall of 1955, the two parties merged to form the Liberal Democratic party (LDP). Almost simultaneously, the left wing and right wing socialist parties united to form the Socialist party (JSP). Thus emerged a situation that Japanese political scientists often call the "system of 1955."[3]

Premier Hatoyama favored rearmament and the removal of Article IX from the Constitution. But constitutional revision was impossible, since the Socialists occupied more than one-third of the seats of the lower house. Besides, it was financially difficult for the Japanese government to expand significantly the size of the defense budget. Partly motivated by a wish to demonstrate to Washington the scope of its efforts toward rearmament, the Japanese government prepared a six-year plan, which envisaged an increase of ground self-defense forces to 180,000 within three years.[4] With this plan in his pocket, Foreign Minister Shigemitsu Mamoru visited Washington in August 1955 to negotiate on such matters as revision of the security treaty and return of Okinawa and the Bonin Islands.

When Shigemitsu proposed revision of the security treaty, however, he met a blunt rejection by Secretary of State John Foster Dulles. Shigemitsu explained that the treaty was thought of as unequal and therefore was not popular among the Japanese. Referring to the Vandenberg resolution, however, Dulles pointed out that the United States could commit itself to defend Japan only within a genuinely collective security arrangement. In such an arrangement, he said, Japan would have to assume military obligations beyond its own territories.[5]

Spurned by Washington, Hatoyama intensified his effort to score a diplomatic point in Moscow. After negotiations for a peace treaty were deadlocked, Hatoyama himself visited Moscow in 1956, where he normalized Japan's relations with the Soviet Union by way of a joint declaration.[6] This opened the way for Japan to join the United Nations in December 1956. When Hatoyama retired after this diplomatic achievement, Ishibashi Tanzan was elected as his successor in December. Like Hatoyama, Ishibashi advocated improvement of Japan's relations with communist neighbors and hoped to develop economic and political relations with the Beijing regime. But he became ill soon after the start of his administration and resigned in February 1957.[7] The premiership was passed to Vice Prime Minister Kishi Nobusuke.

Kishi, a former bureaucrat who had served as a minister in General Tōjō's wartime cabinet, was a statesman of considerable ability. Held in Sugamo Prison after World War II, he had made a phenomenal comeback to become an important political figure in postwar Japan. Kishi was a nationalist, but he was also acutely aware of American power. His vision was of a rising new Japan in a firm partnership with the United States. This partnership would enable Japan to play the role of a major power in Asia. Thus Kishi visited South Asian countries in May 1957 for his first overseas trip as prime minister, and in November, made his second trip to Southeast Asia, which included a visit to Australia and New Zealand.

The itinerary of one of his Asian trips included Taibei where he had talks with Chiang Kai-shek. Kishi emphasized Japan's close ties with Nationalist

China, and although he also favored developing trade relations with the People's Republic, his intimacy with Taibei irritated Beijing. In May 1958, just before general elections in Japan, the Beijing regime suspended all trade with Japan, bitterly criticizing the policy of the Kishi cabinet.[8] This certainly dismayed Fujiyama Aiichirō, who had become foreign minister in July 1957. He entertained an earnest hope to develop Japanese relations with Beijing.[9]

Kishi hoped to put U.S.-Japanese relations on a more equal basis by revising the security treaty, the unilateral character of which he regarded as a legacy of the occupation. Remembering, however, Dulles's cold response to Shigemitsu's plea for revision in 1955, Kishi approached this issue cautiously in public statements.[10] Washington showed a much higher regard for Premier Kishi than it had shown for his two predecessors. He seemed to be more pro-American and more eager than Yoshida to make Japan a positive partner of the United States. He was also relatively young and was expected to continue his leadership role for some years. "Mr. Kishi gives every indication of being the strongest government leader to emerge in postwar Japan," Dulles wrote in a memorandum for President Dwight D. Eisenhower just before Kishi's visit to Washington. "He has emphasized that he desires the establishment of a full partnership with the United States." With his coming to power, Dulles thought, "a period of drift" was over in Japan.[11] Official Washington welcomed Kishi warmly and gave him wide publicity. Dulles remarked that his visit opened a new era in the relations of the two nations, an era that would be much more "on a basis of cooperation than on a basis of the exercise by the United States of unilateral rights."[12]

Dulles understood Kishi's desire to revise the security treaty. "I feel that the time has come," he wrote to Eisenhower, "to take the initiative in proposing a readjustment of our relations with Japan and to suggest to Mr. Kishi that we work toward a mutual security arrangement which could, we would hope, replace the present Security Treaty."[13] When Kishi conferred with Eisenhower and Dulles at the White House on June 25, Dulles said, "We all believe that the important thing is to develop a relationship of real mutuality and real cooperation and our best chance to do that is under the leadership of the present Prime Minister . . . in whom we can have confidence and who has a genuine dedication to the principles of the free world."[14] Eisenhower praised Kishi's public address in Washington and said to him, "Now that you have achieved this personal trust we can move constructively."[15] The only concrete result relating to the security treaty was the decision to set up an intergovernmental committee to study "problems arising in relation to the Security Treaty."[16] But Kishi was impressed by Washington's friendliness and was encouraged by its understanding reception of his ideas for revising the security treaty. Another result of his visit was an agreement on the withdrawal of U.S. ground combat troops from Japan.[17]

A joint committee was soon organized of the Japanese foreign and defense ministers, the U.S. ambassador, and the U.S. commander in the Pacific region. Although the terms of the agreement allowed the joint committee to discuss treaty revision, the committee limited its practice to discussing matters relating to the execution of the existing treaty.[18] Meanwhile, the Ministry of Foreign Affairs was studying how the existing security arrangement would be revised. Anticipating the difficulty of inducing the United States to assume a treaty obligation to defend Japan unless the latter were prepared to assume a similar obligation for U.S. Pacific possessions, Foreign Ministry officials did not plan to revise the treaty itself. They thought of supplementing the treaty with several agreements, which would include an American assurance of military cooperation with the Japanese self-defense forces in case of an act of foreign aggression upon Japan. They also sought an American promise to consult with the Japanese government before undertaking combat operation initiated from Japanese bases and directed outside Japan. Such supplementary agreements, they considered, would be enough to remove basic Japanese grievances. They tended to feel that this was the maximum Japan could hope to achieve.[19] An exchange of letters on September 14, 1957, between Foreign Minister Fujiyama and Ambassador Douglas MacArthur II, clarified the relationship of the treaty with the U.N. Charter and was a step toward piecemeal modifications of the treaty.

In July 1958, Foreign Minister Fujiyama Aiichirō conferred several times with Ambassador MacArthur (nephew and namesake of General MacArthur) on security matters. In their meeting of July 30, MacArthur stated that there were two ways to modify the existing security arrangements: one was to supplement the present treaty by a series of new agreements on particular issues, and the other was to replace it by a new treaty of greater mutuality. Understanding that the Constitution prohibited Japan from sending armed forces overseas, the ambassador asked whether the Japanese government would prefer a new treaty of the mutual assistance type if it was possible to devise such a treaty compatible with the Constitution. After Fujiyama's return from the U.N. General Assembly, he and Prime Minister Kishi held a meeting with MacArthur on August 25, in which Kishi expressed his preference for a new treaty, observing that only a new treaty could put U.S.-Japanese relations on a firm and stable basis.

In early September, Fujiyama left Tokyo for Washington to confer with Dulles. Dulles indicated his willingness to explore the possibility, and joint communiqué, issued on September 11, announced, "It was agreed that the two governments would consult further on this matter through diplomatic channels following Mr. Fujiyama's return to Tokyo."[20] According to Fujiyama's report in the Diet and his later recollection, he outlined for Dulles the main points of revision desired by the Japanese government: (1) the treaty should be revised in such a way as to conform to the new international status of Japan; (2) the United States should assume the obligation to help defend Japan against attack; (3) Japanese obligations should be limited to those compatible with the Constitution; (4) Japan should be consulted before the United States changes the disposition and/or equipment of its forces in Japan, or uses bases in Japan for operational purposes for the peace and security of the Far East; and (5) the treaty should be effective for a limited period.[21] Dulles knew the United States could not expect much from Japan. He told Fujiyama that he was willing to negotiate a new treaty that might require the United States to concede much for an insufficient gain because he regarded the spirit of friendship to be much more important than legal privileges and obligations.[22]

Beginning with the meeting of October 4, in which Kishi himself participated, Fujiyama, MacArthur, and their respective aides met often to discuss treaty revision during the fall. An American draft treaty was offered for discussion, which includes these terms: (1) the treaty would be called the "treaty of mutual cooperation and security" and would define mutual cooperation broadly, including political and economic as well as security matters; (2) the parties, individually and in cooperation with each other, by means of self-help and mutual aid, would maintain and develop their capacities to exercise the right of individual and collective defense against armed attack; (3) each party would agree to recognize that an armed attack against either party in the Pacific area would be dangerous to its own peace and safety and to declare that it would act to meet the common danger in accordance with its constitutional provisions and processes; (4) the existing executive agreement regarding the use of Japanese bases by U.S. forces would be continued under the new treaty; and (5) after ten years, each party could give notice to the other party of its intention to terminate the treaty one year later. The American negotiators also submitted two supplementary documents, one of which provided that prior consultation with the Japanese government was required when the United States made major changes in the deployment of armed forces in Japan or when the United States used bases in Japan for military combat operations not directly related to the defense of Japan.[23] This American proposal showed that the American side had made an effort to consider the Japanese position stated by Fujiyama in his conference with Dulles.

The Japanese negotiators proposed several revisions to the draft. First, they wanted to delete the term "collective defense" from the text, because the Japanese interpreted their Constitution as prohibiting Japan from exercising the right of collective defense. It took some time to explain this to the American side, but finally the phrase was dropped. Second, the Japanese side could not agree to extend the treaty area to include the Pacific region. This extension of the treaty area was a key to the mutuality envisaged by the Americans. Although, the provision did not envision sending Japanese armed forces outside Japan under the existing Constitution, the possibility of such an extension of the treaty area was too drastic for Japan. MacArthur soon understood the political infeasibility for the Japanese government of agreeing to such an extension and appeared ready to begin to persuade Washington on the matter.[24] Prime Minister Kishi and other Japanese officials thought of including Okinawa and Ogasawara (the Bonin Islands) in the treaty area. Kishi defended the idea in the Diet on October 23, but public opinion strongly opposed the inclusion of these islands, and there was doubt about the constitutionality of such an arrangement. Within the government, the minister in charge of the Defense Agency also took a negative attitude. Thus Foreign Minister Fujiyama stated on November 23 that the new treaty would not include these islands, adding that it could therefore be primarily characterized as a kind of base-lease treaty.[25]

In other respects, the American proposal was largely satisfactory to Japanese governmental leaders. It is likely that the Japanese negotiators did not insist on writing the "prior consultation" clause into the treaty itself, satisfied with the American proposal to put it into a supplementary document. Once the U.S. negotiators took an understanding attitude regarding the points to which the Japanese had objected, there emerged a basic agreement on the nature of the treaty. By the time the Japanese government asked the United States to suspend the negotiations temporarily because of disunity within the LDP in late November 1958, basic agreement had apparently been reached. It may be said that the revisions Kishi and Fujiyama intended were less matters of substance than of face and national sentiment. If the United States assumed the obligation to defend Japan against attack, then the security arrangement would no longer be one-sided. If Japan could have a voice regarding certain activities of the U.S. forces stationed in Japan, then its national prestige would be honored and the national feeling satisfied. Such revisions could be carried out by supplementing the existing treaty with joint declarations, but governmental leaders wanted a new treaty precisely because the revisions were matters of face and sentiment.

Kishi's leadership over the party was limited because he was primarily a boss of one faction and had to negotiate with other leaders, those within as well as those outside his coalition. In an effort to weaken faction leaders who were not in partnership with him, Kishi excluded the opposition from the important party posts and largely barred members of their factions from his second cabinet. This move was counterproductive for his leadership, because faction leaders outside his coalition tended to refuse to cooperate in carrying controversial pieces of legislation in the Diet. Their refusal to support the police practice bill in December 1958 is a case in point.[26] Kishi's attempt to enact the bill at that time was a tactical mistake, if his primary aim was the conclusion of a new security treaty. Because there was no national consensus on security matters, and because the Socialists had always mounted spirited opposition to important security bills in the past, he should have carefully mapped out the strategy of overcoming their expected opposition. Although the Socialists had sometimes appeared to support certain kinds of treaty revision, they adopted the policy of outright opposition soon after the beginning of negotiations was announced.[27] He should have avoided raising such a minor, but politically very explosive, issue without the united support of his own party. The issue dramatized disunity within the LDP, provided opposition parties and associations with an experience of vigorous mass protests and a taste of victory, and gave a large segment of the public misgivings about the nature of his policy.

It was when factional cleavages over the police practice bill began to be apparent that Kishi and Fujiyama explained their plan of a new security treaty to the LDP chieftains and asked for their support. Responses were without enthusiasm. Faction leaders did not want to see Kishi's hand strengthened by getting credit for what now seemed to be an easy task. They were also afraid that Fujiyama, a wealthy businessman who had entered politics, might become a powerful leader in the near future, and they did not want to give him an easy diplomatic success. Some faction leaders, such as Ikeda Hayato and Miki Takeo, suggested that it was too early for the government to open such negotiations. Even Kōno Ichirō, an influential boss who was then in partnership with Kishi, caused much trouble for Kishi and Fujiyama by criticizing the treaty plan. Just when they decided to eliminate Okinawa and Ogasawara from the treaty area, Kōno began to argue strongly for the inclusion of these islands. Kōno and his supporters maintained that such an arrangement would strengthen Japan's voice in matters concerning these islands. Some members even declared that the Japanese government should get some promise from the United States regarding the return of these islands to Japan.[28]

After Kishi reshuffled his cabinet in January 1959, hoping to consolidate his power, the foreign minister submitted the so-called Fujiyama Plan to a policy discussion meeting of the party. The plan enumerated the provisions to be written in a new treaty. Because the Fujiyama Plan outlined fairly accurately the major features of the treaty to be concluded the following year, we may assume that U.S. and Japanese negotiators had reached basic agreement on the major features of the new treaty.[29] This illustrates why Fujiyama said several times in the early months of 1959 that the treaty could be concluded very soon. But the plan was not accepted by the party members.[30]

After lengthy discussions between the governmental leaders and the party elders, the two documents, "The LDP's Principles on Treaty Revision" and "The LDP's Principles on the Revision of the Executive Agreement," were approved by the party council in mid-April. The first document accepted the principles enumerated in the Fujiyama Plan. The second document, however, called for negotiating simultaneously for substantial revision of the executive agreement, which Kishi and Fujiyama had wanted to postpone.[31] Although Kishi thus secured the formal support of the party, a number of party members still expressed misgivings on the nature of the projected treaty. For example, Kōno insisted even then that the ten-year term of the treaty was too long. Occasionally others still revealed their lukewarm attitude,[32] but on April 23, Foreign Minister Fujiyama was able at last to reopen negotiations with Ambassador MacArthur. In the fifth meeting, held on May 23, agreement was reached regarding the provisions of the new treaty. Thus Fujiyama was able to outline its details in a public address two days later.[33] The negotiators continued to meet regularly until January 1960, but these meetings were devoted to negotiations for a new executive agreement.[34]

In October 1958, the Socialist party (JSP) decided to oppose the security treaty revision that Kishi intended to negotiate.[35] At that time, the JSP was primarily concerned with blocking the passage of the police practice revisions bill. A national headquarters was established through the JSP's initiative in cooperation with labor and other progressive organizations for the purpose of encouraging and coordinating a mass movement to oppose the bill. When Kishi was forced to back down mainly because of disunity among the LDP, the JSP wanted to switch the focus of the national organization to a mass movement opposing the security treaty revisions. More moderate, less politicized labor organizations did not support the JSP's proposal.[36] But in March 1959 Sōhyō (the Japanese General Council of Trade Unions), the largest labor organization, took the initiative to organize a mass movement against Kishi's security treaty revisions and Japan's security tie with the United States. The JSP, having lost the initiative, decided to join the organization proposed by Sōhyō, and reluctantly agreed to cooperation with the Communists (JCP) in the organization. Because the JCP had considerable influence in peace organizations, it was impossible for the JSP to insist that the JCP be excluded. The JSP did succeed in denying the JCP full membership in the top decision-making body of the organization. The JSP also insisted that the organization be called the National Conference for Joint Struggle against Security Treaty Revisions, limiting its immediate purpose to opposing the treaty revisions the Kishi cabinet was proposing.[37] Although the JSP's ultimate aim was to dissolve Japan's security ties with the United States, it was opposed to including this aim in the name of the new national organization. In this way, the Socialists hoped to win the support of more moderate elements of the public.

Although a national organization was thus established to conduct an anti-treaty revision campaign and coordinate mass movements, there was rivalry and infighting between the Socialists and the Communists. The two parties were different in strength, organization, and ideology. As a parliamentary party, the JSP was by far stronger than the JCP. The JSP was a component of the two-party system created in 1955, although its Diet members were only a little more than half of the LDP's members in the Diet.[38] The JCP, on the other hand, had only one member in the Lower House and another in the Upper House. It had not recovered from the setback it had experienced in the days of underground violence. As a party, however, the JCP had more organizational strength than the JSP.

In elections, the JSP depended on the votes of nonmembers and on organizational and financial help by labor organizations. To block legislation it opposed in the Diet, it had to depend on mass media support and mass movements, and on manipulating factional rivalries within the LDP. The JSP's dependence on labor unions explains why the party had to follow Sōhyō's initiative in organizing national opposition to security treaty revision. The party's dependence upon mass media and public opinion explains why it wanted to delete the phrase "Abolition of the U.S.-Japanese Security System" from the name of the national organization. The Socialists did not want to look overly radical; at the same time they tended to take a tolerant attitude toward radical activist students and workers, for they depended on nonparty activists for mass movement.

The Socialists had their own internal disunity. Intraparty friction between the right and left had continued after their merger in 1955. Because the left wing was strong among the party workers, there had been pressure to keep party discipline along the left-wing lines. Nishio Suehiro was the left wing's major target; when they tried to discipline Nishio for his rightist deviation in the fall of 1959, he and his followers left the JSP with the intention of organizing a new moderate socialist party. He wanted to take all of the right-wing elements from the JSP, but the major right-wing faction, led by Kawakami Jōtarō, decided to remain in the JSP. The Nishio group first organized the Socialist Club in November 1959 and then launched the Democratic Socialist party (DSP) in January 1960. This split of the JSP foretold its gradual decline in the 1960s and 1970s, but the DSP has not made any remarkable growth, either. The birth of the new moderate socialist party did not benefit the Kishi cabinet, because the DSP, which today supports the security treaty, was then opposed to it. The defection of the Nishio group drove the JSP to put more effort into the anti-treaty movement and to look for a chance to bring down Kishi, whom they regarded as the most reactionary of the LDP leaders.[39]

The Communist party had its own mass party organization composed of devoted party members. Their number was not enough to elect communists to the Diet, but they were a powerful asset for the party in conducting a mass movement. Both the JSP and the JCP were opposed to treaty revision, but the JCP emphasized the purpose of abolishing the whole security arrangement with the United States, whereas the JSP emphasized opposition to a new treaty, deferring to the future the dissolution of all security ties with the United States. Behind this tactical difference, there were ideological and strategic differences between them. The Socialists aimed to move Japan toward a neutral position and thus to stimulate a global trend toward peace and disarmament. They wanted to take an equidistant position toward the two superpowers. If they had strong sympathy to the Chinese People's Republic, it was primarily because of their sense of war guilt and their sympathy with the Third World; they had little sympathy with the Soviet Union. They observed that the Kishi government was trying to achieve the status of a more active partner within the anti-communist alliance and that it would create new international tensions in the Far East. Therefore, their target was the Kishi government, not the United States.[40]

The Communists, on the other hand, held that Japan was still under U.S. control and that negotiations for a new security treaty had been initiated by the United States. Therefore, their primary enemy was not the Kishi government but the United States. They wanted to make the mass anti-treaty-revision movement anti-American rather than anti-Kishi. Because their enemy was formidable, the movement must be a persistent one. Thus they were opposed to excesses in violence, especially violence committed by antiparty radical students. The major student organization, *Zengakuren*, was largely controlled by radicals of the Communist League (Bund), who did not follow the JCP.[41]

Coordinated by the National Congress, the anti-treaty-revision movement gradually intensified in 1959. The congress sponsored ten mass-meeting-and-demonstration days in the year.[42] Meanwhile, negotiations between the two governments continued, and in January 1960 complete agreement was reached on the texts of the new security treaty, the revised executive agreement, and other related documents. The new treaty was signed in Washington by Premier Kishi and Secretary of State Christian Herter, who had succeeded Dulles in April 1959.

In the new treaty, as in the old one, the United States was granted the privilege of using facilities and areas in Japan for its military forces for the purpose of "contributing to the security of Japan and the maintenance of international peace and security in the Far East" (Article VI). It had been one of the basic aims of the Japanese government in treaty revision to gain a voice regarding the actions and equipment of the U.S. forces stationed in Japan.

The United States acknowledged this arrangement in a document attached to the treaty. The treaty assigned to the United States an obligation to help Japan defend itself in case of attack, which in turn pledged Japan to act against attack on American forces in Japanese territory (Article V). Japan was to maintain and develop its capacities to resist armed attack (Article II). Although the treaty area was limited to territories under Japanese administration, Japan was committed in some degree to cooperating with American policy in the general area of the Far East: Article IV provided that the two countries would "consult together . . . whenever the security of Japan or international peace and security in the Far East is threatened." Thus the new treaty changed Japan's role from a passive to a more active one in Far Eastern defense.[43]

The vocal public strongly criticized the published treaty. Many were afraid that the new treaty would oblige Japan to develop large-scale armed forces, and they did not show much appreciation for the U.S. commitment to the defense of Japan. The United States promised, in an attached document, prior consultation with Japan on certain activities of U.S. forces using Japanese bases, but the Japanese wanted veto power, not mere consultation. They also contended that the term Far East was not clarified geographically in the treaty. Some considered a ten-year term too long for such a treaty. Many Japanese publicists and intellectuals, who were not nesessarily leaning toward the left, voiced doubts about the wisdom of concluding such a treaty in haste. No major newspaper took a clear stand on the new treaty. Their editorials, however, stated that there were problems to be debated and recommended that the Diet discuss them thoroughly.[44] When the Foreign Minister gave conflicting answers to questions about the geographical definition of the Far East, this episode was given wide publicity in the media.[45] Government spokesmen were failing to convince the public of the merit of the treaty. In an opinion survey conducted in January 1960, 29 percent of those polled regarded the new treaty as "good" and 25 percent regarded it as "bad." In another opinion survey, conducted two months later, those who regarded the treaty as bad increased to 36 percent, while only 21 percent regarded it as good.[46]

Meanwhile, the U-2 incident and the subsequent cancellation of a U.S.-Soviet summit conference increased anxiety over the propsect of a close alliance between the United States and Japan. After the U-2 was shot down in the Soviet Union, it was disclosed that three U-2s were stationed in Japan. American authorities announced that the U-2s operating from Japanese bases had been engaged in weather observation only, and Prime Minister Kishi stated that, as far as he knew, U-2s based in Japan had never invaded the air space of other countries. But most Japanese would not be satisfied with such assurances. The Soviet Union warned of possible retaliation against Japanese bases because U-2 planes had invaded the Soviet Union.[47] The Japanese public was filled with anxiety over the danger accompanying a military alliance with the United States. In the atmosphere of May 1960, risks involved in the treaty, rather than its merits, tended to be dramatized. Opposition to the new treaty was gaining momentum.

Confronted with this, Prime Minister Kishi and most of his party members were determined to extend the Diet session scheduled to end on May 25 and to push the treaty through the lower house quickly, overcoming any possible opposition. The treaty was approved on May 20, but at a cost of great confusion. The opposition parties angrily denied the validity of the endorsement and demanded an immediate dissolution of the Diet. Leading newspapers bitterly criticized the prime minister and his party. The press did not overlook the sitdown tactics taken by the Socialists, but they regarded the tactics of the Liberal Democrats as a far more unpardonable violation of the spirit and procedures of parliamentary democracy. The vocal public was indignant at the extraordinary way in which the government handled such an important issue. Opposition to the treaty itself was now joined by opposition to the open disregard by the government of the spirit of parliamentary democracy. Various groups and associations, mostly nonpolitical, joined in the demand for the resignation of Premier Kishi and the dissolution of the Diet. Antigovernment demonstrations were repeated almost daily in Tokyo, and demonstrations spread into provincial cities. Important labor unions, including the National Railroad Workers Union, began short-hour strikes in protest against the government.[48]

If Kishi had called for a general election in the spring, he would have succeeded more easily in securing the Diet's approval for the new treaty and without much public criticism. Again, he had made a tactical mistake.[49] If Premier Kishi had been willing to postpone the vote on the treaty to the next session and had announced his intention of calling a general election before the vote, he might have secured its approval without bringing on political disaster. But he desired to secure ratification by June 19, the day President Eisenhower was to arrive in Japan. According to the Constitution, a treaty approved by the lower house is automatically given the approval of the Diet after one month, even if it is pending in the upper house. This explains why the Liberal Democrats pushed the treaty through the lower House early on the morning of May 20.

Informed of the political turmoil in Japan, President Eisenhower and Secretary of State Christian Herter considered postponing their visit for about two months until after the Republican national convention.[50] In Tokyo, Ambassador MacArthur told Vice Foreign Minister Yamada Hisanari that he thought postponement "made sense."[51] The Kishi administration, however, strongly desired to have the presidential visit in June as scheduled, and when told of this the president was willing.[52]

Opponents of the prime minister and of the security treaty were against the visit of the president, especially because they now suspected that Kishi would use Eisenhower's visit to escape the current political crisis. When Presidential press secretary James Hagerty arrived in Japan on June 10 to arrange schedule details, he was surrounded at Haneda airport by demonstrators shouting their opposition to Eisenhower's visit. Washington was shocked by this incident and instructed the U.S. embassy to reopen the issue of postponement. Secretary of State Herter noted that the incident had caused "grave misgivings among those who had staunchly supported the visit." It was feared, he stated, "that if a serious incident or rioting should take place when the President was in Japan, there could be a strong revival of anti-Japanese feeling in the United States, with resultant grave adverse effects on Japanese-American relations."[53]

Even before he received this message, Ambassador MacArthur, who had been with Hagerty at Haneda, met with Vice Foreign Minister Yamada on June 11 and warned him that the Japanese government had "the heaviest imaginable responsibility" regarding the presidential visit. The next day he met with Kishi and expressed his misgivings. But Kishi continued to encourage the visit as scheddled, noting a new tone of welcome in the Japanese press.[54] The media, horrified by the prospect of great confusion at the time of the presidential visit, began to call for the public to calm its temper and to welcome the important guest.[55]

The president left Washington for his Far Eastern tour on June 12, but Herter repeatedly directed MacArthur to report Kishi's latest evaluation and also the embassy's own assessment of the feasibility of Eisenhower's visit. As late as June 15, Fujiyama conveyed the administration's desire for the scheduled visit and stressed that the government was taking all necessary measures to guarantee the safety of the presidential party. Thereupon the ambassador cabled that the embassy believed "the balance of advantage clearly lies in going ahead with the visit as planned."[56] But the antigovernment movement was coming to a climax.

That night, student radicals invaded the yard of the Diet building. One female student was killed, and many other students were injured in an ensuing battle with the police. Kishi and his close associates thought of mobilizing ground troops of the self-defense forces to protect the American visitors against possible violence by student radicals. But Akagi Munenori, the minister in charge of the Defense Agency, did not agree to their use for such a purpose. If the self-defense forces were employed to suppress violent but unarmed activists, he feared it would damage their public image.[57] On the following day, having heard the opinion of the chairman of the Public Safety Commission, the Kishi cabinet finally concluded that the government must ask President Eisenhower to postpone his trip to Japan.[58]

The treaty automatically became effective on June 20 without any action being taken by the upper house. The government completed ratification procedures the next day. The United States Senate, which had been watching the situation in Japan, ratified the treaty on June 22. The exchange of ratification documents was made the next day in Tokyo, and the new treaty became effective immediately. Premier Kishi and his cabinet resigned on July 15. Three days later, Ikeda Hayato was elected premier in an extra session of the Diet attended by all parties, including the opposition. The political confusion that had shaken Japan for two months now subsided. The general elections held in November returned the LDP to power with a large majority in the lower house and stabilized Japanese politics.

Given the subsequent history of the security treaty, it may seem rather strange that opposition to the treaty could mobilize such mass protests in early 1960. To be sure, consensus did not exist with regard to security and defense issues, but if Kishi had carefully mapped out his strategy for getting Diet approval of the treaty, he might have gained it without bringing forth such political turmoil. He should have tactfully consolidated his party first. Moreover, he committed several tactical mistakes; his attempt to enact the police practice bill and his failure to call general elections in early 1960 are examples.

There was also the personal factor. As many observers noted, the antitreaty fever was primarily anti-Kishi rather than anti-American. Among the Japanese public there was considerable distrust of Kishi, who had been a member of the Tōjō cabinet. This suspicion and fear, fueled by several international events in the spring of 1960, precipitated the feverish anti-treaty movement.

In the larger historical perspective, the episode of 1960 affected changes since then in Japanese domestic politics, Japan's international circumstances, and the U.S.-Japanese relationship, especially its psychological aspect.

The security treaty revision of 1960 took place when the political system of 1955, an unbalanced two-party system, was about to change. In its place a system emerged that was composed of one dominant conservative party and several small center and left-wing parties. With the advent of center parties, sharp conflict over security and defense issues has been mitigated.

Changes in Japan's international circumstances also alleviated the intensity of domestic conflicts over security issues. Nixon-Kissinger diplomacy toward the two Communist giants drastically changed Japan's international environment. Washington's sudden rapprochement with Beijing was a shock to Tokyo, because relations with China had been a big issue in Japanese domestic politics. The Beijing leaders, however, wanted to improve China's relations with Japan as well as with the United States and began to suggest that they did not oppose U.S.-Japanese security treaty ties. In 1960, such ties had appeared to be incompatible with Japan's friendly relations with the People's Republic, but since 1972, the two have been compatible with each other. This change greatly weakened opposition to security ties with the United States. Although Soviet-American relations changed from détente to a new cold war in the early 1980s, this has not increased opposition to the ties.

The episode of 1960 belonged to an era in which there were wide gaps between Japanese and American power. In 1960 Japan was not a giant in any sense. The Japanese themselves regarded their country as a defeated nation just beginning to rise from the ashes. Thus they retained an inferiority complex. This atmosphere underlay both Kishi's desire to replace the old security treaty with a new one and the anti-security treaty fever as a form of national self-assertion. Along with this inferiority complex, many Japanese, in 1960, revealed a mentality of dependence, which Doi Takeo termed *amae*, toward the United States.[59] They presumed, because of the amae mentality, that Japan could enjoy American kindness whatever they did in opposition to the new security treaty. Their amae expectation was not misplaced. In 1960, the dominant American self-image was still that of the protector of the "Free World." The Americans therefore could be indulgent toward Japan. Not only did official Washington continue to express friendship toward Japan, but the American public also showed few signs of anti-Japanese feeling. The U.S. government attributed everything that happened in Japan to the conspiracy of international communism; and journalists and scholars knowledgeable about Japan explained that most of the demonstrators were not anti-American but anti-Kishi. The American public seemed to be satisfied by these explanations. Such indulgence can no longer be expected in American attitudes toward today's issues in U.S.-Japanese relations.

1. The impact of the peace on Japan's domestic politics was dealt with in detail by two very enlightening articles: Hara Akihisa, "Nichi'Bei anpo taisei to sengo no seiji taisei: Kokusaiseiji to kokunai seiji no renkan kozo—Anpo kaitei zenshi e no sekkin" (The Japan-U.S. security system and Japanese political process), *Kokusai shoka daigaku rons* (Kokusai Shoka University), No.28 (1983): 2-63; Igarashi Takeshi, "Sengo Nihon 'gaiko taisei' no keisei: Tai-Nichi kowa no teiketsu to seito seiji," *Kokka gakkai zasshi* 97, (5-6, 7-8) (1984): 343-409, 453-507 [An English version, "Peace-Making and Party Politics: the Formation of the Domestic Foreign-Policy System in Postwar Japan," was published in *Journal of Japanese Studies* 11, no. 2 (1985): 323-56].

2. For the text of the Security Treaty of 1951, see, for example, J.A.S. Grenville, ed., *The Major International Treaties, 1914-1973* (New York, 1975), 286-87.

3. Nihon seiji gakkai, ed., *55-nen taisei no keisei to hokai* (The emergence and disintegration of the system of 1955) *Nenpo seijigaku: 1977* (Tokyo, 1979).

4. The *Asahi*, March 12M [Morning edition], 15M, August 22M, 1955.

5. The *Asahi*, Sept. 4M, 1955.

6. Donald C. Hellmann, *Japanese Foreign Policy and Domestic Politics* (Berkeley, 1969) analyzes in detail the relationship between domestic politics and Japanese policy toward the Soviet Union. Washington's attitude toward Soviet-Japanese negotiations is discussed by James Morley, "The Soviet-Japanese Declaration," *Political Science Quarterly* 62(1957): 370-79.

7 . Hayashi Shigeru and Tsuji Kiyoaki, eds., *Nihon naikaku shiroku* [A history of the Japanese cabinets], 6 vols. (Tokyo, 1981), Vol. 5, 359-78, especially 373-74. Shiratori Rei, ed., *Nihon no naikau* [The Japanese cabinets], 3 vols. (Tokyo, 1981), vol. 2, 180-85; Tominomori Eiji, *Sengo hoshuto-shi* (A history of the conservative parties in Postwar Japan) (Tokyo, 1978), 81-82.

8. For a general survey of the history of postwar Sino-Japanese relations and relevant documents, see Furukawa Mantaro, *Nicchu sengo kankei-shi* (A history of postwar Sino-Japanese relations) (Tokyo, 1981); and Ikei Masaru, et al., eds., *Sengo shiryo Nicchu kankei* (Documents relating to postwar Sino-Japanese relations) (Tokyo, 1970). The diplomatic and internal political process which led to the breakdown of Tokyo-Beijing relations is analyzed in detail by Kusano Atsushi, "Dai yonji Nicchu boeki kyotei to Nikka funso" (The fourth Sino-Japanese trade agreement and Tokyo's conflicts with Peking and Taipei), *Kokusai seiji* 66(1980): 19-35; and Kishi Nobusuke, *Kishi Nobusuke kaiko roku: Hoshugodo to anpo kaitei* (The memoirs of Nobusuke Kishi: The creation of a United Conservative party and the security treaty revision) (Tokyo, 1983), 365-67, 408-12.

9. "When the issue of treaty revision has been dealt with," Fujiyama often confided to his intimates during his tenure as foreign minister, "China should come next in our domestic agenda." He hoped that, when the Japanese ties with the United States had been reaffirmed by the conclusion of a new security treaty, consensus within the LDP could be secured more easily for his policy of building better relations with the People's Republic. There was considerable difference between Kishi's and Fujiyama's views regarding China policy, which became quite apparent during the 1960s. While Fujiyama was in office, he was preoccupied with the issue of security treaty revision, but he made several attempts to communicate to Beijing his interest in better Sino-Japanese relations. For example, he appointed a China expert to a post in the Japanese embassy in Warsaw and let him contact Chinese diplomats there. See Fujiyama Aiichiro, *Seiji waga michi: Fujiyama Aiichiro kaisoroku* (Politics is my way: The memoirs of Fujiyama Aiichiro) (Tokyo, 1976), 172-75. This author also received valuable information on Fujiyama's ideas from Professor Yamamoto Mitsuru, a colleague at Hitotsubashi, who had covered the Foreign Ministry as a newspaperman when Fujiyama was in office.

10. The *Asahi*, Feb. 8E [Evening Edition], April 22E, 1957.

11. Dulles's memorandum for Eisenhower, "Official Visit to the U.S. of the Prime Minister of Japan, Mr. Nobusuke Kishi, June 12, 1957." *Declassified Documents Quarterly Calalog* (hereafter cited as *DDQC*), Vol. 5 (1979), 195B.

12. Richard D. Stebbins, *The United States in World Affairs, 1957* (New York, 1958), 245.

13. *DDQC*, vol 5, 195B.

14. *DDQC*, vol. 10, no. 2 (1984) 1051.

15. *ibid.*, 1051.

16. For the text of the joint communiqué, see *Documents on American Foreign Relations, 1957*, 320-24. Dulles's memorandum written for Eishenhower before Kishi's visit gives the impression that Dulles was willing to commit the United States to starting nogotiations or "discussions" on treaty revision . He wrote, "this is not the time to negotiate any of the specific provisions of the present treaty. . . . If, however, Prime Minister Kishi concurs in the proposal

that we have discussions looking forward to a common objective of a Mutual Security Treaty or some other mutually satisfactory security arrangement, we should be prepared, subsequent to his visit, to hold discussions with him in Tokyo." (His memorandum, June 12, 1957, *DDQC*). But nothing was mentioned in the joint communiqué regarding the opening of negotiations. Before making a commitment to such a procedure, Dulles had to consult the military, as he told Kishi (Kishi's memoirs, 332). As several documents indicate (*DDQC*, Vol. 6 [1980], 45B, 46ABC), the military was lukewarm on the matter. It is probably the main reason why Dulles avoided any commitment and instead proposed a joint committee.

17. Kishi's memoirs, 331-36; also see Kishi, Yatsugi Kazuo and Ito Takashi, *Kishi Nobusuke no kaiso* (Kishi Nobusuke Remembers) (Tokyo, 1981).

18. Togo Fumihiko, *Nichi-Bei gaiko sanju-nen [My thirty years in U.S.-Japanese diplomacy]* (Tokyo, 1982), 47.

19. *Togo*, 56-59.

20. *Documents on American Foreign Relations, 1958*, 482-83.

21. *Anpo kaitei mondai no kiroku* (Records on the problem of security treaty revision), edited by the research staff of the Cabinet Office and printed for the use of government officials (Tokyo, 1961), 24-26. This is the most useful collection of documents relating to the security treaty revisin of 1960 (hereafter as *Kiroku*). Also useful is Tsuji Kiyoaki, ed., *Shiryo sengo 20-nen-shi: Seiji* (A documentary history of postwar twenty years: politics) (Tokyo, 1966). Among the earlier studies on the security treaty revision of 1960 are George Packard, III, *Protest in Tokyo* (Princeton, NJ, 1966), a study of the anti-treaty revision movement; Robert A. Scalapino and Masumi Junnosuke, *Parties and Politics in Contemporary Japan* (Berkeley, 1962), which discusses in one chapter the domestic aspect of the treaty revision; and I.M. Destler et al., *Managing an Alliance* (Washington, DC, 1976) which used the security treaty revision as one of the three cases to draw general observations on alliance politics between Japan and the United States.

22. Fujiyama's memoirs, 72-73.

23. Togo, 70-73.

24. Togo, 74-78.

25. Togo, 78-80; The *Asahi*, Nov. 24M, Dec. 1M, 3M, 16M, 1958; The *Mainichi*, Nov. 16M, 1958.

26. Watanabe Tsuneo, *Habatsu* (Factions) (Tokyo, 1958), contains a detailed description of actions within the LDP at that time. See also Hayashi and Tsuji, eds., *Nihon naikaku-shi*, 5, 414-15, 422-28; and Shiratori, *Nihon no naikaku*, 2, 205-09.

27. The *Asahi*, Feb. 8E, April 22E, 1957; *Kiroku*, 167-68.

28. The *Mainichi*, Sept. 28M, Nov. 3M, Dec. 7M, 1958; the *Asahi*, Sept. 19M, 30M, Oct. 14, 1958. Later, Ikeda joined the Kishi cabinet and became a supporter of the treaty revision. His initial lukewarm attitude was related to misgivings of his mentor Yoshida about the wisdom of the treaty revision. Miki, on the other hand, remained critical of Kishi's policy and did not vote for the new treaty in the Lower House. Kōno was Kishi's supporter in 1958 in factional politics, but he shifted his position to become one of Kishi's critics in 1959 and 1960.

29. For the text of the Fujiyama Plan, see *Kiroku*, 5-7. See also Fujiyama's memoirs, 88.

30. The *Mainichi*, January 26, February 5, 8, 22, 1959.

31. *Kiroku*, 8-12. Also see the *Asahi*, February 26M, 28E, March 5M, 9M, April 4M, 9M, 11E, 1959; the *Mainichi*, February 1M, 5ME, 6M, 9M, 1959.

32. The *Asahi*, April 11E, 1959; the *Mainichi*, August 3M, 1959; for intra-LDP frictions over the issue of treaty revision, see also Kishi's memoirs, 498-99, 508-09, 532-33, 535; *Kishi Nobusuke no kaiso*, 240ff.; Fujiyama's memoirs, 93-98.

33. The *Asahi*, May 24M, 26M, 1959.

34. *Kiroku*, 62-63.

35. *Kiroku*, 67-68.

36. *Kiroku*, 84.

37. *Kiroku*, 84-86.

38. However, the JSP lost thirty-eight seats in the Lower House and eighteen in Upper House in the fall of 1959 because of the defection of the Nishio faction.

39. *Kiroku*, 313-15.

40. *Kiroku*, 176-83, 222-23.

41. *Kiroku*, 224-66, 266, 291, 293-94.

42. *Kiroku*, 696. This number is based on an estimate by the *Koan chosa shitsu*, which may be translated as the Public Safety Investigation Office.

43. For the text of the new treaty, see *Documents on American Foreign Relations, 1960*, 425-28.

44. For example, see the *Asahi*, January 21M, April 15M, May 13M, 1960; and the *Yomiuri*, February 5M, May 2M, 1960.

45. As for discussions on the definitions of the Far Eastern area, see the *Asahi*, February 10E, 11M, April 15M, 1960; the *Mainichi*, February 9M, 10M, 11E, 12M, 1960; the *Nihon keizai*, April 2M, 1960.

46. A nationwide opinion survey was conducted by the *Asahi* on January 11-12, 1960 (its results were published in the *Asahi*, January 18M, 1960). "Considering everything, do you think this treaty revision is good or bad?" To this question, 29 percent answered "good"; 25 percent answered "bad"; 6 percent gave other answers; 40 percent gave no answer. Another nationwide survey conducted by the *Mainichi* on March 14-16, 1960, the results of which were published in the *Mainichi*, April 5M, 1960, asked, "What do you think of the treaty?" To this question, 21 percent responded "good"; 36 percent responded "bad"; 15.3 percent responded "no interest"; 26.5 percent answered "I don't know."

47. The *Asahi*, May 10E, 11M, 21E, 1960.

48. The *Asahi*, May 20M, 1960; the *Mainichi* and the *Yomiuri*, May 20M, 1960; *Kiroku*, 148-50.

49. In his memoirs, Kishi says that he wanted to hold general elections in February 1960, but he was strongly advised against it by LDP's secretary general. He regrets that he lost this chance to call general elections to establish the legitimacy of his mandate. Kishi's memoirs, 533-34.

50. Herter to MacArthur, No. 2763, May 23, 1960, *Declassified Documents Reference System: Retrospective Collection* (hereafter cited as *DDRS*), 635A.

51. MacArthur to Herter, No. 3871, May 26, 1960, *DDRS*, 635C.

52. Herter to MacArthur, No. 2795, May 26, 1960, *DDRS*, 635D.

53. "Chronology of Ambassador MacArthur's Discussion with Prime Minister Kishi and Other Japanese Officials on the President's Visit to Japan," memorandum prepared by G. Graham Parsons for Herter, June 27, 1960, *DDRS*, 637A.

54. "Chronology of Ambassador MacArthur's Discussion . . . ," 637A.

55. The *Asahi*, June 12M, 14M, 1960; the *Mainichi*, June 11M, 12M, 13M, 14M, 1960; the *Yomiuri*, June 12M, 14M, 15M, 1960; and the *Nihon keizai*, June 11M, 16, 1960.

56. "Chronology of Ambassador MacArthur's Discussion . . . ,"637A.

57. Akagi Munenori, *Watakushi no rirekisho* (My life history) (Tokyo, 1973).

58. The *Asahi*, June 17M, 1960.

59. Doi Takeo, *The Anatomy of Dependence* (an English edition of his *Amae no kozo*) (Tokyo and New York, 1973).

5

Southeast Asia in U.S.-Japanese Relations

AKIO WATENABE

In August 1955, the world consisted of eighty-two independent countries, of which sixty-nine existed before World War II (Japan, China, Thailand, and Nepal included) and thirteen were postwar creations (Republic of Korea, Philippines, Pakistan, India, Burma, Ceylon, Indonesia, South Vietnam, Cambodia, and Laos among them).[1] These fourteen countries (four old and ten new) formed, for the first time in history, an Asian international society of independent nations.

The emergence of this Asian international society was a direct result of the Japanese war in the Pacific and Asia. Japan contributed to the emergence of this society first by its militaristic expansion and then by its defeat. Nothing was certain, however, about Japan's relations with Asia even after the conclusion of the San Fransisco peace treaty in September 1951. Japan was, more than anything else, a former enemy not only to most of the Asian countries but also to the rest of the world. In addition, Britain and other European countries were not sure about their future in Southeast Asia. Asian peoples had just realized their cherished dreams of independence or were on the verge of their fulfillment, but political situations in many of their countries were almost boiling. All of these conditions made Asia an ideal arena for new competition between the United States and the Soviet Union.

Against this background, it is remarkable that Japan successfully restored its former influence in Asia. The economic dependence of many Asian countries on Japan today is so great that some people argue that Japan has realized the dream of a Greater East Asia Coprosperity Sphere, despite its wartime defeat. How has this process come about? What factors have determined Japan's role in postwar Asia? What role did the Japanese themselves envisage for their country after their defeat? How did the Americans respond to the Japanese desire in the early postwar years? This essay will outline changing American attitudes toward the question of Japan's role in Asia and will discuss reactions of Japanese policymakers to shitfting international circumstances with particular reference to U.S.-Japanese relations in Southeast Asia.

A position paper of the Japanese government "On the promotion of economic cooperation with Southeast Asian Countries" (20 May 1953) characterizes the economic status of Asian countries as follows:

> Southeast Asian countries did not òccupy a very large place in world trade in 1949 with its share in the exports being 9.6 percent (as compared with 13.1 percent in 1937) and in the imports 10.9 percent (9.3 percent in 1937). However, with regard to such special products as rubber, tin, tea, vegetable oil, and jute, they used to get an exclusively large share in world exports, and there existed before the war so-called triangular patterns of trade in which Southeast Asian countries had a favorable balance of trade with the United States, which had a favorable balance with Europe and Japan, both of which in turn had a favorable balance with Southeast Asian countries. This structure of triangular trading relations has decomposed after the war, however, because the recovery of economy in Southeast Asia was slow and also because man-made substitutes for their products such as nylon and synthetic rubber contributed to a decline of their exports, with the result that they have now a trade deficit with the United States.[2]

The author of this position paper was obviously concerned with the changes brought about by various developments during and after the war to the traditional structure of Asian international trade. Before we analyze the attempted response to these changes by American and Japanese policymakers, it may be appropriate to have a brief look at the triangular trade patterns that existed between Southeast Asia, the United States, and Western Europe (plus Japan) before the Pacific war. The multiple relationships between Asia, the United States, and Europe in 1913, 1928, and 1938 may be represented by the three diagrams in the accompanying figure, in which each vector indicates the amount of trade surplus from one area to another, in terms of $10 million (new dollars, i.e., 1934 to 1971). In 1913, India provides a typical example of the triangular trade: it earned foreign money by selling its products to the United States (and Europe and Japan as well), which enabled it to buy manufactured goods from the United Kingdom. While India's case remained unchanged in 1928, a similar pattern emerged also with Southeast Asia, whose exports to the United States showed a marked increase, helping finance its imports of manufactured goods from the United Kingdom. In 1938, the effects of the Great Depression were such that imports from the United Kingdom into Asian countries remarkably decreased. Japanese trade with Southeast Asia

Multiple Trade Relationships between Asia, the United States, and Europe

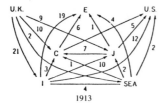

1913

C = China
E = Europe
I = India
J = Japan
SEA = Southeast Asia
US = United States

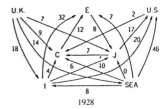

1928

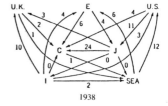

1938

Source: Mukai Jūichi, "Ajiya no bōeki kōzō to kokusai shūshi" (Trade structure of Asia and its international balance), in *Ryōtaisenkanki no Ajiya to Nippon* (Asia and Japan in the interwar period), ed. Ōno Ichiichiro and Yoshinobu Shuku (Tokyo, 1979), 57; the article relies largely on three works published by the United Nations in Geneva: *Europe's Trade* (1941), *The Network of World Trade* (1942), and *Industrialization and Foreign Trade* (1945).

was more or less balanced in those days, and its place in the Asian trade is not therefore visibly expressed in these diagrams.

The continuous decline of British trade and the gradual rise of Japanese trade (and American as well) during the interwar period can be seen in table 5.1, which shows the changing pattern of Southeast Asian (and Indian) imports from major industrial centers during that period.

In short, the triangular trade relationship which grew into existence in the 1910s and 1920s was seriously paralyzed by the Great Depression; in the United States there was a sudden decrease in demand for the raw materials that Southeast Asian countries produced. The shrinkage of trade surpluses of these countries led inevitably to a decline in their purchasing power for manufactured goods. In the ensuing fierce competition among the industrial countries for markets, Japan, which was more quick than others to recover from the depression, fared relatively well. These developments formed the background for the trade frictions between Japan and the United Kingdom and some other European countries during the 1930s.[3] The revival of the world market for Southeast Asian products as a result of the war boom in the latter part of the 1930s made it appear that the triangular trade of the good old days, with Japan playing a more important role than before, was coming again, but the outbreak of war in the Pacific gave the finishing blow to any dream of restoring the old patterns of triangular trade.

Table 5.1. Percentage Shares of Major Industrial Centers in the Imports of Southeast Asia and India

	Year	Japan	U.S.	U.K.	Europe[a]
India	1913	2.6	2.5	60.7	8.7
	1928	5.8	6.2	43.6	17.2
	1938	11.0	7.5	36.1	17.8
	1978	7.7	11.9	(8.2)	29.5
SEA	1913	2.9	6.9	14.3	20.7
	1928	5.5	12.0	12.6	20.4
	1938	8.4	16.6	11.0	21.6
	1978	24.6	14.2	(4.3)	14.7

Sources: Figures for the prewar years are from Mukai Jūichi, "Ajiya no bōeki kōzō to kokusai shūshi" in *Ryōtaisenkanki no Ajiya to Nippon*, ed. Ōno Ichiichiro and Yoshinobu Shuku (Toyko, 1979), 58-63. Those for 1978 are from International Monetary Fund, *Direction of Trade Statistics*, 1976-82.

[a]For 1913, includes Germany, France, and Holland; for 1928 and 1938, the three above plus Austria, Belgium, Luxembourg, Czechoslovakia, Italy, Sweden, and Switzerland; for 1978, the nine EEC countries.

It would be tempting to conclude that the economic friction between Japan and the European colonial powers (the United States included) was one of the reasons for Japan's decision to enter into the war in 1941. It seems more logical, however, to argue that Japan was, with little preparation, plunged into the task of building a Greater East Asian Coprosperity Sphere, an impossible task in the eyes of any sensible man. Without the participation of other industrial nations and especially that of the United States, how could a still weak Japan afford to economically support the vast area of Southeast Asia? Japan, by itself, could not, absorb all the products of Southeast Asian countries, which were suddenly deprived of a large proportion of their traditional markets in the United States and Europe. If for this reason alone, the concept of an East Asian Coprosperity Sphere as an exclusive economic zone was doomed to failure. Japanese administrators in the occupied areas were forced to adopt an industrialization policy to supply necessary goods to the local population as well as to the occupying army. There was little possibility for the success of the industrialization policy pursued under these extremely unfavorable circumstances. The Japanese concept of the East Asian Coprosperity Sphere was premature in the sense that it lacked sound economic foundations.

The chief concern of economic policymakers for postwar Japan was clearly how to provide the Japanese people with food and clothing. What importance

did they give to Japanese access to raw materials and markets in East Asia
for that purpose? A report prepared by a group of economists for the Ministry
of Foreign Affairs immediately after Japan's surrender estimated the effects
of the loss of the former spheres of influence upon the Japanese economy:

> Foreign territories and spheres of influence had been for some time
> brought into a division-of-labor relationship with our country, whereby
> they not only supplied us with food (rice, soy beans, grain, sugar, etc.)
> and industrial raw materials (iron ore, coal, salt, cotton, etc.), but also
> served as markets for our textiles and other industrial products, while
> at the same time becoming outlets for our excess population. In recent
> years particularly, industrial diversification underwent a marked devel-
> opment; in the so-called Japan-Manchukuo-China Comprehensive De-
> velopment Plan, projects were laid out for the distribution of industries
> in accordance with the suitability of the various regions involved. For
> example, steel and light metal foundries and electric power stations
> were concentrated in outside territories and in Manchukuo and north
> China, where natural resources are plentiful. Large amounts of capital
> were invested for this purpose. Though the construction of various in-
> dustrial facilities was closely linked to military aims, in the world of
> the future, the foundation for the development of a peaceful Japanese
> economy will be greatly weakened by the loss of profits from industrial
> diversification within spheres of influence, unless it becomes possible
> to trade freely, without regard for national boundaries.[4]

Apparently it was primarily continental Asia that the authors of this report
had in mind when they referred to former Japanese spheres of influence,
although they did not draw a clear line between continental and Pacific Asia.
In refuting the argument that severe limits should be placed upon Japan's
access to resources and markets in East Asia in order to prevent it from
regaining a predominant position in Asia, the report maintained that to hold
Japanese economic strength at an artificially low level would not only "reduce
the Japanese people to extreme penury" but also "hamper the economic recovery of other regions in East Asia (*tōa*)."

The report went on to elaborate the ideal relationship between Japan and
East Asia, taking China as an example.

While China would be able to export such products as silk, tea, pighair,
tung oil, carpets, tungsten, etc., the earnings accruing from these exports
would be small. To Japan, however, China can supply the most needed
materials, such as salt, soy beans, coal, and iron ore, without depriving

itself of the amount demanded for its own needs. In return, Japan can supply China with manufactured goods, in particular, machinery and chemicals. As for Japan, given a rather limited amount of exportable products to American and European markets, it would be impossible to finance its imports unless it could find markets for its manufactured goods in Asia (tōyō). Even if Japanese industrial products may compare unfavorably in quality with those of the United States and Europe, they would be welcomed to the Chinese consumers because of their low price. Therefore, both from the Chinese and the Japanese viewpoints, it would be only natural that China import Japanese industrial products. . . . A similar relationship can be also applied to Korea, French Indochina, and other countries in Asia (tōyō). The recovery of Japanese industry would contribute to the prompt industrialization and the substantial improvements of living standards of East Asian peoples. It would be most desirable, therefore, not to hold Japanese economic development in check but to promote vigorously the industrialization of Asia as a whole, including Japan. Moreover, if a poor and populous Asia succeeded in industrialization, it would provide the United States and Europe with vast markets and thus contribute greatly to the prosperity of the entire world.[5]

It is not known how the occupation authorities responded to this concept of Japan's role in postwar Asia. From the very early days of the occupation it was clear that the rehabilitation of Japanese commerce and industry would be essential if the victorious countries wanted to avoid assuming the onerous responsibility of supporting a defeated Japan for an indefinite period of time. A logical conclusion would be to allow Japan to participate in international trade. If a rigorous pruning or even a complete elimination of those Japanese industries supposed to contribute to war-making potential was desirable on security grounds, light industries, in particular textiles, would be the inevitable answer to the Japanese economic problem. Even Great Britain, which was averse to seeing the resumption of full-grown Japanese competition, would be ready to leave Southeast Asian markets for cheap Japanese piece goods as long as it was successfully engaged in more lucrative trade in Latin America.[6]

The most benign vision of Japan's role in postwar Asia among the victorious countries, however, was far from the view entertained by Japanese economic planners of the day. They tended to emphasize long-term prospects for sophisticated products such as machinery and chemicals rather than short-term prospects for products such as textiles and other consumer goods.[7] One of the reasons given was that industrialization in many "backward" countries

(India and China, in particular) was expected to proceed to such an extent that, although their light industries would become competitive with those of Japan in due course, a great demand would be created for capital goods. Japanese machinery would have to compete with American or European products, but according to the Japanese economic planners, the existing socio-economic conditions in Asian countries would be more favorable for relatively cheap Japanese machinery than for sophisticated and costly Western machinery.

Another point emerging from the arguments of the Japanese economic policymakers is their concern about the choice between access and possession. According to them:

> The tendency toward American domination of the world economy is destroying autarchy and making possible a system of international trade that can be carried on with a minimum of barriers. This will lead toward full employment and higher standards of living throughout the world. . . . There is some doubt as to the extent to which the defeated nations and the backward nations will be allowed to share the profits of increased world trade, and the effectiveness of the new system will to some degree be reduced so long as the Soviet Union and those in its sphere of influence do not participate, but at all events, this trend in the postwar world economy bodes well for the future of Japan, which is highly reliant upon trade for its subsistence.[8]

Implied in this line of argument is the notion of the economic vulnerability of Japan. In 1938 the Japanese minister of foreign affairs, Arita Hachirō, was reported to have stated that if free access to foreign markets and raw materials were denied Japan, it would be necessary for Japan to "acquire certain access to necessary raw materials" by possessing its own spheres of influence[9] The policymakers of the postwar Japanese economy were now saying that, given the failure of the old method of acquiring access to markets and resources, the only conceivable way would be to have a chance to participate in "a system of international trade that can be carried on with a minimum of barriers." This is why they welcomed what they thought was the American approach to "one world." And this is one of the important sources of the globalism which was to characterize Japanese thinking in the postwar period. Although the concept of free trade requires globalism, the immediate concern of Japanese economic planners was whether Japan would be allowed access to markets and raw materials in Asia.[10]

The United States also had its view of Japan's role in postwar Asia.[11] Willian Sebald, chairman of the Allied Council for Japan, stated in 1947 that the reconstruction of Japanese industry would be indispensable for the Far

East, adding that full rehabilitation had to wait for the resumption of free trade, which was to come after the peace settlement with Japan. General Chang Chen, Chinese representative to the council, emphasized the importance of mutually beneficial arrangements between China and Japan, suggesting that China would be ready to supply an increasing amount of raw materials to Japan, but added that, given the poor state of production facilities in China after many years of war, Japan should first assist China in reconstructing mines, factories, and transportation.[12]

By the spring of 1947, officials in the various agencies of the U.S. government who were concerned with Japan came to subscribe to the idea that Japanese industrial capacity could and should be utilized for the positive purpose of economic recovery of the entire region of Asia. There were differences, however, among the State and Defense departments, the Economic Cooperation Administration (ECA), and the General Headquarters in Tokyo about the way in which this could be brought about. Apart from the ordinary interbureaucratic rivalry over the pursestrings, they differed in substance about the connection between China (continental Asia) and Southeast Asia (Pacific Asia) and about the relationship between economic and military approaches. In short, the dispute was between those who insisted that the Communists should be contained on the Asiatic continent and those who thought that they should be contained on its periphery. The former favored an active intervention in Chinese affairs even by military means and were opposed to opening a commercial window with China. The latter argued for a policy of securing Southeast Asia for the West, while encouraging the new forces in China to look west by maintaining certain social and economic contacts with them. On the whole, the moderates in the State Department and the army, including General MacArthur, prevailed over the militant faction until the outbread of Korean hostilities.

What implications did these developments have for Japan's role in Asia? First, irrespective of the differences among U.S. policymakers about specific aspects of the containment policy, they all agreed on the strategic importance of Southeast Asia in United States policy vis-à-vis the Soviet Union. The economic backwardness and anti-European nationalism in many countries of the region provided, it seemed, an ideal opportunity for the Soviet design of expanding its own influence. The Japanese experience in Southeast Asia before 1941 was now considered a valuable asset that could be utilized by the United States for the purpose of promoting political stability and economic prosperity in Asia. The prewar triangular patterns of the Asian trade were thus rehabilitated at least in the papers of the U.S. government, although one particular side of the triangle, that connecting Southeast Asia with Europe, now seemed precarious.

Second, although the emphasis in U.S. policy toward Asia shifted clearly from China to Japan, it still remained ambivalent about whether Japan could be maintained without China—an element that seemed an essential condition for its economic viability. It was now U.S. policymakers who asked the same question that had intrigued Japanese economic planners in 1945. The authors of *The Basic Problems of Reconstruction of The Japanese Economy* raised the question of whether Japan could achieve a self-sustained economy without its former colonies and spheres of influence, which had provided about 30 percent of its imports (mostly raw materials) and 37 percent of its exports before the war.[13] In the same vein, American policymakers now asked themselves with whom Japan could integrate in Asia, after the loss of Manchuria, China, Korea, Formosa, and Sakhalin which had supplied Japan before 1941 with about 35 percent of its raw materials and absorbed 40 percent of its exports.[14]

The answer the Americans gave to that question was also similar to the one given by the Japanese: an uninterrupted access to Asian markets and raw materials would be essential for Japan. Well before the Japanese defeat and the Cold War, an American expert on Japan wrote, "The real issue with respect to Japan's economic future is rooted in postwar international commercial policy. *If* the United Nations move toward lessened impediments to international trade rather than in the direction of intensified economic nationalism and super-protectionism, Japan—without colonies—can live and prosper" (emphasis in original).[15]

The new problem was, however, that the likely form of impediments to international trade was neither the exclusion of the defeated nations (as the Japanese feared) nor the revival of economic nationalism of the 1930s (as envisioned perhaps by both American and Japanese analysts), but communist expansion through Asia. The Americans, fearing communist domination of the entire region of Asia, deemed it essential to secure Southeast Asia as a vital segment in a "great crescent" of containment that ran from Japan through island and mainland Southeast Asia, India, and Australia.[16] The question remained, however, whether continental Asia was already out of the reach of Western influence. No final answer was given to this question until the outbreak of the Korean War.

An ambitious idea for an Asian version of the Marshall Plan, which would attempt to secure not only Southeast Asia but also at least parts of continental Asia, gradually lost ground to the more modest version of containment. According to the latter approach, a commercial window with mainland China should be kept open in the expectation that Beijing, even under a communist regime, might take a course independent of Moscow. It was therefore permissible for Japan to have a certain level of commercial relations with China, although an excessive dependence of her economy on the Asian continent would be dangerous. Japan should be encouraged to cultivate its economic relations with Southeast Asia, maintaining at the same time low-key trade relations with China. As a result of this policy, the volume of Japanese trade with China in 1950 rose to $59 million despite the victory of the Chinese communists in October 1949.[17]

Thus, in the evolution of American thinking about Japan's role in Asia, a distinction existed between Southeast and Northeast Asia even before the victory of the communists on the Asian continent. Although Southeast Asia was regarded as the natural frontier for Japanese economic expansion, China (or Northeast Asia in general) was not completely excluded in the American concept of an Asia with which Japan could integrate economically. But American policymakers placed greater emphasis on Japan's regional role in Southeast Asia. It was often ambiguous whether keeping communism out of Southeast Asia was the end and Japanese economic recovery was the means for it or vice versa. American policymakers around 1950 were haunted, as the Japanese war planners before 1941 had been, by the idea that Japan was so economically vulnerable that it had to be assured access to markets and raw materials in that part of Asia within its own political influence.

The outbreak of war in Korea in June 1950 changed the political and ideological context in which Japan's relations with Southeast Asia were discussed. With regard to China, it shifted the advantage within the U.S. government from the moderate to the militant faction. China, at that time, was clearly designated as an enemy to the West with whom trade was explicitly prohibited. Following the American ban on the China trade, Japan's Ministry for International Trade and Industry adopted measures in October 1950 to strengthen the embargo of strategic materials to China.[18] In December the GHQ issued a directive by which all trade with China was prohibited. These developments obviously added great weight to the argument that the Japanese would need to be assured markets and raw materials in Southeast Asia.

The war also brought about a very important change in the general conditions surrounding the Japanese economy. The effects of the war on the economy were indicated dramatically in the sharp increase of Japanese dollar exports: the first half of 1950 (i.e., before the effects of the war had appeared) witnessed nearly a 30 percent increase in dollar exports as compared with the preceding six months, and the second half saw as much as a 54 percent increase over the preceding half-year period. This trend continued into the following year although at a declining pace (a 33 percent and a 4.7 percent increase during the first and the second halves).[19] The offshore procurements—special demand procurement orders (*tokuju*) placed by the U.S. forces in Japan in order to support the fighting efforts in Korea—played an extremely large role in these developments. The dollar earnings accrued from special demand procurements accounted for 19.3 percent of the total figures of exports and 14.8 percent of the total dollar earnings of Japan in 1950. The comparable figures for the following year were 45.6 percent and 26.4 percent.[20]

Although these developments helped to fill the chronic dollar gap in Japan, their effects were temporary. In fact, the economic boom caused by the Korean War began to subside in 1952 when an agreement for a ceasefire in Korea appeared imminent. Japanese exports saw a 1.4 percent decline during the first half of 1952 and a 13.7 percent decline during the latter half as compared with the preceding six months.[21]

It was under these circumstances that a new scheme, "U.S.-Japan Economic Cooperation," was discussed in the early months of 1951 among U.S. and Japanese officials who were closely involved in Japan's economic policy.[22] The program was intended to prolong the spending of U.S. dollars in Japan for military purposes even after the immediate procurement needs related to the Korean War ceased to exist. For this purpose economic policymakers in the GHQ in Tokyo recommended to Washington that Japan's industrial capacity and manpower should be mobilized to the fullest extent possible in support of the free world's military efforts in Asia. Military and economic rationales were thus closely combined in the concept of economic cooperation under which Japan was expected to receive special procurement orders. This explains the continued dollar earnings from procurements, which increased rather than decreased after the Korean ceasefire.[23]

Southeast Asia weighed very much in the concept of U.S.-Japanese Economic Cooperation. According to a GHQ position paper entitled "Japan's Economic Recovery and Future Progress Toward Economic Cooperation with the United States" (27 June 1951):

> Japan has considerable excess industrial capacity and manpower available for use in support of the free world economic programs. In terms of index numbers on the industrial activity index it is about 50 points. In terms of the value of additional manufactured products it is about $2.7 billion per year. From this capacity it should be possible to accrue at least $1.0 billion in the form of special procurement—increasing current special demand procurement to five times the present level. It is clear that American policy is now dedicated to the fullest possible utilization of this surplus capacity.
>
> Utilization of this surplus capacity is limited currently by the availability of the necessary raw materials. Imported raw materials and food valued at about $3.2 billion will be required for capacity operations. This compares with estimated imports for 1951 amounting to $1.9 billion. . . . Ideally, Japan's position today can best be alleviated by find-

ing new or underdeveloped sources of supply within economic shipping distances which might be paid for in whole or part with finished products needed in the source areas.[24]

The same document went on to describe the historical interest of Japan in developing raw material sources and Japan's exploration of sources in Southeast Asia before 1941. In short, the program's intent was to combine Japan's surplus industrial capacity with the underdeveloped sources of raw materials in Southeast Asia for the purpose of supporting American military efforts there.

Various steps were taken to implement this idea in 1951 and 1952. For example, contact was made with Japanese engineers who had worked or surveyed the mines in Southeast Asia before and during the Pacific War. On the request of the GHQ, they submitted Southeast Asian development projects. A Japanese export bank was established in February 1951 to aid in financing such projects. Experts were sent from Japan to the countries in the region (forty-three to Taiwan, thirty-six to Pakistan, fourteen to Thailand, six to India, five to Indonesia, two to Burma, and one to Ceylon by the end of February 1952). Preliminary negotiations for projects of mineral and marine resources development were under way in early 1952 with the Philippines, Goa, Taiwan, Indochina, India, Burma, and Macao.[25]

It is probable that the concept of economic cooperation was virtually a joint product of American and Japanese economic policymakers concerned with the long-term prospects for Japan's economic self-reliance.[26] The Economic Stabilization Board of the Japanese government stated in February 1952 that Japan should establish a viable economy as quickly as possible by, among other steps, "promoting and tightening her economic cooperation with the United States, Southeast Asian countries, and other democratic countries in order to contribute to their defense production and economic development."[27]

The wording of this document closely resembles that of the American officials of the day. It is questionable, however, to what extent the Japanese committed themselves to the underlying philosophy of the U.S. policy. Two things at least are worth mentioning. First, the Japanese talked about the necessity for the strengthening of the defense production of Southeast Asian countries and the self-defense power of Japan itself, but apparently with certain reservations. It is well known that Prime Minister Yoshida offered stubborn resistance to John Foster Dulles's pressure for larger defense efforts on the part of the Japanese government. Finance Minister Ikeda Hayato presented Japan's case when he met with Walter Robertson in October 1953.[28] It is significant that the ESB document cited above did not mention defense production in Southeast Asia when listing the concrete measures to be taken.

It simply said, "Japan will cooperate more actively with the economic development of Southeast Asia along the lines of the economic assistance programs of the United States and the economic development programs of Southeast Asian countries and thereby increase the imports of goods and materials from this area and improve the balance of sterling trade."[29] One may conclude that the Japanese were interested in purely economic aspects of the U.S. security program and other related programs in Asia, giving only lip service to American beliefs about the military-strategic significance of those programs.

The second point is concerned with the China problem. Given the widespread feeling of Japan's economic insecurity in anticipation of the end of American tutelage, many Japanese economic policymakers were unsure whether raw materials and markets for their industrial products in Southeast Asia would be a sufficient replacement for Chinese markets. They were also well aware of the strong suspicion, if not outright hostility, among Southeast Asian peoples toward Japan. Therefore, while accepting the idea that cooperation for economic development in Southeast Asia would be desirable in the interest of political stability of the region as well as for a self-sustained economy of Japan, Japanese policymakers recognized that such a policy ought to be based on the "principle of mutually beneficial cooperative relationship" and that importance to be given to Southeast Asian development projects should be balanced against the long-term prospects for Chinese markets. They were far from being naïve about the American willingness to support Asian development genuinely for economic purposes, reminding themselves of the probable financial burden that would rest on their own shoulders for any successful implementation of economic cooperation with Southeast Asia.[30]

A similar view was expressed in a book by two prominent Japanese experts on the Asian economy. They criticized the current trend of thought in which Southeast Asia was pictured from an outsider's viewpoint, primarily as raw materials sources or markets for Japanese goods. They specifically mentioned the oft-quoted phrase, "economic development of Southeast Asia as an integral part of U.S.-Japanese economic cooperation," which had also, according to them, a similar connotation. The authors of the book were circumspect about, if not opposed to, the integration of the Japanese economy with Southeast Asia. They thought that Japan could do without Chinese raw materials except for one important item—coal. They thought that the time would come "in several years or in less than two decades" when a substantial amount of coal had to be imported from abroad; then "Chinese resources would again assume a very important role in Japanese industry." Japanese industrial products would have to face severe competition from American and European products in Southeast Asian markets where Japan was only temporarily enjoying favorable conditions in price and quantity because products of the United States and Europe were directed to other areas in the wake of the Korean War.[31]

The idea of economic integration of Japan with Southeast Asia was envisaged by some who entertained an ambitious idea of securing a great crescent of Asia for the West by combining Japan's industrial capacity with raw materials in Southeast Asia. But that was only part of the picture. At least from the Japanese viewpoint, the idea that Japan could and should have a role in economic development in Asia was older than U.S. containment policy. When amalgamated with the American version, the Japanese concept of its role in Asia still maintained Japanese characteristics. China was excluded by circumstances, not design, and Southeast Asia failed to satisfy Japan's immediate economic needs. It was some years later that the Japanese economy began to have a significant impact on economic development in the region. The immediate answer to Japan's economic needs had to be found in the opening of markets in advanced industrial countries. After the mid-1950s, Japanese economic policymakers adopted a new, two-front strategy: producing capital-intensive goods that were exportable to developing countries on the one hand (this part of the strategy was a continuation of the old concept of Japan's regional role), and producing labor-intensive goods exportable to advanced countries on the other.[32] The success of this new strategy depended, of course, on the attitudes of the other industrial countries, especially the United States. What fate this new strategy was to have belongs to a different story. Suffice it to say that it did succeed, and that consequently the Japanese economy became closely involved in the global, rather than merely regional, network of economic interdependence. Japan's regional role, which began to assume some importance after the late 1960s, should, therefore, be examined in that perspective.

1. The Communist portions of the four divided countries (Vietnam, Korea, China, and Germany) and Mongolian People's Republic are not counted for the purpose of this paper.

2. Keizai shingichō, chōseibu, "Tōnan ajiyashokoku tono keizaiteikei no sokushin ni tsuite," 20 May 1953, 4.

3. Hosoya Chihiro (ed.), *Taiheiyō-ajiya-ken no kokusai keizai funso-shi 1922-45* [A history of international economic conflicts in Pacific-Asia: 1922-45] (Tokyo, 1983).

4. Gaimushō chōsakyoku, *Nihon keizai saiken no kihonmondai* [Basic problems for the reconstruction of Japanese economy], (September 1946), 42.

5. Ibid., 89-90.

6. An article by Sydney Cambell of Reuters, quoted in Shimamoto Tōru, *Nihon keizai no saiken* [The reconstruction of Japanese economy] (Tokyo, 1948), 158–59. For a broader survey

of British opinion of Japan in the early postwar period, see Gordon Daniel, "Britain's View of Postwar Japan, 1945-49," in Ian Nish, ed., *Anglo-Japanese Alienation 1919-1952* (Cambridge, 1982), 257-78.

7. Gaimushō, *Nihon Keizai*, 138-42, 10-11. See also Shōzaburō Sakai, "Nihon sangyō saihensei no kadai" [Problems for restructuring Japanese industry], in Hamano Ichirō, ed., *Nihon keizai saiken no riron* [Theory of Japanese economic reconstruction], (Tokyo, 1948), 288-302.

8. Gaimushō, *Nihon Keizai*, 88.

9. U.S. Department of State, *Foreign Relations of the United States, Japan, 1931-1941*, vol. I, 802. This passage of Mr. Arita's statement is quoted in Harold G. Moulton and Louis Marlio, *The Control of Germany and Japan*, (Washington, DC, 1944), 78.

10. I have discussed the same topic in a somewhat different perspective in "From Bitter Enmity to Cold Partnership, 1945-52," in Nish, *Anglo-Japanese Alienation*, 229-55.

11. For a more detailed account of this subject, see Michael Schaller, *The American Occupation of Japan*, (New York, 1985). This author has also benefited from reading Michael Schaller, "Japan, China and Southeast Asia: Regional Integration and Containment, 1947-1950," a paper presented to the Norfolk Conference in 1982 on the occupation of Japan.

12. *Asahi Shinbun*, October 2, 1947. See also Asakai Kōichirō, *Shoki tainichi senryō seisaku* [Allied Policy toward Japan in the Early Years of Occupation], (Tokyo, 1979), vol.2, 259-65.

13. Gaimushō, *Nihon Keizai*, 41. Included in these areas were Korea, Taiwan, Sakhalin, the South Sea mandated islands (*nanyō*), Manchuria, the leased province of Kwantung, and China proper.

14. Schaller, "Japan, China and Southeast Asia," 11.

15. Moulton and Marlio, *Control of Germany and Japan*, 84.

16. Policy Planning Staff (PPS) file 51, as quoted by Michael Schaller, "Securing the Great Crescent: Occupied Japan and the Origins of Containment in Southeast Asia," *The Journal of American History* 69(2) (September 1982): 402.

17. Hagiwara Tōru, *Nihon gaikōshi* [Diplomatic History of Japan], vol. 30, (Tokyo, 1972), 412.

18. Ibid.

19. Ōkurashō Zaiseishishitsu, comp., *Shōwa zaiseishi: shūsen kara kōwa made* [A history of finance in the shōwa period: From the surrender to the peace treaty], vol. 19: *Statistics* (Tokyo, 1978), 107.

20. See Nakamura Takafusa, "Nichibei keizai kyōryoku kankei no keisei" [The formation of economic cooperation relationship between Japan and the United States], in Nakamura, ed., *Kindai nihon kenkyū*, vol.4, *Taiheiyō sensō* [A study on modern Japan, vol.4: The Pacific War] (Tokyo, 1983), 284. Nakamura used both broad and narrow concepts of special demand procurements. Figures cited here are in the broad sense, namely figures which include spending for private consumption by U.S. military personnel and their familites in Japan in addition to military orders in the strict sense.

21. Ōkurashō, *Shōwa*, 107.

22. See Nakamura's essay, cited in n. 20; also Hagiwara, *Nihon gaikōshi*, 99-106.

23. These post-Korean War procurements were called "new special demand procurements" (shin-tokuju) and contributed to 63.9 percent of Japan's total exports and 36.8 percent of its total foreign exchange earnings in 1952. The comparable figures for 1953 were even larger: 70.0 percent and 38.2 percent. After 1954 the importance of procurement earnings began to decline, but their accumulated amount during the period 1950 to 1957 came to $5.2 billion. This figure should be compared to $2 billion, the total amount of U.S. aid to occupied Japan. See Nakamura, *Nihon gaikōshi*, 284-85.

24. The National Archives, Record Group 331, Box 8355. The author of this document is unknown. Judging from the content and the date, however, it was probably written by someone who worked for the Economic and Scientific Section of the GHQ in Tokyo. The Economic Cooperation Program started officially in June 1951.

25. Keizai antei honbu (Economic Stabilization Board), "Tōnan ajiya keizai kaihatsu ni taisuru kyōryoku ni kansuru genjō no setsumei" ("An explanation of the present state of affairs concerning economic cooperation with regard to Southeast Asian economic development), 27 February 1952. See also ESB, "Interim Progress Report on Southeast Asian Development," 4 January 1952. I have been unable to identify those Japanese engineers and other experts who were mobilized for these projects.

26. See Senga Tetsuya's interview in Osanai Hiroshi and Kondo Kanichi, eds., *Sengo sangyōshi e no shōgen* (Testimony on history of postwar Japanese industry) (Tokyo, 1978), 217. Mr. Senga was an executive officer of the Federation of Economic Organizations (Keidanren) at that time.

27. ESB, "Establishment of a Viable Economy and Promotion of Economic Cooperation," 12 February 1952, 1.

28. Miyazawa Kiichi, *Tokyo-Washington no mitsudan* [Secret talks between Tokyo and Washington], (Tokyo, 1956), 250-54.

29. ESB, "Establishment of a Viable Economy," 2, 7.

30. ESB, "Tōnan ajiya keizaikaihatsu ni taisuru kyōryoku sokushin no tameno mondaiten" [Some problems in the way of the promotion of cooperation with Southeast Asia for economic development], 25 February 1952, 1-2.

31. Ōkita Saburō and Hara Kakuten, *Ajiya keizai to nihon* [Asian economy and Japan], (Tokyo, 1952), 1, 179-80, and 183-84. Okita was among the authors who wrote the Gaimushō report on "The Basic Problems of Reconstruction of Japanese Economy" and was an ESB official at the time of writing this book in 1952. He left the ESB to take up a post in the ECAFE (Economic Commission for Asia and the Far East) at Bangkok in April 1952.

32. This strategy is known as the "Okita Plan." See Okita Saburō, "Watashi no rirekisho" (The course of my life), 23d in the series, *Nihon Keizai Shinbun*, July 1981.

6

Decline of Relations during the Vietnam War

WALTER LAFEBER

At the beginning of the 1960 to 1975 era, expert observers characterized United States-Japan ties with the term "inevitable harmony," or "a sense that Japan's future was inseparably linked to that of the United States." At the end of the era, Theodore Draper; a respected analyst, condemned the lack of "mutuality and reciprocity" in the relationship, then concluded that "the Japanese 'alliance' is either a courtesy title or a convenient fiction."[1] After allowing for overstatement, Draper's words indicated what had happened to the relationship during the years of the U.S. involvement in Vietnam. By 1975 the ties between the two nations approached a historical norm, a norm that was closer to the relationship of the 1920s or the pre-1904 years than the relationship of 1945 to 1960.

Some acute observers anticipated the change. In 1964 the U.S. Department of State, with the aid of the American embassy in Tokyo, compiled a secret policy paper on "The Future of Japan." It prophesied the following:

> Looking ahead over the next ten years, we can expect to find our-
> selves dealing with an increasingly strong, confident and nationalistic
> Japan. Pro-Western, conservative elements will probably retain control
> at least until 1969 or 1970, possibly alternating power thereafter with
> socialist governments of considerably more moderate hue than today's
> Japan Socialist Party. . . . Japan's economic and security relations with
> the U.S. will remain vitally important to it—and scarcely less so to
> us—but the relationship will become less predominant in Japan's foreign
> relations and more pragmatic as Japan seeks its own way in the world
> and attempts to reduce its present extraordinary dependence on the
> U.S. China will remain an area of potential policy difference with us,
> but with the odds against a major split on recognition and other basic
> issues, partly because of the broad consensus in Japan in favor of self-
> determination on Taiwan. . . .

It is difficult to see how Japan's minimum economic goals can be attained unless Japan is afforded opportunity to expand its sales in the U.S. market at least in proportion with the growth of the U.S. GNP. . . . This will require firm Executive Branch resistance of American industry demands for curtailment of Japanese imports. . . . It is only less important that when the U.S. must act contrary to Japanese trading interests, time and effort be taken to put the best possible face on the action . . . instead of the Japanese learning of the matter for the first time through Washington press announcements, as so often in the past.

An attempt to predict Japanese developments ten years ahead should allow sufficient of the saving element of the earthquakes and typhoons that mark the natural scene.[2]

Remarkably prophetic, especially on problems of trade, China, and prior notice, the paper did miss several "earthquakes" that soon shook the relationship. The State Department notably failed to emphasize the two problems that climaxed in the Nixon shocks of 1971 and pushed relations to a postwar nadir: Vietnam and Okinawa.

These four policy issues (trade, Southeast Asia, China, Okinawa) reshaped the traditional postwar relationship between Washington and Tokyo during the 1960 to 1975 years. The pivotal turns in that course can be traced by examining the four issues during two crucial junctures: 1965 to 1968 and 1969 to 1973.

As John Kennedy escalated the American effort in Vietnam, the United States ambassador to Japan, Edwin O. Reischauer, understood that "inevitable harmony" was giving way to a more painful "slow equalization of the partnership," and, as he recalled, "I began using the word partnership" to describe the process.[3] Having survived the uproar over the security treaty fight in 1960, the relationship soon centered not on large strategic policy issues, but on trade and less important diplomatic problems. Kennedy helped salve the wounds of the 1960 debate less by taking an active part in decision making (astonishingly few references to Japan exist in the memoirs and histories of his presidency), but by being personally popular among Japanese and allowing experts such as Reischauer to handle relations. In Japan, Prime Minister Ikeda Hayato similarly healed the fissures by adopting a so-called low posture that created few political headlines and focused on economic development. By 1963 Ikeda's Liberal Democratic party won a resounding electoral victory. In 1964 his country ranked sixth in world economic productivity, and during the next three years Japan's economy passed West Germany, Great Britain, and France to place just behind the two superpowers.[4]

The effect on U.S.-Japan trade began to gain attention about 1965, just as

Americans began to die in Vietnam in large numbers. A trade balance long favorable to the United States turned unfavorable; by 1968 the U.S. deficit had quadrupled the deficit of 1967. An internal State Department history summarized the results: "Of these [problems], one of the most important was the coincidence of Japanese economic and trade growth with the worsening of the U.S. balance of payments. The United States, therefore, while keeping Japan's unique circumstances in mind, encouraged Japanese efforts to achieve a greater sense of independence, and began to look to Japan to implement its new position in the Free World by assuming duties and responsibilities commensurate with its strength.[5]

The State Department believed, in other words, that Japan would not use its new wealth to help in Vietnam. The problem went deeper. If the Vietnam War had not occurred, the trade turnaround would still have happened; the aging United States industrial plant would still have been on a collision course with the newly restructured Japanese economy. Washington officials grew bitter as Japan maintained high trade and investment barriers.[6] On a visit to Washington, Foreign Minister Miki Takeo responded by criticizing American business, especially textiles and steel, for retreating to a 1930s kind of protectionism that thwarted Japanese trade.[7]

Vietnam, however, sharpened the growing animosity. The Japanese, in American eyes, never really understood how the conflict influenced the Tokyo-Washington relationship. But as early as November 1966, U.S. financial experts noted that although Japan's economy had slumped in 1965, its growth rate leaped from 2.7 percent to 7.5 percent in 1966—helped by nearly $1 billion spent in Japan by the United States for goods needed in the Vietnam effort.[8]

Resolving structural problems developing in the "partnership" was subordinated to a Vietnam struggle that soon consumed Washington's attention. Memoirs from the Johnson administration contain few more references to Japan than do those of the Kennedy years. The president seemed interested in his most important Asian ally almost solely because of the help it might give in Vietnam.[9] Johnson, however, never consulted with Satō Eisaku, Ikeda's successor, before deciding to bomb North Vietnam in 1965 or to escalate the ground fighting.[10] Satō, who agreed with Johnson's policies more than did other leaders of the Liberal Democratic party, publicly went along with the United States escalation.

Severe doubts quickly appeared, however. One American involved in Vietnam planning, James C. Thomson Jr., recalled that "A Japanese, early on, told me a wondrous thing that made my hair stand on end. . . . 'We tried that twenty years ago, and it was a terrible mistake to do.' "[11] Others objected publicly. Matsumoto Shigeharu, chairman of the International House of Japan, wrote in *Japan Quarterly* during early 1966, "As the domestic situation stands in Japan at the moment, a war between America and Communist China would split the nation in two, one half pro-American and the other antiwar, with a danger of disturbances approaching a civil war in scale."[12] Reischauer believed affairs had reached the point where he had to announce that the loss of Japan would be more serious to U.S. interests than the loss of Vietnam. He delayed leaving Tokyo in mid-1965, as he had planned, to spend another year smoothing over growing cracks in the relationship.[13]

Washington's public statements did not lessen the tension. Assistant Secretary of State William P. Bundy condemned Japanese conservatives for displaying too much "tolerance" for Communists in Vietnam, China, and at home. Another State Department official, Douglas MacArthur II, announced that Japan's two largest newspapers had been "infiltrated" by Communists, a charge the State Department had to retract. A great architect of the postwar alliance, Yoshida Shigeru, declared from retirement that racism distorted the American view of Asian realities.[14] When Johnson thought of planning a visit to Japan in late 1966, the reaction from Tokyo was immediate: "inconceivable."[15] By 1968, what had once perhaps been inadvertence had become policy: the U.S. embassy in Tokyo advised that on Vietnam strategy Japan should be ignored.

As Matsumoto observed, the two nations differed over how United States policy might affect China. In 1964, the People's Republic (PRC) had exploded a nuclear device. National Security Council Asian experts warned NSC adviser McGeorge Bundy that although "Satō is a high-posture man, ready to lead Japan toward a long-term UK-type dependability as a US ally," the "*key issue on Satō's mind is Communist China.* . . . He is willing to play along with us on China," but only if Washington had a tenable long-term plan; he wanted no more "cliches [that] he has heard before."[16] During a visit to Japan in 1964, George Kennan had been struck over "the extent to which Communist China now dominates the external horizon of Japanese opinion," Japan's desire for better relations with the PRC, and "a perfectly natural desire among the Japanese to escape at least partially from the cloying exclusiveness of the American tie."[17]

Kennan's analysis raised few echoes in Washington. Lyndon Johnson escalated the U.S. commitment in Vietnam precisely to contain China. When State Department officials at the desk level moved to open consideration of relations with the PRC, Secretary of State Dean Rusk, in Thomson's words, refused "to move one inch on China policy."[18] When Kennan publicly suggested a relaxation of both the American view of China and the U.S.-Japan security arrangement, the Johnson administration quickly informed the Japanese that any "general concept of [U.S.] disengagement in this area" is nothing

more than "beautiful dreams," to use Reischauer's words.[19] Privately, Reischauer warned Vice President Hubert Humphrey that China was the "deeply
disturbing thing. This lurks behind all [the Japanese] think about Vietnam."[20]

With the explosion of the Chinese nuclear device and growing Japanese
doubt about U.S. policy, momentum grew in Satō's government during late
1964 and 1965 to establish official diplomatic relations with the PRC.[21] Trade
between the two Asian powers grew until Japan became China's premier
trading partner in 1966.[22] Rusk tried to keep his policy on course by assuring
Foreign Minister Shiina Etsasaburō that despite the Chinese nuclear success,
"The United States in no sense limits its commitment to Japan in terms of
the weapons employed. It would be literal madness for anyone to contemplate
the use of nuclear weapons or nuclear blackmail against Japan. The United
States considers its security arrangements with Japan entirely valid without
regard to the nature of weapons used."[23] Security, however, was not the main
problem; apparently no serious discussions were held about modifying the
1960 arrangements, although Tokyo officials sent up trial balloons about
curing "nuclear allergy."[24] Politics and trade, however, were quite different
issues.

The United States tried to hold the line politically (especially by preventing
formal Tokyo-Beijing relations and PRC entry into the United Nations), while
surrendering to the inevitable Japanese-Chinese trade ties. Some U.S. officials
(although apparently not Rusk) even thought this approach could be turned
to their advantage. In a discussion with Miki Takeo, secretary general of the
Liberal Democratic party, on January 13, 1965, Vice President-elect Humphrey laid out the more flexible line. The United States would oppose recognition of the PRC or its admission to the U.N., Humphrey began, but he
understood personally that Japan would develop economic relations with the
Chinese "even if we didn't like it." He only worried about the conditions:
"For example, it would be injurious to our position in the world for Japan to
give more favorable credit and terms to Communist China than to England,
the Philippines or to us." Through trade, moreover, "Japan could act to reduce
some of the aggressive, militant spirit of Communist China." Speaking individually, as he stressed he was doing, Humphrey concluded that "Japanese
trade with the Mainland could be a positive factor." Miki nicely replied "that
Japan thought about its trade with Communist China in exactly the way Vice
President-elect Humphrey had stated."[25]

The deal thus emerged that Japan could profit economically as long as it
cooperated politically and followed a trade policy of playing no favorites.
Neither part of that deal helped the effort in Vietnam. Rusk told Johnson on
the eve of Satō's visit in November 1967 that the United States wanted larger
pledges for economic aid, postwar rehabilitation, "international police-

keeping," and double the $100 million Satō already was giving the Asian Development Bank. Rusk also wanted the Japanese to ease pressure for the return of Okinawa, at least until U.S. security in Southeast Asia improved.[26] Satō finally agreed with Johnson's public communiqué summarizing their talks that attacked the "present intransigent attitude" of the PRC. The prime minister then told a Diet committee in Tokyo that he could "neither affirm nor deny" that China had aggressive tendencies, and he repeatedly denied that his government viewed the PRC as a "hypothetical enemy."[27] Satō took this position although 1967 marked a low tide in Sino-Japanese affairs, especially in the trade area, where the Cultural Revolution caused a downturn.[28]

Rusk was not pleased by Japan's performance, even though Japan had tried to help some in Vietnam by urging Soviet officials to restrain Ho Chi Minh.[29] Writing to Johnson in 1967, Rusk lamented the lack of a "more mature and responsible attitude on the part of Japan towards the threat posed by Chinese Communists and by the internal instability of the countries on the periphery of China." Rusk now sounded quite different about the security pact arrangement than he had when talking with Shiina two years before: the Japanese should understand that American support "for our own commitments in Asia" could depend on Japan's becoming more responsible in the region.[30] The developing American view was summarized in *The Nation* of January 15, 1968: "It seems the Japanese Governments have made an important distinction between the safety of Japan and the containment of communism."[31]

Rusk and Johnson were particularly bitter that Japan had not been a better partner in regional security and development. A fundamental reason for the original American involvement in Vietnam between 1949 and 1954 had been the assumption that Vietnam had to be held as part of a security package (including capitalist economic development) for the entire region—especially for Japan. Only by keeping Southeast Asian markets open could the United States prevent intolerable Japanese-Chinese relations.[32] In 1963, Zbigniew Brzezinski, at the start of a long fascination with Japan, hoped that "Japanese resentment against the United States for impeding trade with China might be overcome" if Japan assumed "regional responsibility for guiding and inspiring the development of Asia."[33]

Walt Whitman Rostow, of the State Department's Policy Planning Staff (and soon to become Johnson's National Security Advisor), broadened Brzezinski's approach. In March 1965, he explained to Johnson how the United States could resolve the dilemma of growing, narrow nationalisms while preserving American preeminence: "It is our interest in each of the regions of the free world to assist in the development of local arrangements which, while reducing their direct dependence on the United States, would leave the regions open to cooperative military, economic, and political arrangements with the

U.S. This requires of us a systematic policy designed to strengthen the hand of the moderates in the regions and to reduce the power of extremists— whether those extremists are Communists or ambitious nationalists anxious to take over and dominate their regions."[34]

Rostow's formula strikingly resembled the Nixon Doctrine of four years later. More immediately, it served as a rationale for escalating the effort in Vietnam. Rostow later believed that the turning point for Asian regionalism was Johnson's speech at the Johns Hopkins University in April 1965 when the president both announced the military escalation and pledged a massive regional development effort in Southeast Asia. An Asian Development Bank appeared, the Asian and Pacific Council (ASPAC) met for the first time, and the Association of Southeast Asian Nations (ASEAN) revived in 1965.

Rostow hoped Japan would help lead the movement as "a way of moving out from the home islands in a setting of multilateral institutions which dimmed painful memories of . . . Japanese imperialism."[35] Satō cooperated by contributing $200 million to the Asian Development Bank. Foreign Minister Miki apparently coined the phrase "Asia-Pacific Concept" to replace the bad connotations of "Greater East Asia Coprosperity Sphere." (Miki further clarified his position by calling the Vietnam conflict "a civil war," apparently to Satō's displeasure, not to mention Rusk's.[36]) Tokyo's initiatives pleased Washington. In September 1965, Fukuda Takeo, minister of international trade and industry, told Reischauer that he wanted to discuss Japan's aid to Southeast Asia and "Japan's access to U.S. capital sources." Reischauer responded warmly.[37] Records of the ensuing conversations in Washington are apparently not declassified, but the Fukuda plan resembles the Lamont-Kajiwara deal that opened New York bank resources for Japanese development of Manchuria after World War I.

The Lamont-Kajiwara agreement never fulfilled American hopes, and neither, for the Johnson administration, did Japan's contribution to regionalism in the 1960s. The Satō government joined ASPAC only on the understanding that it would not become involved with anti-Communist or anti-Beijing policies.[38] Japan's contribution to the Asian Development Bank increased only after fervent pleas from Johnson. Japanese investment in Southeast Asia did increase; by 1967 Japan's auto companies had gained control of the Thai market and textile investments expanded through the region. But such investment was not what Americans had in mind when they called for Japan to take a lead. They wanted a major, ongoing contribution to security, particularly in Vietnam, and particularly after the British announced in early 1968 that they would withdraw their military forces from Malaysia and Singapore by 1971. Japan instead, in Washington's view, only moved to develop their assets and dominate Southeast Asia's trade.[39]

In retrospect this offensive can be seen as part of a global Japanese economic effort that appeared in the mid-1960s; prominent authorities in Japan emphasized that the nation must increasingly act globally and not become overly dependent on a single region such as Southeast Asia.[40] Such a perspective, however, did nothing to help Johnson and Rusk in Vietnam. In their view not even appeals to Satō himself (which Johnson made personally[41]) produced the needed results.

As trade and the Vietnam War shaped Washington's view of Satō's policies, the issue of Okinawa molded much of Japan's view of U.S. intentions.[42] The U.S. embassy in Tokyo reported that a reliable public opinion poll revealed that only the nuclear test ban issue concerned as many Japanese as did the Okinawa reversion question.[43] Satō, moreover, was clearly determined to regain the Ryukyus and the Japanese population on those islands.[44]

The only real question became the date when the United States would return the Bonins and Okinawa. Middle-level experts on Japan in the State and Defense departments understood; they had long been preparing a position on reversion.[45] But as the Vietnam bloodshed increased, they encountered opposition from top policymakers. Okinawa had become a massive logistics center, important less for the nuclear weapons stored there (although these deeply disturbed Japanese opinion), than because the base gave the United States a vastly larger capacity to fight non-nuclear wars in Southeast Asia.[46] Rusk agreed with the policy, but it was the Defense Department that led the fight to retain Okinawa. Secretary of Defense Robert McNamara urged Johnson in September 1967 to tell Foreign Minister Miki bluntly that the bases "are there at least as much for the protection of the Japanese as they are for the defense of the United States," and Japan should therefore share "the very heavy political and economic costs of providing security to the area."[47]

While the Vietnam struggle continued, however, the Okinawa problem could not be resolved. During the Satō-Johnson summit in late 1967 the Bonins were returned to Japanese administrative control (the United States retained two bases). Although important, the gesture was less crucial than the Okinawa problem. A 1967 public opinion poll revealed that for the first time in years the United States was not the country best liked by Japanese; they preferred Switzerland.[48] Inside Satō's Liberal Democratic party dissidents led by Nakasone Yasuhiro and Fujiyama Aiichirō argued that the prime minister's public willingness to support Johnson's policies on Vietnam and China harmed Japanese interests.[49] The president meanwhile suffered a fatal political defeat when the North Vietnamese launched their Tet offensive in February 1968. He took himself out of the election campaign and made a serious offer to open negotiations with Ho Chi Minh. Amid these rapid changes, Satō reportedly told his cabinet that he no longer considered binding the Yoshida Letter assurance that Japan would not work out long-term economic ties with the PRC.[50]

Both the new president, Richard Nixon, and his national security advisor,

Henry Kissinger, realized that Johnson's Vietnam policies had hit dead end. They planned to remove U.S. ground troops from the country, but they were not about to abandon either South Vietnam or larger American commitments in Asia. They believed U.S. power and influence could be recaptured by manipulating a new triangular relationship with Russia and China. American commitments to Asia could meanwhile be maintained with the help of other regional powers, especially Japan.[51]

At Guam in mid-1969, the president outlined a policy that became known as the Nixon Doctrine. While depending on Asian allies to assume more of the responsibility for containing communism in the region, the United States would reduce its present forces, particularly in Southeast Asia, but maintain its treaty commitments by providing a nuclear shield for friends and furnishing military and economic aid to allies.[52] Lowering the American profile in Asia could also paradoxically strengthen the United States position in countries such as Japan. Marshall Green, assistant secretary of state for East Asian and Pacific affairs, explained why in a long memorandum sent to Nixon in the spring of 1969: "As long as the war in Vietnam continues, it will be difficult to decrease the official American presence in such countries as Japan, the Philippines and Thailand. We must nevertheless bear in mind that an excessive U.S. presence in East Asia presents a serious political liability not only in terms of our relations with the countries concerned but also prospectively in terms of weakening governments we seek to strengthen."[53] Green emphasized the 6,000 excess U.S. intelligence personnel in Japan. Nixon wrote across the top of Green's report, "This is Great." The president was willing to make tactical retreats for the sake of strategic advances. As he had written in his 1967 *Foreign Affairs* essay:

> During the final third of the twentieth century, Asia, not Europe or Latin America, will pose the greatest danger of a confrontation which could escalate into World War III. . . .
>
> The United States is a Pacific power. Europe has been withdrawing the remnants of empire, but the United States, with its coast reaching in an arc from Mexico to the Bering Straits, is one anchor of a vast Pacific community. Both our interests and our ideals propel us west-ward across the Pacific, not as conquerors but as partners.[54]

United States forces dropped rapidly in number (including a reduction of 12,000 in Japan between 1969 and 1971), but as Muraoka Kunio, of the Japanese Diplomatic Service, saw clearly, "There is nothing in the Nixon Doctrine to suggest a drastic decline of the United States interest in Asia."

Under the doctrine, Muraoka observed, the importance to Americans of "maintaining friendly relations with Japan cannot be overestimated."[55]

Muraoka's analysis signaled how power was shifting, regardless of Nixon's and Kissinger's intentions. The United States might ultimately use nuclear weapons to enforce containment, but short of that it would have to depend on such allies as the Japanese to maintain a containment policy in a post-Vietnam era. Nixon, however, refused to follow the policy to that conclusion. He and Kissinger could never bring themselves to recognize the shifting of this power. They consequently held back from transferring real security tasks to Japan.[56] Nixon held these tasks tightly, both to maintain unilateral United States freedom of action and to give him the high cards for playing the new game with the Soviets and Chinese. Secretary of Defense Melvin Laird visited Japan in 1971 and mused publicly that his hosts should undertake greater defense efforts. He even reportedly declared he would look with "equanimity" on Japanese development of nuclear weapons.[57] That view certainly did not mesh with Nixon's policy. He never wanted Japan to share control of a nuclear shield long held by the United States. The president did not even want Japan to undertake a significant, public, conventional buildup. When Chou En-lai accused Kissinger of "tempting Japan into traditional nationalist paths," the American vigorously and convincingly denied it. The U.S. security arrangement of 1960, Kissinger argued, contained Japan's traditional "nationalism," and—he added ingeniously—the surest way to tempt Japanese nationalism would be to trigger competition for Tokyo's favor between China and the United States.[58]

The Japanese did not see the situation so clearly. In 1970, the government published its first postwar White Paper on defense that suggestively mentioned an "autonomous" defense policy that could somehow develop under the 1960 arrangements. With the project fourth buildup of the defense forces for 1972-1976, Japanese military spending was to grow into the seventh largest defense budget in the world. Nevertheless, the fourth buildup also demonstrated, in Muraoka's words, "heavy dependence" not only on United States power in case of nuclear threats, but for "any major conventional assault on Japan."[59] A highly knowledgeable former State Department official, moreover, doubted that the Japanese civil service, despite its "high competence" in other areas, had the background, incentive, or personnel to deal with "increasingly complex matters" in the strategic-military realm.[60]

The Vietnam tragedy thus forced Nixon to undertake a tactical retreat to more traditional American policies in Asia. These policies would have surfaced whether or not the Vietnam War had occurred. They were either historic American approaches or policies that could be seen developing out of changes in the region that appeared as early as 1957-1960 and included the Sino-Soviet split and Japan's new economic prowess. In the end, Nixon never could come to terms with the Vietnam conflict. But neither could he come to terms with a new Japan that was evolving outside the Vietnam context, for he wanted the Japanese somehow to help enforce the Nixon Doctrine but not to build a military force that could threaten either the United States' unilateral activity in the region or the restraints long imposed on Japan's nationalism. Because of that contradiction, Nixon and Kissinger no more came to terms with Japan militarily and politically than they did economically.

Nixon's decision to reduce the land war and, over the much longer term, the air war in Vietnam made American administrative control over Okinawa expendable. That view was reinforced by a comprehensive analysis of U.S.-Japan relations that Kissinger organized and drove through the bureaucracy (over strong Pentagon opposition) during his first days in the White House.[61] Proud of his ability to distinguish the big picture from relatively minor details, Nixon pledged the return of Okinawa to Japan's control during his summit meeting with Satō in the autumn of 1969. The president wished only to maintain bases for conventional U.S. forces; not even the right to store nuclear weapons—a concession demanded by the Pentagon—was retained, although as the 1960 security pact provided, such weapons could be reintroduced on Japanese soil under joint consultation arrangements.

But Nixon did want another detail. He privately asked Satō for assurance that Japanese textile exports to the United States would be limited. The president could thus fulfill a campaign pledge made in southern states where the textile industry floundered. Kissinger's notes show that Satō agreed. The official Japanese position was, however, that the prime minister would have to negotiate the issue in Tokyo. Back home Satō confronted textile and political interests that prevented granting Nixon's request. The president became furious. By 1971, after nearly two years of fruitless talks, he threatened cutting off Japan's textile exports to America by invoking the 1917 Trading with the Enemy Act. That threat, the Nixon "shocks" of 1971, an imposed U.S. deadline, and back-channel diplomacy by Kissinger and Satō's aides finally resolved the issue in October 1971.

The relationship, whose balance-wheels both sides had taken too much for granted, was now strained by long-term changes in Japan and the United States. Nixon did not understand the demands of Japanese politics, but the prime minister did not understand that this time the United States intended to discipline an economic power that Americans were beginning to view as "Japan, Inc."[62] A campaign promise had turned into a policy principle for Nixon. He refused to allow the belance-wheels of time and patience, which both sides had exhibited until this time, to resolve the issue. By 1971 Nixon had run out of both time and patience in this and other crucial foreign policy areas.

By 1971, the textile problem was, in Nixon's mind, less a part of the Okinawa issue and more a part of a general crisis. The U.S. economy, undermined by accelerating inflation and growing lack of competitiveness among some of its major industries, stumbled toward its first unfavorable balance of merchandise trade since the 1890s. Nixon cared less about historical precedent than he did about what the turn portended for the U.S. capacity to maintain costly worldwide commitments. The United States no longer had the capability of paying for the kind of containment policy it had followed even before 1961, not to mention afterward.

The reasons for this growing incapability related to the new complexities of the post-1960 world, a relative decline in U.S. productive capabilities, rising competitiveness of Japanese and European industry, and responsibilities at home assumed by Johnson's Great Society program. The costs of Vietnam only exacerbated this new situation. Nixon, however, had an immediate problem: he was running for reelection in 1972 and, in the early stages of the campaign, planned to cap his career with summits in China and the Soviet Union. To reverse the American decline, he refused to reduce overseas commitments or obligations at home, but determined to make the allies—especially Japan—pay more for both the commitments and obligations.

The Japanese were obvious targets. As the textile imbroglio exemplified, Americans saw them as unfairly threatening basic U.S. industries. As the dollar became overvalued and the entire postwar economic structure that rested on the dollar began to crumble, Nixon asked leading competitors to revalue so that breathing room could be found. Germany did so after 1969, but Japan did not. By 1971, Secretary of Commerce Maurice Stans reportedly declared, "The Japanese are still fighting the war, only now instead of a shooting war it is an economic war. Their immediate intention is to try to dominate the Pacific and then perhaps the world."[63] One observer has noted that Stans's image of Japan "was frozen somewhere in 1942,"[64] but Stans was, after all, a high-ranking member of the Nixon administration and a close personal associate of the president. His views, only slightly discounted, represented a consensus in the administration. One State Department briefing paper reportedly went further by terming Japan a "potential enemy."

Japan's sin was not in refusing to build nuclear or even larger conventional forces, but in not sufficiently helping the United States to pay for American nuclear and conventional forces strung around the world. In Nixon's eyes, this sin ramified when he could neither end the Vietnam War on his terms nor stop the decline of the U.S. economy. His careful delineation, in his publicized 1971 speech at Kansas City, that Japan had to be seen as one of the "five great economic super powers," made sense only as a signal to Japan to act like both an economic superpower and an American ally. The president (not to mention his national security advisor) seldom preoccupied himself with economic issues unless they directly related to his geopolitical concerns. Nixon revealed that linkage precisely in the Kansas City speech when he declared that "economic power will be the key to other kinds of power, the future of the world in other ways in the last third of this century." When the Japanese either missed or ignored this signal, Nixon moved to wring concessions by declaring economic war. He imposed a 10 percent surcharge on imports until Japan agreed to revalue, set a deadline for concluding the textile deal on his terms, and announced his trip to China that would radically change the traditional U.S. relationship with Asia.

C. Fred Bergsten wrote at the time that "the new economic approach, coupled with the coming presidential visits to Peking and Moscow, produced the most bizarre U.S. foreign policy imaginable: war on our friends, concessions to our traditional adversaries."[65] Nixon, however, explained the apparent contradiction in his 1972 foreign policy report. He declared that the "shocks" were regrettable, but they "only accelerated an evolution in U.S.-Japanese relations that was in any event overdue, unavoidable, and in the long run, desirable" because the relationship had to become a "more mature and reciprocal partnership."[66]

Nixon's words (the 1972 report was actually written by Kissinger) assumed that the U.S.-Japanese relationship of 1945 to the early 1960s had been an exception in the century-old history of the two nations' ties. Americans and Japanese were returning to a more normal set of relations, the kind that characterized their bilateral dealings in the interwar years or before World War I—only this time-U.S. officials determined to keep the dominant military power of the relationship in their own hands. The Vietnam War had only sharpened and intensified the effects of this change until the results had to be dealt with in 1971.

Unsurprisingly, Tokyo officials read the shocks differently. The post-1945 ties with the United States had been based, in Muraoka's words, "on total confidence." The announcements of Nixon's visit to Beijing and the imposition of the New Economic Plan undercut that confidence because in neither instance had Japan been consulted.[67] The Japanese embarked on a more independent foreign policy. Ignoring U.S. protests, Satō dispatched two of his top department chiefs to discuss affairs with Hanoi just before Nixon was to arrive in China. Satō also suddenly established diplomatic relations with Outer Mongolia, a Soviet-controlled country on China's borders; that move occurred just four days before U.S. officials flew to Tokyo to brief the Japanese on the Nixon-Mao summit. Japan also improved relations, especially in the economic area, with Russia and China, while retaining U.S. military protection. But that protection was somewhat less important, for as Japan exploited the Sino-Soviet rift economically, so Tokyo was left without an immediate military threat to worry about. The Japanese were maneuvering profitably in Nixon's five-power world.[68] Nor, after the president's New Economic Plan of 1971, could Americans complain as effectively about Japan's mercantilistic tactics for capturing foreign markets and protecting its own.

In 1973, Kissinger could declare (unilaterally and from New York City) that it was to be "The Year of Europe and Japan" in U.S. foreign policy, but in reality 1973 became the year of the Middle East and Watergate. The Middle East conflict and resulting oil embargo by Arab and Iranian producers forced Japan to make its first major open break with the United States in the post-1945 era. As a 1971 staff study informed Kissinger, a rise of energy prices "would affect primarily Europe and Japan and probably improve America's competitive position."[69] (Such a comment and its policy implications were probably unthinkable in Washington as late as 1965.) Japan rejected the U.S. position on Israel and moved closer to the Arabs, who provided 80 percent of Japan's oil imports. In a larger framework, Tokyo's new policies not only attempted to break with American policy in the Middle East, but sought to become less dependent on United States economic—especially energy—policies in general. Americans were no longer viewed as the reliable suppliers of the early 1960s. The 1971 shocks, a unilaterally imposed embargo on American soybean exports to Japan, policy in the Middle East, and an independent, aggressive Japanese economic offensive in Southeast Asia to replace the departed Americans transfigured a relationship that was already changing when Nixon entered office.[70]

As Kissinger tried to control the effects of these changes in his "Year of Europe and Japan" approach, another group attempted to improve Japanese-United States ties through a Trilateral Commission. Studies in 1971-72 by Zbigniew Brzezinski and the Brookings Institution influenced David Rockefeller, chairman of Chase Manhattan Bank, to establish the Trilateral Commission so that shattered ties could be renewed among Japan, Western Europe, and the United States. But it also aimed at nothing less than what one member called "a new world order," with the three industrial power blocs forming the foundation for that "order."[71]

Trilateralism, however, never could create such a new order. Japan's relations with Western Europe, for example, could not approximate the importance of ties with the United States or, increasingly, even the new ties with Southeast Asia. Tokyo officials, moreover, prevented the commission from issuing consensus statements on security issues—despite Kissinger's 1976 declaration that "security is the bedrock of all that [the industrial democracies] do."[72]

In 1975, Kissinger glossed over these problems by announcing that the "strains" of 1971 "are behind us. . . . U.S.-Japanese bilateral relations, I am pleased to say, have never been better in 30 years." In the same speech, however, Kissinger more accurately indicated why the relations could not be as good as they were before the mid-1960s: "a new international environment" had developed, "a world of multiple centers of power, of ideological differences both old and new, clouded by nuclear peril and marked by the new imperatives of interdependence."[73] To deal with this new world, both nations had to work within an arrangement that was no longer fully acceptable to either side: Japanese economic power was a constant irritation in American debate and policymaking, while dependence on U.S. security arrangements created doubt in Japan. The 1977 Japanese White Paper on defense for the first time expressed public doubts about the U.S.-Soviet strategic balance.[74] A relationship once characterized by terms such as "harmony" and "partnership" had changed to "competition."[75] The "earthquakes" and "typhoons" that struck the U.S.-Japanese relationship between 1960 and 1975—not the artificial atmosphere of 1945 to 1960—portended the future of the relationship as they also reflected the more distant, pre-1931 past.

1. The "inevitable harmony" analysis is in Priscilla A. Clapp and Morton H. Halperin, "U.S. Elite Images of Japan: The Postwar Period," in *Mutual Images: Essays in American-Japanese Relations*, ed. Akira Iriye (Cambridge, Mass., 1975), 210-11; Theodore Draper, *Present History* (New York, 1983), 51-114.

2. U.S. Department of State, "Department of State Policy on the Future of Japan," NSC Country File, Japan, Lyndon B. Johnson Library, Austin, Texas (hereafter cited: LBJ Library). The author thanks David C. Humphrey of the LBJ Library for his advice and efforts in making available newly declassified material.

3. Oral History Interview of Edwin O. Reischauer, 8 April 1969, LBJ Library, 6.

4. I.M. Destler, Fukui Haruhiro, and Satō Hideo, *The Textile Wrangle: Conflict in Japanese-American Relations, 1969-1971* (Ithaca, NY, 1969), 25-26; Edwin O. Reischauer, "Our Dialogue With Japan," *Foreign Affairs* 45 (January 1967): 215-17.

5. U.S. Department of State Administrative History, "East Asia: Japan," Chapter 5, 15-16, LBJ Library.

6. *New York Times*, 6 July 1967, 49; *Department of State Bulletin*, 9 October 1967, 453.

7. *Department of State Bulletin*, 9 October 1967, 457.

8. *Wall Street Journal*, 11 November 1966, 22.

9. "Memorandum for the President," from Francis M. Bator, 16 June 1965, NSC Country File, Japan, LBJ Library; Richard J. Barnet, *The Alliance. America, Europe, Japan, Makers of the Postwar World* (New York, 1983), 270.

10. Oral History Interview of Reischauer, 6-7.

11. Oral History Interview of James C. Thomson, Jr., 22 July 1971, LBJ Library, 54.

12. *Japan Quarterly*, 13(1) (January-March 1966), 17-26.

13. Oral History Interview of Reischauer, 9-10; *New York Times*, 22 January 1966, 1.

14. Barnet, *The Alliance*, 270.

15. John K. Emmerson, "Japan: Eye on 1970," *Foreign Affairs* 47 (January 1969): 357; George R. Packard, III, "Living with the Real Japan," *Foreign Affairs* 46 (October 1967): 200-201.

16. "The Week that Was," Chester L. Cooper and James C. Thomson, Jr., to McGeorge Bundy, 7 January 1965, NSC Country File, Vietnam, vol. 25, 114, LBJ Library.

17. George F. Kennan, "Japanese Security and American Policy," *Foreign Affairs* 43 (October 1964): 14-22.

18. Oral History Interview of Thomson, 17, 40.

19. Reischauer to Secretary of State, 24 September 1964, NSC Country File, Japan, LBJ Library; Oral History Interview of William P. Bundy, 1969, vol. 1, 36, LBJ Library.

20. "Breakfast at Embassy-Tokyo, Dec. 28, 1965," in Jack Valenti—Notes Taken at Various Meetings during 1965 and 1966, Office Files of the President, LBJ Library.

21. "Prospects for New Japanese Prime Minister," Thomas L. Hughes to the Acting Secretary, 10 November 1964, NSC Country File, Japan, vol. 2, LBJ Library.

22. *Far Eastern Economic Review*, 28 September 1967, 629.

23. "Memorandum of Conversation," 12 July 1965, NSC Country File, Japan, vol. 2, LBJ Library.

24. "Special Report: Japan Rethinking Security Policy," Central Intelligence Agency, 29 April 1966, NSC Country File, Japan, vol. 2, LBJ Library; *Washington Post*, 18 December 1967, A16; *New York Times*, 24 December 1967, 1; Reischauer to Secretary of State, 24 February 1966, NSC Country File, Ryukyus, LBJ Library.

25. "Memorandum of Conversation," 13 Jan. 1965, NSC Country File, Japan, vol. 2, LBJ Library.

26. "Memorandum for the President," from Rusk, 10 November 1967, NSC Country File, Japan, vol. 2, LBJ Library.

27. Emmerson, "Japan: Eye on 1970," 356-57.

28. *Far Eastern Economic Review*, 28 September 1967, 595.

29. Reischauer to Secretary of State, 24 February 1966, NSC Country File, Japan, vol. 2, LBJ Library.

30. "Memorandum for the President," from Rusk, 4 September 1967, Central File, LBJ Library.

31. W. Macmahon Ball, "Japan in Asia's Future," *The Nation* (15 January 1968): 84.

32. Michael Schaller, "Securing the Great Crescent: Occupied Japan and the Origins of Containment in Southeast Asia," *Journal of American History* 49 (September 1982): 392-414.

33. Zbigniew Brzezinski, "Threat and Opportunity in the Communist Schism," *Foreign Affairs* 41 (April 1963): 525.

34. W.W. Rostow, *The Diffusion of Power. An Essay in Recent History* (New York, 1972), 426-30.

35. Rostow, especially 429-30; U.S. Department of State Administrative History Chapter 7, Part B: "East Asian Regionalism," LBJ Library.

36. *New York Times*, February 13, 1967, 8; Ball, "Japan in Asia's Future," 83.

37. Reischauer to Secretary of State, 15 September 1965, NSC Country File, Japan, vol. 2, LBJ Library.

38. Ball, "Japan in Asia's Future," 83; Packard, "Living with the Real Japan," 197-98.

39. *U.S. News and World Report*, July 24, 1967, 90-91.

40. Bernard K. Gordon, "Japan, the United States, and Southeast Asia," *Foreign Affairs* 56 (April 1978): 579-82.

41. "Memorandum for the President," from W.W. Rostow, 13 November 1967, NSC Country File, Japan, vol. 3, LBJ Library.

42. The Okinawa issue is well analyzed in Watanabe Akio, *The Okinawa Problem* (Melbourne, 1970), 167-68, especially for the impact on the alliance.

43. Reischauer to Secretary to State, 26 June 1966, NSC Country File, Ryukyus, LBJ Library.

44. "Okinawan Developments Affect Japan," Thomas L. Hughes to the Acting Secretary, 10 July 1964, NSC Country File, Ryukyus, LBJ Library.

45. I.M. Destler, "Country Expertise and U.S. Foreign Policymaking," in M.A. Kaplan and Kinhide Mushakoji, eds., *Japan, America, and the Future World* (New York, 1976), 134-35.

46. Philip W. Quigg, "Japan in Neutral," *Foreign Affairs* 44 (January 1966): 258.

47. "Memorandum for the President," from Robert S. McNamara, 30 August 1967, President's Confidential File, CO 141, LBJ Library; Reischauer to Secretary of State, 24 May 1966, NSC Country, Japan, vol. 2, LBJ Library.

48. Packard, 200.

49. *New York Times*, 5 April 1968, 9; *Christian Science Monitor*, April 16, 1968, 1.

50. *New York Times*, 7 April 1968, 9.

51. These arguments are detailed in Seymour Hersh, *The Price of Power* (New York, 1983).

52. Henry Kissinger, *White House Years* (Boston, 1979), 220-25; Leslie H. Brown, *American Security Policy in Asia*, Adelphi Papers, no. 132 (London, 1977), 1-8.

53. Quoted in Tad Szulc, *The Illusion of Peace. Foreign Policy in the Nixon Years* (New York, 1978), 107.

54. Richard M. Nixon, "Asia after Viet Nam," *Foreign Affairs* 46 October 1967): 112.

55. Muraoka Kunio, *Japanese Security*, Adelphi Papers, no. 95 (London, 1973), 5-6.

56. A good contemporary analysis is in Robert E. Osgood, "The Diplomacy of Allied Relations: Europe and Japan," in Osgood, et al., *Retreat From Empire? The First Nixon Administration* (Baltimore, 1973), 194-98.

57. Brown, *American Security Policy*, 7.

58. Kissinger, *White House Years*, 334.

59. Muraoka, *Japanese Security*, 3-4; Brown, *American Security Policy*, 9.

60. Brown, *American Security Policy*, 4.

61. Roger Morris, *Uncertain Greatness: Henry Kissinger and American Foreign Policy* (New York, 1977), 103-04.

62. This discussion is based on Morris, *Undertain Greatness*, 104-05; and Destler, Fukui, and Satō, *Textile Wrangle*, 8, 40, 292-93, 329, 316-17.

63. Destler, "Country Expertise," 142.

64. Barnet, *The Alliance*, 308.

65. C. Fred Bergsten, "The New Economics and U.S. Foreign Policy," *Foreign Affairs* 50 (January 1972): 208-09. The Nixon quote and a good analysis within the context of later shocks are in *New York Times*, 23 Jan. 1972, 5.

66. This report is summarized in Osgood, 197; this discussion has been informed by David P. Calleo, *The Imperious Economy* (Cambridge, Mass., 1982).

67. Muraoka, *Japanese Security*, 2.

68. Muraoka, *Japanese Security*, 12, 16, 20; Szulc, *Illusion of Peace*, 528.

69. Barnet, *The Alliance*, 328.

70. *New York Times*, 28 August 1972, 14; and 6 April 1975, F9; Brown, *American Security Policy* 12. On the changing U.S.-Japanese position in Southeast Asia, see Gordon, "Japan, the United States, and Southeast Asia," 585; Brown, *American Security Policy* 11-12; *New York Times*, 28 August 1972, 14.

71. Jeremiah Novak, "The Trilateral Connection," *The Atlantic Monthly*, 240 (July 1977): 57.

72. Richard H. Ullman, "Trilateralism: 'Partnership' For What?" *Foreign Affairs* 55 (January 1977): especially 3-18.

73. *Department of State Bulletin*, July 7, 1975, 1-2.

74. Gordon, "Japan, the United States and Southeast Asia," 579-81.

75. Clapp and Halperin, "U.S. Elite Images of Japan," 218.

PART TWO

The United States
and Japan in the
World Economy

Using the case studies of Part One as their starting point, the next group of essays examines how Japan has performed in the economic arena since its leaders succeeded in integrating the country into the U.S.-led world economy on their own terms, and how their very success has created havoc with "the American system."

Okimoto and Krasner (chapter 7) offer several theoretical (predictive) models for Japan's reaction to the disruption its booming economy caused in the structure of the economic regime, i.e., rules of the game that are central to the American system. They concede that Japan, under pressure from the United States, has greatly liberalized its trade policies since the 1960s, but contend that these changes have had meager outcomes. Especially in areas in which the United States has demonstrated a competitive advantage in trading with third countries, Japan continues to buy less than would be expected. Okimoto and Krasner offer several explanations, stressing the need for greater attention to the private sector. Although they indicate that American demands have been essential to obtain even modest results in Japan, their analysis suggests that current protectionist trends in the United States could conceivably lead to the disastrous economic nationalism of the 1930s—rather than to active Japanese leadership in a restructured liberal trading system.

Kanemitsu (chapter 8) provides a particularly valuable statistical profile of Japan's trade relations, especially with the United States, as they have evolved since 1955. His data dovetail neatly with the changing pattern of political power—Japan's movement, as he suggests, from protegé to partner—described in earlier chapters. Kanemitsu's tables and his explanations of them allow the reader to be more sanguine about the working of the principle of comparative advantage than Okimoto and Krasner suggest. The jury is still out on the issue, but there are indications that Japanese are more optimistic these days than Americans about how well free trade works, much like the British and the Americans in their days of hegemony, as noted by Okimoto and Krasner. Kanemitsu also touches on another area of growing American concern, Japan's role as an exporter of capital. He notes that as savings mount, public consumption in Japan still does not offset the high rate of savings, and more and more money will be available to buy property in the United States.

Feldman's essay (chapter 9), highly technical though it is, describes and explains the liberalization of Japanese capital markets as the economy gained strength and its would-be managers gained confidence. A major opening of the capital markets occurred in the mid-1960s, as the success of Japan's high growth strategy became evident, and regulation all but disappeared in 1980. Feldman's analysis, consistent with that of Okimoto and Krasner, suggests that liberalization came only after regulation proved successful—that is, when it was no longer needed. Japan was responding less to external pressures or any objective sense of fairness than to confidence that protection of its capital market was no longer necessary. But like Kanemitsu's discussion, Feldman's offers hope that institutional mechanisms are sufficiently flexible to enable Japan to accommodate its partners in the world economic system.

All three essays demonstrate the superb strategy pursued by Japan's leaders in the reconstruction of the country's postwar, postoccupation economy. They protected their industries and their markets and moved shrewdly and aggressively to expand their exports. They were slower than some Americans to perceive the extent of their success, but by the mid-1960s they initiated a process of liberalization in trade practices and capital markets that continues to this day. Japanese political leaders and state economic managers are responsive to the needs of their trading partners, but the outcome of liberalization to date has been disappointing to potential American exporters—as perhaps it always will be.

7
Japan's Evolving Trade Posture

STEPHEN D. KRASNER
and DANIEL I. OKIMOTO

Japan has experienced more dramatic levels of economic growth than any other major industrialized country. One-twentieth the size of that of the United States at the end of the Second World War, Japan's economy increased to one-half that of the United States by the early 1980s. Its products jumped from 3.4 percent of world exports in 1963 to 7.5 percent in 1982,[1] and its exports dominated several fast-growing and important industrial sectors. Its intrusion into the world economy has generated conflict to the extent that Japan has been accused of protecting its domestic economy while preaching international liberalism. Import-impacted industries of other countries have demanded protection; trading partners have pressed for greater access to the Japanese market.

This essay is an effort to describe and explain Japan's trade posture. A country's trade posture has two components: policies related to both tariff and nontariff barriers and international regimes, and actual outcomes with regard to the movement of goods. Three major trade postures can be described, although these do not exhaust the logical possibilities: myopic self-interest is characterized by only the most grudging and minimal changes in national policy, indifference or hostility toward liberal international regimes, and limited access for foreign products; selective accommodation is characterized by reactive concessions in trade policy, indifference or limited support for international regimes, and selective change in trade outcomes; active cooperation is characterized by extensive national liberalization, strong support for and leadership in international regimes, and significant changes in actual outcomes, that is, the actual movement of goods.

A country with a trade posture of myopic self-interest aims at maximizing its national objectives over the short and medium term. There is little or no concern about system stability and few connections are made between issue areas. Myopically self-interested states act as free riders whenever possible.

Given a liberal international system, such a state will pursue protectionist policies (to maximize either static utility or dynamic growth), abandoning them only to avoid foreign retaliation or when domestic industries are so competitive that foreign products cannot compete. Ineffective liberalization—policy modifications that do not lead to changes in outcomes—may be used to mollify trading partners. Little support or leadership is provided for international organization.

A country with a posture of selective accommodation acts as a follower in a liberal regime but not as a leader and it accedes to foreign pressures for policy change. These changes are accompanied by alterations in the actual flow of goods, but the state does not take a leadership role in maintaining international regimes, nor does it alter policies in areas where it is not under pressure.

A country with a posture of active accommodation is concerned with system maintenance. It is a strong supporter of liberal regimes and may choose to lift restrictive measures even without explicit pressure from trading partners. Policy changes lead to changes in actual outcomes. Short-run economic interests are subordinated or sacrificed for long-run objectives including systemic stability.

In sum, the three ideal-typical postures identified above can be differentiated along two dimensions, policy and outcomes. Policy can be more or less liberal with regard to eliminating domestic barriers to trade. Given a liberal regime, the very removal of such barriers is a major act of support for the regime. In addition, a state may play a more or less active role in international organizations, and outcomes may be more or less open with regard to the actual flow of goods.

Each of these ideal-types can be explained by one or more systemic level theories that has been applied to the area of international trade. Systems level analyses can be complemented by national level arguments that focus upon political structure, interest group activity, national values, and electoral incentives as a more detailed guide to sectoral variation.[2] These arguments can be illustrated with reference to Japan.

Various realist or structural analyses of the international economy, especially the theory of hegemonic stability, imply that Japan has and will pursue a policy of myopic self-interest. The theory of hegemonic stability maintains that an open global economic system is associated with a hegemonic distribution of power. Only a hegemonic state has the ability and interest to create and maintain such an environment. The hegemon is a leader in international organizations, tolerates free riders, and acts as a lender of last resort. As the power of the hegemon declines, the global economic system becomes more closed. The hegemonic state itself adopts more protectionist measures as increasing international competition raises the costs of openness. It becomes more reluctant to tolerate free riders and less willing to bear disproportionate costs for regime maintenance. Other states are unable to step into the breach because they cannot allocate the costs of providing collective goods or co-ordinate their policies, given differing national objectives. Hegemonic sta-bility theory argues that the two most dramatic examples of policy liberalization and openness with regard to outcomes—the middle of the nine-teenth century and the period from 1945 to 1970—are associated with he-gemonic states, Great Britain and the United States. As British power faded at the end of the nineteenth century and American power since 1970, inter-national economic transactions have become more restricted.[3]

Hegemonic stability theory implies that Japan's position in the international system would encourage a policy of myopic self-interest. Over the years, the ratio of the U.S. Gross National Product (GNP) to that of Japan has steadily decreased. In 1955, the GNP ratio was 10.59; ten years later it had almost halved (6.17). By 1970, it had dropped to 4.19 and declined still further to 3.12 by 1975. In 1981, the ratio was 2.15.[4] During the early postwar period Japan was so small that acting as a free rider was the optimal policy. Japanese contributions to system stability, had they been attempted, would have had little impact. Protectionism maximized short- and medium-term national in-terest because it provided static benefits for the terms of trade and dynamic benefits by protecting new industries until they became internationally com-petitive.[4]

Japan's position relative to that of the United States has changed rapidly over the postwar period. Once only 5 percent the size of its American coun-terpart, Japan's economy mushroomed to over 40 percent the size of the U.S. GNP by 1980. The decline in American power was visible across a number of specific issue areas, most notably oil. Hegemonic stability theory associates such weakening in power capabilities with less regime stability and more protectionism. Secondary powers cannot stem this tide. As the system moves toward greater closure, there is little incentive for countries like Japan to liberalize. Japan is not strong enough to act as a leader. Conciliatory policies would not necessarily be reciprocated by Japan's trading partners because of domestic interest group pressures. Because no state can be sure that the game will continue to be played by the same rules, the most prudent course is to act in terms of short- and medium-term national goals. Although this might mean occasional accommodation to foreign pressures in order to avoid costly consequences, it would preclude any leadership role or general liberalization. In sum, hegemonic stability theory suggests that Japan has pursued, and will continue to pursue, a policy of myopic self-interest because in the early post-war period it was small enough to act as a free rider and in more recent years it has not been large enough to stabilize the system in the face of declining American hegemony.

The theoretical underpinnings for the second ideal-type trade posture, selective accommodation, are derived from modified structural discussions of international regimes and from game theoretic analysis of iterative prisoner's dilemma. Regimes are principles, norms, rules and decision-making procedures around which actor expectations converge. Regimes coordinate the behavior of individual actors: they lower the likelihood of disputes by enhancing the flow of information and therefore reduce suspicions of cheating; they lessen the intensity of conflicts by providing for dispute settlement procedures; when differences cannot be reconciled, they may specify appropriate levels of retaliation, making it less likely that conflictual behavior will spread from one dispute to another.[6]

Once regimes are in place they are likely to persist even though the power configurations that led to their creation may have changed. Actors are uncertain about alternatives. Existing regimes establish salient solutions for a known set of problems. Vested bureaucratic interests and institutions develop around established principles, norms, rules, and decision-making procedures.

Since 1945, international regimes have been created for many important issue areas. The problems most directly addressed by these regimes were those of the 1930s, especially beggar-thy-neighbor practices, including competitive devaluations, import quotas, and high tariffs. The exchange rate system specified by the Articles of Agreement of the International Monetary Fund and the liberal trading order embodied in the General Agreement on Tariffs and Trade (GATT) were efforts to prevent a repeat of the depression years. Issues that had not been salient in the 1930s, including industrial policies, international capital flows, and domestic financial structures, were not directly addressed by the postwar international economic regimes.

Arguments based on the significance of international regimes suggest that Japanese behavior would change, but primarily in those areas covered by explicit agreements. As a major beneficiary of the postwar system, Japan would have some stake in maintaining existing regimes. Japanese policymakers would be concerned about the consequences of violating explicit rules. Japan might not only react to pressures and complaints concerning violations of existing rules, but even take an active and initiatory role in supporting ongoing regimes.

However, an analysis of international regimes grounded in a realist framework would be skeptical about the prospects for altering Japanese behavior in areas not covered by explicit rules and decision-making procedures. General principles and norms would not provide clear guidelines under conditions of clashing national interests. Attempts to create new rules of the game with specific prescriptions and proscriptions would be very difficult in the absence of a hegemonic leader. Thus, while Japan would be accommodating, perhaps even initiatory, with regard to issues covered by existing rules of the game, little progress could be expected in other issue areas. If nonregime-governed issues grew more salient, tension and conflict would increase even though Japan's trade posture adhered to existing rules.

A game theoretic perspective also suggests that Japan's trade posture would evolve toward selective accommodation. However, this approach points to changes in Japanese trade posture over time as opposed to across-regime- or nonregime-governed issues. As pressure from Japan's trading partners increased, Japan would adopt increasingly liberal policies. Trade posture is seen as analogous to the game of prisoner's dilemma. The optimal outcome for a player occurs when that player cheats (protects) and the other player cooperates (liberalizes). However, if both players cheat (protect), they are worse off than if they had both cooperated (liberalized). For instance, if one trading nation can impose an optimal tariff on its trading partners, it will be better off than under a situation of free trade. However, if its trading partner retaliates, then both are likely to finish in worse condition than if they had adopted a policy of mutual cooperation leading to free trade.

In single play prisoners dilemma, the logical outcome is mutual cheating; however in iterative prisoners dilemma, mutual cooperation is more likely. In a fascinating exercise, Robert Axelrod invited players to submit strategies for an iterative prisoners dilemma game. These strategies were then played against each other. The winning strategy was TIT FOR TAT. TIT FOR TAT is a strategy in which a player cooperates on the first move and then does whatever the other player did on the last move. A player using TIT FOR TAT never defects first, retaliates immediately, and is quick to forgive when the opponent switches from defection to cooperation.[7]

If a player is sure the game will continue, then TIT FOR TAT will be a stable solution for any set of cardinal values in conformity with the conditions for a prisoner's dilemma payoff matrix. Each player begins by cooperating, and cooperation continues. If the game will end at some point, then the rationality of continuing to play TIT FOR TAT, as opposed to some other strategy, such as ALL DEFECTION. depends upon the relationship of the values of the payoff matrix and the probability that the game will end. Even under conditions of mutual defection, it is still possible to move to a TIT FOR TAT strategy, provided there is a clustering of individuals playing TIT FOR TAT. If such a cluster is large enough, it can displace the strategy of ALL DEFECTION.

The implications of this analysis for current behavior in the area of international trade are quite sanguine. Charles Lipson has argued that, because trading relations can be characterized as an iterative prisoner's dilemma, the prospects for cooperation are high.[8] The number of plays can be increased by disaggregating transactions into smaller parts. More significantly, the costs of making a mistake (cooperating when the other player defects) are not high, at least relative to the costs of making a mistake in the international security arena. There is also more transparency in international economic environments than in security ones; cheating can be discovered more easily. Hence the mutual distrust that undermines strategic and military cooperation is less of a problem in the area of trade because of repeated plays, transparency, and small differences between the pay-offs for cheating instead of cooperating.

A game theoretic analysis suggests that Japan would alter its international economic posture in response to pressure from trading partners. Changes would not be isolated. Cooperation in one play of the game would lead to cooperation in others. Even making the most generous assumptions about American policy through the 1960s with regard to tolerating Japanese protectionism and the most cynical ones about Japanese policy, the logic of an iterative prisoner's dilemma situation suggests that mutual cooperation would emerge once the United States began to demonstrate that it was prepared to retaliate against Japan. This argument is more sanguine about the prospects for a liberal order than is modified realism with its emphasis on regimes. Cooperation cumulates over time; eventually it becomes active rather than selective as each player comes to understand that defection will always be punished leaving both worse off. In the long run, a game theoretic approach suggests that Japan would adopt a trade posture of active cooperation.

There are other arguments that also imply that Japanese policy would evolve toward active cooperation even in the shorter run. Japanese accommodation need not necessarily be explained by pressure from economic partners or be limited to issue areas covered by existing regimes. The two other approaches which suggest an evolution toward active cooperation for Japan are liberal, or Grotian, theories emphasizing the mutual benefits of interdependence and a realist, or structural, argument stressing the stability that arises out of a structure of mutipolarity.

A liberal or Grotian perspective sees both national and subnational actors linked by a web of interdependence created by ongoing transaction flows. These flows are not hostage to changes in international power distributions. They are not constantly threatened by cheating, either, because custom and habit have evolved over time into internalized norms or because rational calculation, based on full confidence in the continuity of the system, dictates cooperative behavior.

Since 1960, there has been a significant increase in the relative importance of trade for all major countries except Japan. The income elasticity of trade has been greater than unity. Taking 1963 as equal to 100, the volume of world trade had increased to 300 by 1982 (it had peaked at 305 in 1980) while the volume of world production had increased to only 223. The value of world exports increased from $154 billion in 1963 to $1,845 billion in 1982.[9]

For Japan, exports plus imports as a percent of Gross Domestic Product (GDP) declined slightly from 21.2 percent in 1960 to 20.3 percent in 1970, but then rose to 30.1 percent in 1981.[10] Trade is critical for some sectors of the Japanese economy. Japan is more heavily dependent on raw material imports than is any other major industrialized country. Some of the most dynamic firms in the Japanese economy have regarded exports as a critical part of their overall strategies. Many Japanese corporations have become more active direct foreign investors since the late 1960s. The international capital market has become a more important source of funds. Thus, liberalism would see Japan as a country whose public and private actors have a high stake in the stability of an open international economic system. The interests of many groups in Japan, both inside and outside the government, depend upon the vitality of this system. As Japan's capabilities increase, it would play a more active role in preserving and even improving the ongoing order. In sum, Japan would be an active and positive player in the global political economy.

A second argument that suggests optimistic prospects for a liberal world trading system, with high levels of active cooperation from Japan as well as from other major countries, emphasizes the mutual interests of states functioning in a multipolar system. A group of countries that are relatively equal in size and relatively highly developed have an incentive to support an open trading system because the benefits of openness, as measured by the relative gains from trade, economic security, and the absolute gains from trade, are likely to be greater than the costs incurred in negotiating and maintaining such a system. This logic has been most thoroughly elaborated by David Lake. Lake argues that the present international structure is not analogous to the 1930s. (He defines structure in terms of a state's relative share of world trade and labor productivity.) In the 1920s, the decline of Britain's technological prowess and share of world trade resulted in a structure in which there was only one supporter for a liberal system, the United States, and no hegemon. Such a structure is likely to lead to protectionism. In contrast, the late 1980s and beyond will be a period of "mutual supportorship" in which there are several countries, including Japan, with high and relatively equal levels of productivity and shares of world trade. Under these conditions supporters recognize that protectionist initiatives will lead to retaliation reducing the utility of all actors. There is strong incentive for major industrialized market economy states to continue to adhere to liberal policies. In particular Japan, according to Lake, is now becoming a "supporter" rather than a "spoiler" because its labor productivity is approaching that of the United

States, Germany, and France. Barring protectionist moves by trading partners, Japan ought to continue to pursue a more open and liberal trade posture.[11]

None of these approaches has paid much attention to the possibility of a divergence between policies related to tariff and nontariff barriers and international organizations, and actual outcomes, that is, the pattern of trade flows. They have focused on one or the other of these variables or tacitly assumed that the two elements of trade posture would move in the same direction. A state that lowered its trade barriers would be supporting a liberal regime and would experience an increase in its imports. A state that imposed trade barriers would experience lower levels of imports and would weaken the liberal international trade regime by violating its norms and rules. As we will demonstrate in the case of Japan, there is not always congruence between policy and outcomes; policy changes are not necessarily accompanied by changes in the actual outcome of international commodity movements.

The Japanese have adopted a trade posture that is consistent with selective accommodation. The pattern of change in Japanese policy can be explained by a strategy of TIT FOR TAT in an iterative prisoner's dilemma game. In general, one would expect that conflicts resulting from what could be regarded as unfair export practices to be more easily reconciled than those arising in relation to imports. So long as trading partners do not object to dumping, subsidizing, or export downpours, there is little incentive for exporters to change their behavior. However, threats to retaliate against such practices are, once they are voiced, likely to be highly credible. The pattern of interest group pressure in importing countries, where established industries are losing their markets, creates incentives for public officials to act. If exporters have any foresight, and if they can coordinate their behavior so that the collective choice problems associated with a reduction in sales can be overcome, conflicts generated by exports are likely to be resolved through a pattern of selective accommodation.

This supposition is borne out by Japanese responses to American complaints concerning export behavior. Japan's political system makes alteration of export behavior easier as a means of reducing bilateral frictions than accommodation on the import side of the trade equation. MITI, for example, has become noticeably more responsive to foreign outcries of Japanese dumping. Whereas it might have turned a deaf ear to the same complaints in the past, MITI is now trying hard to prevent dumping because of the tense and volatile atmosphere abroad caused by the influx of Japanese products. In sectors where formal complaints have been filed or at least threatened, MITI has made it a practice to issue "administrative guidance," warning the industry in question against dumping. Such warnings are then followed by careful monitoring of production costs and export prices and volumes. Plainly, MITI is worried about inflaming anti-Japanese sentiments and triggering retaliation for violations of internationally accepted codes.

Dumping is especially hard to control, because of the intensity of price competition in Japan. Even under close MITI monitoring, dumping can still occur as an extension of cutthroat pricing practices at home. Because MITI would like to lower political temperatures on the export side, where it has the administrative clout to regulate trade behavior (so that pressures can be relieved on the import side, where accommodation is constrained by the closeness of the LDP's ties to noncompetitive industries outside MITI's jurisdiction), it has tried to stop excessive price competition from being carried out across national borders. The irony is that MITI must be circumspect in its handling of this problem, because it is liable to face charges of price fixing and restraint of trade by the U.S. Justice Department and Federal Trade Commission if it extends too visible a hand. In the case of 64K RAM exports, this is precisely what happend; MITI's attempt to curb price cutting out of deference to warnings from the U.S. Department of Commerce only led to the threat of a law suit by the Justice Department for violations of antitrust. Nevertheless, as indicated by the decline in the number of dumping charges, MITI's admonition—on top of vocal American complaints—seems to have had some effect. Japanese companies are more careful about following aggressive pricing strategies that raise questions about dumping.

Another area where the Japanese have come to exercise more self-restraint is in their old strategy of export-lead recovery from cyclical recession. Since the mid-1970s, the Japanese have come to understand that the export market is no longer as elastic as it used to be and that any attempt to export one's way out of recession is apt to be viewed abroad as trying to foist off unemployment. Here again, MITI has had to monitor the flow of exports during cyclical recessions. American companies, which continue to lose ever larger shares of their own markets to Japan, find it hard to believe that any kind of self-restraint is being exercised; but relative to market shares that the Japanese feel they could win if they were perfectly unencumbered, some degree of self-restraint can be seen to be at work.

Japan's exercise of self-restraint—dictated by pragmatic calculations of the costs and benefits of nonrestraint—are particularly evident in what is perhaps the most significant realm of change in Japanese export policies, namely the acceptance of voluntary export restraints (VERs) and orderly market agreements (OMAs) covering several key export commodities such as steel and automobiles. In 1983, these commodities accounted for over 40 percent of Japan's total exports to the United States. The Japanese feel that, were it not for VERs and OMAs, their products could capture much larger shares of the American market.

Why, then, were these industries willing to accept VERs? In three of the four cases, acceptance generated considerable conflict in Japan before the affected industries finally acquiesced to foreign demands. Probably the main reason why, in the cases of steel and automobiles, Japanese manufacturers relented to U.S. demands was because the United States represented such a big and indispensible market. They were realistic enough to realize that if VERs were not accepted, ceilings would be placed on Japanese exports any-way, and the United States might also take retaliatory action. Under such circumstances, Japanese steel-and automakers had almost no choice but to concede. It is doubtful that MITI by itself could have forced the auto industry to accept VERs, whatever the degree of emphasis it placed on the importance of maintaining harmonious U.S.-Japan relations.[12] Japanese companies were determined to resist, invoking the shibboleths of free trade, but eventually gave in when they realized that the costs of defiance would outweigh the benefits.

Having grudgingly accepted VERs, however, Japanese manufacturers dis-covered that higher profits could still be made. Automakers simply shifted the mix of exports to higher priced models. Under the trigger price mechanism (based on the average, not marginal, costs of steel for the world's most efficient producer), Japanese companies reaped the windfall benefits of selling the same steel that they would have sold anyway, only at higher prices. Unlike European steelmakers, the Japanese chose not to expand their share of the U.S. market appreciably under the trigger price system, because their export earnings did not suffer, and they wanted to avoid creating any further friction with the United States.[13]

Although the United States succeeded in forcing Japan to swallow voluntary export restraints, the United States may have been the one to incur the heaviest, long-term costs of this coercion. The costs have included, for example, Ameri-ca's retreat from the principles of free trade, stronger and more insidious inflationary pressures, and protection for inefficient industries with no incen-tives, much less guarantees, for the recovery of competitive strength. Beyond buying time, and mollifying politically powerful interest groups, how much has the United States gained?

Viewed in long-run perspective, one can argue that Japan has been the prime but inadvertent beneficiary from VER arrangements. Every time the United States has forced a VER on Japan in one product market, Japan has responded by shifting its mix of exports to products of higher value. And as the overall volume of trade has risen steadily, Japan's relative share has more than kept pace. U.S.-imposed VERs, in short, have hastened the evolution of Japanese exports from relatively low value-added textiles to steel, consumer electronics, various machinery, automobiles, computers, office equipment, and other high value-added technology products. By protecting its declining industries, America has inadvertently provided a catalyst for the rechanneling of Japanese exports from declining, smokestack sectors into the high growth, high technology sectors—precisely the direction toward which Japan's comparative advantage has been shifting anyway. By accepting American VERs and modifying their export behavior, the Japanese managed to deflect pressures on their own home markets and at the same time advance their long-term industrial interests.

That it has worked to Japan's advantage, ex post facto, should not detract from the significance of Japan's willingness to accommodate U.S. demands at what was perceived to be some sacrifice. In terms of the Axelrod TIT FOR TAT strategy, Japan adopted a cooperative strategy in spite of America's latest moves of noncooperation. Indeed, the irony of America's swing away from openness toward selective protection—at precisely the time when it was demanding that Japan move in the opposite direction—was not lost on the Japanese. Japan's immediate reasons for cooperating stemmed more from the threat of negative sanctions than from positive inducements. The unanticipated, long-run rewards for cooperative behavior—conflict avoidance and larger profits—came later.

Selective accommodation to foreign pressures turned out to be not very damaging to Japanese national interests; indeed, in almost every case, the benefits have far outweighed the costs. Under these circumstances, being flexible, accommodating, and cooperative is easy, because it involves little or no self-sacrifice.

Japan's trade posture with regard to imports presents a more complicated picture because of the incongruity between policies and outcomes. Japan has made sweeping changes in the area of removing formal trade barriers. The number of items covered by Japanese quota restrictions fell precipitously from 466 in 1962 to 27 by 1983, bringing Japan not only in line with, but actually below, most OECD countries (France had 46 items on its list of residual import restrictions). Of the 27 items, 22 (or over 80 percent) cover agricultural products, the only area where formidable import quotas have remained in place.

Japan has also altered nontariff barriers in other areas. In accord with codes established during the Tokyo round of multilateral trade negotiations, Japan made substantial changes in customs procedures and industrial standards. The cumbersome procedures used by Japan and reluctance to accept the results of standards tests conducted in other countries had led trading partners to complain that these were devices used by Japan to exclude foreign products. Japan also entered into extensive negotiations with the United States regarding government procurements, especially as related to the communications in-

Japan's Offsetting Responses to Liberalization

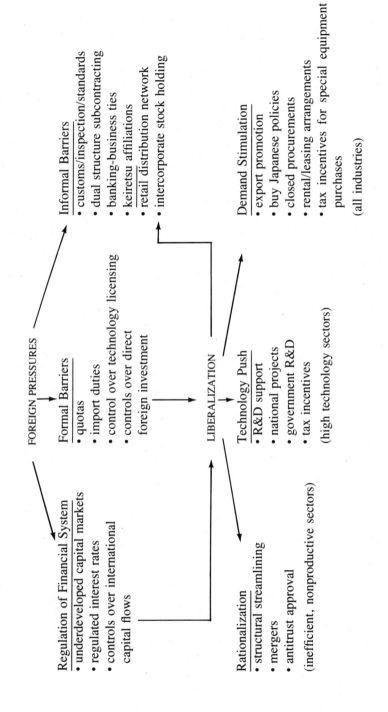

dustry. Hence in many, if not all, areas of nontariff barriers to trade, Japan's policy has become markedly more liberal since the 1960s.

Japan's average duty rates also have fallen sharply. In 1963, average duties stood at 7.3 percent for all imports and 20.9 percent for dutiable imports; by 1981, these rates had dropped to 2.5 percent and 4.3 percent, placing Japan among the lowest in the world (lower than the United States and much lower than Europe). The duty rate for small cars plummeted from 40 percent in 1968 to zero by 1980; similarly, duties for color televisions and machine tools disappeared; computer peripherals fell from 22.5 percent to 6.0 percent in 1983. For semiconductors, the United States and Japan agreed to abolish all tariffs by 1987. Except for agriculture, therefore, Japan has rolled back formal tariff barriers and quotas farther than any other country, including the United States.

We should note, however, that Japan dragged its feet on trade liberalization and conceded only when it no longer could hold foreign governments at bay. By the 1970s, roughly the time when Japan moved in line with other advanced industrial states in terms of formal trade bareriers, most sectors of the Japanese economy had long graduated from "infant industry" status.

Furthermore, it is also possible to argue that what appeared to be selective accommodation was actually nothing more than myopic self-interest. If Japanese industries had already developed the capacity to compete, then lifting formal barriers was not consequential, especially not with nontariff barriers continuing to impede access as a de facto second line of defense. Even for industries such as computers and semiconductors, which appeared badly over-matched against foreign Goliaths like IBM, there were third-line defenses, consisting of "lateral steps" that could be taken to soften the impact of liberalization. The repertoire of compensatory measures included, research-and-development (R&D) subsidies, national research projects, special tax provisions, preferential loans, guaranteed procurements, mergers, and structural rationalization.

The liberalization of discrete aspects of trade may not accomplish much in isolation because of the interchangeability of policies that have similar functions. When the Japanese government abolished formal barriers, exposing industries like semiconductors to potential foreign domination, it was able to mitigate the trauma by shifting from tariff protection to R&D subsidies and joint national research projects designed to hasten the industry's development (see figure). The "technological push" worked, helping to bring the Japanese semiconductor industry from far behind to the forefront of technology in an astonishingly short period of time.

From the standpoint of the specific rules of the GATT regime, the substitution of R&D subsidies for tariffs and quotas has been a step in the right

Table 7.1. Imports as Percentages of Japanese Domestic Supply

Industry	1970	1972	1974	1976	1978	1980
Agriculture, forestry, and fishing	16	15	18	16	13	17
Mining and quarrying	59	60	76	79	69	80
Manufacturing	3	3	4	3	3	4
Transport and communications	6	6	9	10	7	10
Total: All industries	5	4	7	6	4	7

Source: Derived from figures in U.N., *Yearbook of National Account Statistics*, various years.

direction. But this step was taken in response to foreign pressure, not initiated by Japan. Japan's trade policy has been consistent with both myopic self-interest and selective accommodation. A more refined judgment requires an assessment of actual trade flows. If policy liberalization is accompanied by increased imports, then Japan's behavior must, at the least, be seen as selective accommodation.

We have noted that, since the mid-1960s, the Japanese government has made substantial modifications in its trade policies. The modifications can be explained by a variety of factors: strong American pressures, the maturation of Japanese industrial structure and financial markets, changes in the international system and an awareness that Japanese policies had to be brought into closer alignment with the country's growing power. These factors have forced Japan to alter policies formulated during an earlier era of infant-industry protection. Aside from lingering barriers in certain specific areas, no one can deny the trend toward policy liberalization.

Beyond the unmistakable trend, however, we must ask whether changes at the policy level have resulted in changes in actual outcomes. If the answer is yes, then Japan's trade posture can be seen as one of active cooperation or at worst as selective accommodation. If, on the other hand, the answer is either no or unclear, then a number of alternative explanations can be offered, ranging from clever manipulation by Japanese policymakers to the more benign conclusion that policies have little to do with outcomes or that there are temporal lags between policy change and behavioral outcomes.

The aggregate evidence shows only modest movement toward greater openness in the Japanese economy. Looking at foreign imports as a percentage of total domestic supply for several major industries, we see only limited increases from 1970 to 1980 (see table 7.1). Another aggregate indicator of openness is foreign trade as a percent of gross domestic product. For all industrialized market-economy countries, trade as a percentage of aggregate

Table 7.2. Manufactured Imports as Percentages of GDP

Country	1970	1980	Percentage Increase
Japan	2.41	2.87	19
U.K.	10.16	16.03	57
Italy	7.96	12.70	59
France	9.23	13.09	42
Germany	10.41	15.03	44
U.S.	3.48	5.73	64
Canada	16.40	20.20	23

Source: Derived from figures in World Bank, World Tables, 3d ed., Comparative Economic Data, Table 6 and country pages, Economic Data Sheet I, using current prices.

economic activity remained more or less constant from the mid-1950s through the 1960s but rose sharply during the 1970s with exports and nonfactor services for all countries increasing from 13.4 percent of GDP in 1970 to 19.8 percent in 1981 and imports from 12.9 percent to 20.1 percent.[14] Japan's experience is not exceptional, with exports rising from 10.8 percent of GDP in 1970 to 15.5 percent in 1981, and imports from 9.5 percent to 13.6 percent. This amounts to a 54 percent increase in the share of imports as a percentage of GDP for Japan, as compared with increases of 10 percent for the United Kingdom, 32 percent for Canada, 51 percent for Germany, 59 percent for France, 67 percent for Italy, and 92 percent for the United States.[15] For Japan, however, this increase is unimpressive given the sharp escalation of energy prices and Japan's heavy dependence on energy imports. In 1982, mineral fuels, including oil, gas, and coal, accounted for nearly 50 percent of Japan's total imports. One would have expected that Japan's trade ratio, more than that of countries less dependent on imported energy, would have reflected OPEC price hikes, particularly since it would have had to expand exports to pay for the rising costs of imports.

The import of manufactures into Japan was low in 1970 and has not increased much despite changes in policy. The government has liberalized trade, investment, and capital market policies, but the importance of manufactured imports has not grown. Table 7.2 shows manufactured imports as a percentage of GDP in 1970 and 1980. Not only are the absolute figures much lower for Japan, but the level of increase in the 1970s is lower than that of other major industrialized countries. Table 7.3, illustrating manufactured imports as a percent of total imports, shows this pattern continuing into the early 1980s, after the second oil shock.

Table 7.3. Manufactured Imports as Percentage of Total Imports

Country	1972	1974	1976	1978	1980	1982
Japan	29	23	20	22	18	20
United States	68	55	54	54	49	58

Source: Derived from figures in GATT, *International Trade 1976/77, 1980/81, 1982/83,* country pages, appendix tables.

The low level of Japanese manufactured imports is particularly striking in sectors where other countries, particularly the United States, are generally recognized as having a competitive advantage. This is brought out by table 7.4, which presents figures for all three-digit SITC (Standard International Trade Classification) numbers beginning with the digit 7, which designates machinery, for all categories in which the United States and Japan were among the ten largest exporters in 1982 and either the United States or Japan was among the twenty largest importers. Figures are presented for American and Japanese shares of exports and imports for all market economy countries, and for Japanese and American sales to third markets, that is, American exports excluding sales to Japan and Japanese exports excluding sales to the United States. This gives some measure of the competitiveness of Japanese and American products in third markets where they compete head to head. In all cases where complete data are not available, it is because Japan is not among the top twenty importers. (Smaller importers are not listed in the U.N. *Yearbook of International Trade Statistics.*) It is very unlikely that the inclusion of a more complete set of data would alter the general conclusions that can be drawn from the table, since Japan is not a major importer of any of the products for which data are missing.

The most obvious conclusion suggested by the share of exports and imports of the United States and Japan (columns 3-6) is that the United States is a major importer as well as a major exporter for most categories of goods. Although Japan is a major exporter of many categories of machinery, it is not a major importer of any; the highest percentage of imports accounted for by Japan in any category is 5.50 percent (SITC 714, engines and motors). This is also the only category in which the aggregate share of Japanese imports exceeds that of exports. In most cases Japanese exports were more than ten times greater than imports.

Columns 7-9 provide some indication of the competitiveness of American and Japanese products in third markets, column 9 shows the ratio of U.S. exports to Japanese exports in third countries. Japanese exports exceed American exports in only five of twenty-three categories for which data are available (as indicated by a figure of less than 1.00 in column 9). American products are competitive with Japanese products in third country markets. However, as columns 10-12 indicate, American products do not sell very well in Japan compared with sale of Japanese products in the United States. American sales in Japan exceed Japanese sales in the United States in only five categories (as indicated by a figure greater than 1.00 in column 12).

Column 13 provides an indication of how well American products sell in Japan compared with their sales in third markets. This column reports the ratio of the figures in column 12 to those in column 9. This figure would be equal to 1.00 if the ratio of American sales in Japan to Japanese sales in America was the same as the ratio of American sales in third markets to Japanese sales in third markets. For example, if the United States sold ten times more electrical machinery than Japan in third markets, and also sold ten times more electrical machinery in Japan than Japan sold in the United States, then column 13 would equal 1.00. In other words, sales in third-country markets are taken as a predictor of sales for American and Japanese products in each other's markets. Figures less than 1.00 indicate that the United States is selling less than would be predicted on the basis of sales in third-country markets; figures greater than 1.00 indicate that it is selling more. As the numbers in column 13 indicate, there is not one instance in which the United States is selling more in Japan than would be predicted on the basis of sales in third-country markets. In most cases, it is selling less than one-fifth, in many cases less than one-tenth. Even assuming that sales to Japan should be 50 percent less than would be predicted on the basis of sales to third markets (because the Japanese market is about half the size of the U.S. market), most American products are still substantially underrepresented in Japan. The best showing for the United States is SITC 728 (other machinery for specialized industry) in which sales of U.S. products in Japan compared with Japanese products in the United States are 90 percent of what would be predicted on the basis of performance in third markets. It is very unlikely that the inclusion of numbers for the missing entries in column 13 would alter the overall conclusions that can be drawn from the table, because these are all categories in which Japan is not among the top twenty market-economy importers.

American producers find it much harder to penetrate the Japanese market than Japanese producers to penetrate the American market, compared with their relative performance in third countries. Tables 7.1 through 7.4 suggest that Japan's trade policy changes in the 1960s and 1970s have not had much impact on actual outcomes. The data presented here can, of course, only suggest this because the level of imports might have been even lower had

Table 7.4. Japanese and U.S. Trade in Machinery, 1982

SITC Number (1)	Description (2)	United States		Japan		US Exports Excl Japan (000 US $) (7)	Japan Exports Excl US (000 US $) (8)	7:8 (9)	US Exports to Japan (000 US $) (10)	Japan Exports to US (000 US $) (11)	10:11 (12)	12:9 (13)
		% Exports to Mkt Econs (3)	% Imports fr Mkt Econs (4)	% Exports to Mkt Econs (5)	% Imports fr Mkt Econs (6)							
712	Steam engines, turbines	37.08	6.64	18.84	<1.54							
713	Intrnl combus pstn engn	26.60	15.95	13.08	<1.17							
714	Engns & motors	37.08	17.86	1.40	5.50	2,925,723	11,250	26.2	198,662	18,161	10.90	.41
716	Rotating elec plant	19.53	7.25	17.10	1.85	1,304,411	1,144,863	1.14	22,635	167,897	.13	.11
718	Oth power genratg mach	5.88	4.56	7.14	2.06	89,487	93,953	.95	2,706	18,026	.15	.16
722	Tractors non-road	24.21	15.01	15.01	<1.31							
723	Civil engrg equip, etc.	43.01	5.89	11.65	<1.27							

| | | United States | | Japan | | | | | | | | |
| | | % Exports to Mkt Econs | % Imports fr Mkt Econs | % Exports to Mkt Econs | % Imports fr Mkt Econs | US Exports Excl Japan (000 US $) | Japan Exports Excl US (000 US $) | 7:8 | US Exports to Japan (000 US $) | Japan Exports to US (000 US $) | 10:11 | 12:9 |
SITC Number (1)	Description (2)	(3)	(4)	(5)	(6)	(7)	(8)	(9)	(10)	(11)	(12)	(13)
724	Textile, leather machnry	7.82	12.81	14.70	<1.83							
725	Paper, etc. mill machry	14.20	9.45	4.86	<1.69							
726	Prntg bkbndg mach pts	20.08	13.96	6.09	3.07	615,245	134,220	4.58	29,308	61,359	.47	.10
727	Food machry non-dom	18.33	6.11	2.58	1.72	358,657	44,747	8.01	358,657	7,046	1.40	.17
728	Oth machry for spec indus	16.36	9.40	8.42	2.77	1,999,484	1,018,398	1.96	232,575	130,751	1.77	.90
736	Metal wrkg mach tools	12.68	18.58	14.83	2.82	1,108,271	821,785	1.34	75,686	562,650	.13	.10
737	Metal wrkg mach	17.60	8.07	9.52	<1.57							

Table 7.4. Cont'd

SITC Number (1)	Description (2)	United States		Japan		US Exports Excl Japan (000 US $) (7)	Japan Exports Excl US (000 US $) (8)	7:8 (9)	US Exports to Japan (000 US $) (10)	Japan Exports to US (000 US $) (11)	10:11 (12)	12:9 (13)
		% Exports to Mkt Econs (3)	% Imports fr Mkt Econs (4)	% Exports to Mkt Econs (5)	% Imports fr Mkt Econs (6)							
741	Htg coolg equip	21.25	5.56	19.49	<1.79							
742	Pumps for liquids, etc.	22.47	9.44	10.72	1.95	1,163,028	495,379	2.34	29,986	73,753	.40	.17
743	Pumps centrfuges, etc.	22.77	11.31	11.42	2.38	1,752,777	765,629	2.28	86,182	159,960	.53	.23
744	Mech handlg equip	15.40	7.91	14.81	<1.72							
745	Nonelec mach tools	19.38	10.21	6.77	1.87	1,161,816	318,763	3.64	1,161,816	318,763	.56	.15
749	Nonelec mach pts, acc	12.63	9.14	13.57	2.18	1,762,796	1,570,368	1.12	62,137	390,175	.16	.14
751	Office mach	10.40	24.49	43.43	1.12	560,109	14,561,719	.38	28,579	1,002,031	.02	.07
752	Auto data proc equip	36.42	6.46	9.39	4.13	4,881,754	728,925	6.70	395,011	631,935	.62	.09

		United States		Japan		US Exports Excl Japan (000 US $)	Japan Exports Excl US (000 US $)	7:8	US Exports to Japan (000 US $)	Japan Exports to US (000 US $)	10:11	12:9
SITC Number	Description	% Exports to Mkt Econs	% Imports fr Mkt Econs	% Exports to Mkt Econs	% Imports fr Mkt Econs							
(1)	(2)	(3)	(4)	(5)	(6)	(7)	(8)	(9)	(10)	(11)	(12)	(13)
759	Office, ADP mach pts access	43.08	18.88	8.47	3.07	4,157,218	411,709	10.10	408,660	486,483	.84	.08
761	TV recvers	5.66	16.94	35.20	<1.48							
762	Radio receivers	2.91	32.20	46.63	.94	149,350	1,496,609	0.10	550	904,804	.0006	.006
763	Sound recorders	4.28	26.69	75.94	<.080							
764	Telecom equip pts, acc	22.45	23.75	17.23	2.01	3,213,936	2,889,554	1.11	161,279	1,507,691	.10	.10
771	Elec power machy	10.19	14.49	17.60	2.91	350,764	541,683	.65	11,219	83,658	.13	.20
772	Switchgear, etc. parts NES	15.44	10.38	12.83	2.63	1,891,448	1,382,343	1.36	104,891	276,577	.38	.29

Table 7.4. Cont'd

| | | United States | | Japan | | US Exports Excl Japan (000 US $) | Japan Exports Excl US (000 US $) | 7:8 | US Exports to Japan (000 US $) | Japan Exports to US (000 US $) | 10:11 | 12:9 |
| | | % Exports to Mkt Econs | % Imports fr Mkt Econs | % Exports to Mkt Econs | % Imports fr Mkt Econs | | | | | | | |
SITC Number (1)	Description (2)	(3)	(4)	(5)	(6)	(7)	(8)	(9)	(10)	(11)	(12)	(13)
773	Elec distrb equipment	11.99	9.82	18.43	<1.52							
774	Electro med Xray equip	33.99	19.45	9.01	5.46	925,322	212,933	4.34	109,514	61,228	1.78	.41
775	Hshold type equip	8.77	11.67	14.09	<1.39							
776	Transistors, valves, etc.	28.40	29.19	17.24	4.77	4,207,802	1,890,958	2.23	216,330	795,115	.27	.12
778	Electrical mach	17.60	13.72	17.29	2.71	2,300,017	1,755,359	1.31	128,883	631,376	.20	0.1
781	Pass motor veh excl buses	5.23	34.92	29.82	0.57	3,116,486	8,210,502	.37	45,546	9,804,613	.004	.01
782	Lorries spcl mtr veh	9.75	19.68	26.88	<1.14							

		United States		Japan								
SITC Number (1)	Description (2)	% Exports to Mkt Econs (3)	% Imports fr Mkt Econs (4)	% Exports to Mkt Econs (5)	% Imports fr Mkt Econs (6)	US Exports Excl Japan (000 US \$) (7)	Japan Exports Excl US (000 US \$) (8)	7:8 (9)	US Exports to Japan (000 US \$) (10)	Japan Exports to US (000 US \$) (11)	10:11 (12)	12:9 (13)
783	Road motor veh	9.79	8.00	14.18	<1.12							
784	Motor veh prts, access NES	25.51	13.40	8.44	<.81							
785	Cycles, etc. motrzd or not	2.49	26.88	66.49	<.93							
786	Trailers, non-mot veh	7.48	2.52	10.73	<1.42							
791	Railway veh	16.40	5.88	10.42	<1.63							
792	Aircrft etc.	44.61	13.24	0.60	3.76	10,980,430	35,608	308.37	906,372	123,236	7.35	.02
793	Ships, boats etc.	8.72	2.62	39.34	<1.61							

Source: Derived from figures in U.N., *1982 Yearbook of International Trade Statistics*, Vol. 2, ST/ESA/STAT/SET.G/31/Add.1 (New York, 1984), 1130-1218.

these policy changes not been made. We have not attempted the much more complex counterfactual analysis that would be required to more effectively substantiate our argument.

An examination of Japan's trade posture, including both state policies and actual outcomes, does not lead to a straightforward conclusion that Japan has become more open or liberal. There is no doubt that Japanese trade policies have changed. Behavior has also changed but in more ambiguous ways. Japan has accommodated to foreign pressures to control export surges. Although this posture is consistent with selective accommodation explained by a TIT FOR TAT strategy, it has not been particularly painful. Japan has become more involved in world trade, but the increase is smaller than that of any other major industrial state, and smaller than might have been expected. In particular, the ratio of manufactured imports has not increased substantially, and in some areas of high technology where the United States is usually recognized as being highly competitive, such as office and telecommunications equipment, the import ratio has been relatively low and has even declined in contrast to patterns in the United States and the European community.

To explain this disjunction between policies and actual outcomes, several alternative interpretations can be offered. First, it may be that Japanese policymakers have only consented to liberalization in those areas where Japanese producers have been able to compete. Where domestic companies have not been internationally competitive, policymakers have found ways of insulating them from more efficient foreign producers; this is especially conspicuous in highly politicized sectors like agriculture, food processing, and construction. For infant industries with great growth potential, import protection, as an integral part of industrial targeting, can confer dynamic advantages over foreign competitors under conditions of imperfect competition. One might call this a strategy of calculated ineffectuality under the guise of liberalization.[16] Prima facie evidence for this interpretation can be found in the persistent inability of foreign producers to take full advantage of their comparative advantage in some industrial sectors.

A second interpretation of the disjunction between policy and outcomes is that barriers to outside entry arise out of the structure of the private sector as opposed to deliberately ineffectual public policy choices. Changes in trade policies have had only a marginal impact because of impediments embedded in the structure of Japan's domestic economy. The multilayered system of retail distribution, featuring close ties between buyers and sellers, for example, makes it unusually difficult for outsiders to break in. The interlocking network of ownership among Japanese corporations often disposes them to do business with closely related domestic firms, even when foreign firms are able to offer competitive prices. During the forty years of postwar recovery and growth, Japanese companies have spun out intricate webs of interdependence, risk diffusion and sharing, and common interests and goals based on long-term interactions and mutual trust. Such deeply embedded institutional impediments as subcontracting networks, *keiretsu* affiliations (industrial groupings like Mitsubishi and Sumitomo, centered on a lead bank or major manufacturer), and the value placed on implicit long-term business transactions are not readily amenable to government-ordered change. Japan's economy clearly does not function in the classical Adam Smith mode. Although it is certainly market-based, like that of the United States, Japan's economy is permeated by a maze of formal and informal organizational networks that structure and shape the market process.[17] In commercial transactions, short-run market calculations—such as comparative prices and noniterative bidding—are not the sole determinants of business decision. Other considerations—long-standing business ties, financial interdependence, intercorporate stockholding, *keiretsu* membership, and subcontracting networks—enter into the complex calculus as factors of often overriding importance.

Organizational factors fit into a broader concept of market behavior in that they take consciously into account many relevant long-term considerations that transcend immediate price signals As Williamson and Coase have pointed out, trying to minimize long-run transaction costs (e.g., poor quality, opportunism, constant monitoring, costly litigation) is highly rational from the standpoint of corporate strategy.[18] For U.S. firms, breaking into Japan's structured but highly competitive market, therefore, poses far greater inherent difficulties than the reverse—Japanese companies seeking to establish footholds in the less structured, more decentralized U.S. market.

A third possible interpretation is that public policies have only a limited impact on outcomes. Basic underlying factors like national ratios of total savings versus dissavings or factor endowments and geographic distance may be the prime driving forces behind trade patterns, including the percentage of manufactured imports. A state can regulate the influx of foreign products by imposing quantitative restrictions, but whether it can adopt policies that automatically raise import levels is not clear. If foreign producers are not competitive, the removal of tariffs or nontariff barriers will not have any effect. Given Japan's factor endowments and its geographic distance from trade partners, it can be argued that the observed pattern of trade, including the percentage of manufactured imports, is consistent with what would be predicted from a conventional Heckscher-Ohlin-Samuelson analysis.

A fourth possible interpretation is that there are lags between policy changes and trade outcomes. Foreign exporters, unable to crack the Japanese market in the past, may be reluctant to take full advantage of greater opportunities now opening up. They may find that they have to adapt their products to Japanese tastes and offer the kind of after-service that Japanese customers demand. Often they will have to be prepared to absorb short-term losses in order to establish long-term market footholds. It may also take some time before Japanese consumers and industrial customers become accustomed to purchasing foreign goods. All this suggests that the effects of policy liberalization may only be registered some time later, after adjustments are made on both sides.

These explanations are not mutually exclusive. Of the four explanations for the disjuncture between policy and outcomes, only the third has been tested systematically. Using a modified version of the Hecksher-Ohlin-Samuelson model, Gary R. Saxonhouse has found that the ratio of Japanese manufactures falls well within the normal range, given its resource base and location.[19] Neither the first nor the second is amenable to quantitative testing, and empirical data for the fourth is unavailable, because verification of the time-lag hypothesis lies presumably in the future.

This is not to say, however, that the third approach is immune from criticism or that it is most persuasive. The Hecksher-Ohlin-Samuelson model sheds light only on the relative composition of imports at a specific point in time, given broadly defined factor endowments. It does not say anything about absolute levels of trade, much less account for trade imbalances. It cannot say much more than that Japan will import raw materials and export manufactures, but the latter may be textiles, automobiles, or computers. Nor does it deal with a variety of political forces that have a direct bearing on trade. Exactly how much it tells us about the relationship between public policies and trade outcomes is, therefore, open to question.

In spite of the measurement difficulties and the obvious problems of making aggregate inferences from microlevel factors, we believe that the second interpretation—private sector impediments—deserves more attention than it has received. Interviews with foreign businessmen who have tried to export into Japan indicate that the barriers posed by Japan's extra-market institutions and practices constitute serious bottlenecks, especially in such areas as marketing (e.g., retail distribution, sellers of intermediate goods, and buyers of end-user products), direct foreign investments (e.g., corporate mergers and acquisitions), and public policies (e.g., close government-business cooperation). *Keiretsu* groupings, the role of giant trading companies, close banking-business relations, industrial policy, the complex set of relationships between individual bureaucracies, the LDP, and interest groups, and extensive intercorporate stockholding—to say nothing of distinctive cultural values and business practices—undoubtedly make Japan far harder for Americans to penetrate than the American market is for Japanese to break into. In Oliver Williamson's terminology, hierarchical or organizational factors are more widespread in Japan than in the United States.[20]

As Japan's economy develops and is exposed increasingly to the forces of internationalization, such organizational factors may recede in importance. Should that happen, private sector barriers to foreign penetration will be reduced. However, as market trends are likely to be limited by the inertial weight of the extant system, trade tensions between Japan and other industrialized states will persist. Changes in trade policies have served to alleviate but not eliminate such tensions. To resolve conflicts in the future, Japan's trade partners will insist that greater progess be made with respect to actual outcomes.

Japan and the United States are the two major economic powers in the noncommunist world. The extent to which they can cope with their international trade conflicts will have an important impact on the larger system of world trade. The analysis presented in this essay suggests, although it cannot firmly conclude on the basis of available evidence, that differences in domestic economic structures will become an increasingly important consideration in international trade disputes. So long as tariff or nontariff barriers were so high that they blocked the import of goods, domestic structures were irrelevant. However, as formal state barriers to trade have been lowered these domestic structures have become more important determinants of trade flows. The current international regime for trade offers no guidance for dealing with such issues. It tacitly assumes that all countries have more or less similar domestic political economies; that international rules will have the same impact in different states.[21] If, however, the removal of formal trade barriers opens markets in one country because its firms act as if they were in an auction market, while leaving markets inaccessible in other countries whose firms act as if they were in customer markets, friction is bound to result. This friction may be lessened by changing domestic political economic structures in one or more countries, by expanding the scope of the international regime by drafting rules that apply to these new problems, or by limiting the amount of economic interaction. All of these alternatives will require initiatives that move beyond the postwar liberal system so carefully created and nurtured by the United States.

1. General Agreement on Tariffs and Trade (GATT), *International Trade for 1982/83* (Geneva 1983), Table A 23.

2. For an analysis of Japanese trade policy which explicates sectoral variations in terms of electoral coalitions and bureaucratic behavior see Daniel I. Okimoto, "International Trade and Trade Policy in Japan," unpublished paper prepared for the Japan Political Economy Research

Conference, Vol 2, Honolulu, Hawaii, July 1984. See also D.I. Okimoto, *Between MITI and the Market,* (Stanford, Calif., forthcoming), chapter 4.

3. The classic discussion of the importance of a hegemon for maintaining an open international order is Charles Kindleberger, *The World in Depression* (Berkeley, 1973). For discussions of the relationship between hegemonic interests and the creation of an open regime see Robert Gilpin, *U.S. Power and the Multinational Corporation* (New York, 1975) and Stephen D. Krasner "State Power and the Structure of International Trade," *World Politics* 28 (1976).

4. World Bank, *World Tables*, 3d ed., vol. 1, 238-39, 247-57.

5. Avinash Dixit and Albert S. Kyle, "On the Use of Trade Restrictions for Entry Promotion and Deterrence," Discussion Papers in Economics No. 56, Woodrow Wilson School of Public and International Affairs, 1984.

6. This definition of regimes is from Stephen D. Krasner, "Introduction: Regimes as Intervening Variables," in Krasner, ed., *International Regimes* (Ithaca, N.Y., 1983). The most extensive discussion of the impact of regimes on behavior can be found in Robert O. Keohane, *After Hegemony: Cooperation and Discord in the World Political Economy* (Princeton, N.J., 1984).

7. Robert Axelrod, *The Evolution of Cooperation* (New York, 1984).

8. Charles Lipson, "The Transformation of Trade: The Sources and Effects of Regime Change," in Krasner, *International Regimes*, 233-71.

9. GATT, *International Trade 1982-83*, Table Al.

10. World Bank, *World Tables,* 507.

11. David A. Lake. "Beneath the Commerce of Nations: A Theory of International Economic Structures," *International Studies Quarterly* 28 (June 1984); and David A. Lake, "International Economic Structures and American Foreign Economic Policy, 1887-1934," *World Politics* 35 (1983).

12. Amaya Naohiro, *Nihon kabushiki kaisha*: *Nokosareta sentaku* (Japan, incorporated: Remaining options) (Tokyo, 1982), 55-100.

13. Hugh Patrick and Sato Hideo, "The Political Economy of United States-Japan Trade in Steel," in K. Yamamura, ed., *Policy and Trade Issues of the Japanese Economy* (Seattle, WA, 1982), 197-238.

14. World Bank, *World Tables*, 3d ed., vol. 1 (Washington, DC, 1983): 503.

15. World Bank, *World Tables,* 507.

16. See, for example, James C. Abegglen, "Narrow Self-Interest: Japan's Ultimate Vulnerability?" in Diane Tasca, ed., *U.S.-Japanese Economic Relations* (New York, 1980), 21-31.

17. Imai Ken-ichi and Itami Hiroyuki, "The Firm and Market in Japan: Mutual Penetration of the Market Principle and Organization Principle", unpublished paper, August 1982.

18. Oliver E. Williamson, *Markets and Hierarchies* (New York, 1975); Ronald Coase, "The Nature of the Firm," *Economica* (1937): 386-405.

19. Gary Saxenhouse, "Evolving Comparative Advantage and Japan's Import of Manufactures," in K. Yamamara, ed., *Policy and Trade Issues of the Japanese Economy* (Seattle, 1983), 2:39-70.

20. Williamson, *Markets and Hierarchies*.

21. Judith Goldstein and Stephen D. Krasner, "Unfair Trade Practices: The Case for Differential Response," *American Economic Review* 74 (May 1984): 282-87.

8

U.S.-Japan Trade Relations, 1955-1982

HIDEO KANEMITSU

Throughout the period from 1955 to 1982, a close political and economic interdependence existed between the United States and Japan, but the characteristics of their interdependence underwent substantial changes. The span of years may be divided into three periods.

Period I (1955-64) may be characterized as one of patron-protégé relations, in which the United States gave unilateral support and protection as a powerful patron of Japan and helped it enter the postwar international community. The United States strongly endorsed Japan's membership in GATT in 1955 and in OECD in 1964. In the latter year, Japan was asked to become an IMF Article 8 nation, symbolizing its status as a developed industrial country. Throughout this period Japan was almost totally dependent upon the United States for both exports and imports. Though the United States also needed Japan's political and economic stability in the Far East, the relationship between the two countries was overwhelmingly one-sided. Japan's goal was to develop and stabilize its economy above everything else. Indeed, after renewing the security treaty with the United States in 1960, Japan's major concern was exclusively focused on its domestic economic growth while maintaining its external equilibrium. The Japanese economy expanded rapidly; its real Gross National Product (GNP) grew at a rate of about 10 percent, compared with 3.2 percent for the United States. Japan's trade expanded still faster; its exports grew at a rate of 13 percent and its imports at 12 percent, while United States exports and imports grew much more slowly, at a rate of 5 percent. Throughout the period, Japan's merchandise trade balance had a chronic deficit averaging about $800 million annually. On the other hand, the United States enjoyed a merchandise trade surplus averaging about $4.5 billion. Japan's trade deficits with the United States also continued at an annual average of about $500 million until 1964.

Period II (1965-73) was a historic one for the Japanese economy. Japan succeeded in achieving spectacular economic growth (approximately 10 percent of real GNP growth per year). In contrast, the U.S. economy grew at a much slower rate of 3.4 percent in real GNP, which was lower than the average growth rate (4.4 percent) of the industrial countries in the world. Japan expanded its exports at a rate of more than 20 percent and its imports at approximately 19 percent per year. During the same period. The U.S. import expansion rate (approximately 15 percent) was much higher than its export expansion rate (about 11 percent), indicating a downward trend in the U.S. Merchandise trade surplus. On the other hand, Japan had a surplus in its merchandise trade balance for the first time since the end of World War II. Since 1965, the bilateral trade balance between the United States and Japan has continued to create a considerable trade surplus for the latter. Globally Japan had arrived at the stage of a secular surplus on current account, which enabled it to become a long-term capital export country.

In 1971, the United States had a trade deficit for the first time in this century. Since then, the U.S. trade deficit has continued to increase except in 1973 and 1975. During the period of 1965-73, the United States was the only major industrial country involved in a large-scale war. In the international monetary sphere, the so-called dollar shortage in the 1950s evolved into a dollar glut and finally the gold convertibility of the U.S. dollar was suspended, marking the end of the era of the Bretton Woods System.

In contrast to the international position of an overvalued Japanese yen in Period I, the IMF par value of the Japanese yen (360 yen per U.S. dollar) was considered to be grossly undervalued. But the Japanese government was quite reluctant to recognize this currency realignment until the end of Period II in 1973. Unquestionably, Japan made a great effort to maintain close ties with the U.S. leadership in connection with international currency crises and the settlement of the Kennedy Round at the GATT multilateral trade negotiation. From this standpoint, Period II can be described as one of a leader-follower relationship between the United States and Japan. Though conflicts on trade issues were by no means lacking between the two nations, such as the textile negotiations in the early 1970s, both the United States and Japan came to recognize valuable benefits arising from mutual trade expansion.

Period III (1974-82) started with the first oil crisis; then, in 1979-80, the second oil crisis delivered another serious blow to the world economy. The overall performance of the Japanese economy, which depended so heavily on imported foreign oil, was affected acutely by these energy crises. This was reflected principally in Japan's balance of payments deficits, first a $4.7 billion deficit in 1974, then an $8.7 billion deficit in 1979, and a deficit of over $10 billion in 1980. In 1974, Japan experienced a decrease in its real GNP (minus 1.2 percent in real GNP growth) for the first time since the end of

World War II. In fact, during this period, Japan's GNP growth rate declined sharply to the level of 4.7 percent per annum, which was less than one half of the annual rate of the previous period. Though Japan maintained its export expansion rate at approximately 15 percent in value terms, its growth rate in volume dropped substantially to only 7 percent, less than one-half that of the previous period. Japan's import growth rate also was reduced considerably from 15 percent in Period II to 2.3 percent in volume.

During the same period, the United States also experienced a slower growth of its real GNP at a rate of 2.2 percent per annum, but its export growth rate increased slightly from 11 percent in Period II to 12.6 percent in value terms. The U.S. import growth rate (14.8 percent) was still higher than its export growth rate, a trend continuing from the previous period. Moreover, the gap between Japan's export expansion with the United States was widening in this period, which accelerated the deficit trend of the U.S. merchandise trade balance. Indeed, Japan's export expansion rate (about 17 percent) was increasingly larger than its import expansion rate (about 12 percent) with the United States throughout this period.

The tensions in the economic relationship between the United States and Japan gradually mounted, and perhaps the U.S. government for the first time came to recognize a rival relationship with Japan. Thus, Period III can be characterised as the period of competing partners between the United States and Japan. This competitive relationship was exemplified when the U.S. government strongly requested that the Japanese government take specific actions in order to cope with the problem of sharing the oil deficits in 1976-77. The United States and Japan in Period III faced constant conflicts, particularly in the area of international trade and investment. Trade frictions involving exchange rate misalignment and Japan's import restrictions became rampant against the background of the huge U.S. trade deficits and Japan's trade surplus, especially in 1977-78 and 1981-82. In fact, the bilateral trade imbalance between the United States and Japan constituted the most fundamental cause of the U.S.-Japanese economic conflicts, which became political issues in the United States as well as in Japan.

The United States and Japan as competing partners do not yet have an equal status when considering international security, where the United States has maintained an overwhelming superiority in a worldwide context. In contrast, Japan purposely and stringently restricted it military role in the international community in the post–World War II era.

From 1955 to 1982 world exports (excluding the centrally planned economies) expanded at a remarkable pace of 13.3 percent annually. World exports excreased approximately twenty times, from $85 billion in 1955 to $1,663 billion in 1982. During the same period, U.S. exports expanded at an annual rate of 11.5 percent, increasing approximately fifteen times, from $14.3 billion in 1955 to $212.2 billion in 1982. At the same time, Japan's exports expanded at an annual rate of 18.6 percent, much larger than the world export expansion rate. Japan's exports increased about seventy times, $2 billion in 1955 to $139 billion in 1982. As a result, the United States decreased its export world share from 16.8 percent (1955) to 12.8 percent (1982), while Japan's export world share increased from 2.4 percent (1955) to 8.4 percent (1982).

On the other hand, the United States expanded its imports at a much faster rate (13.6 percent per annum) than its export expansion rate. Thus, the United States increased its imports approximately twenty-one times, from $11.4 billion in 1955 to $244 billion in 1982. Japan's imports also expanded at a remarkably high rate of 17.2 percent per annum; thus, Japan increased its imports approximately fifty-three times, from $2.5 billion in 1955 to $132 billion in 1982. Accordingly, the United States slightly increased its import world share from 12.8 percent (1955) to 14 percent, while Japan's share increased from 2.8 percent (1955) to 7.6 percent (1982).

We observe that the U.S. export expansion rate, 11.5 percent, was much slower than its import expansion rate, 13.8 percent. Japan had just the opposite case in the same period, that is, its export expansion rate, 18.6 percent, was higher than its import expansion rate, 17.2 percent. Consequently, the United States increasingly reduced its trade surplus and eventually generated trade deficits, while Japan clearly maintained trade surpluses during this period. Indeed, these contrasting trends in the United States and Japan started around 1964-65, a critical period for U.S.-Japan trade relations.

During the same period, Japan's exports to the United States expanded at an annual rate of 18.6 percent, which is exactly the same expansion rate of Japan's total exports to the whole world. On the other hand, Japan expanded its imports from the United States at an annual rate of 13.9 percent, which was lower than Japan's global import expansion rate, 17.2 percent. Thus, the difference between Japan's export growth rate and import growth rate with the United States is much greater than the difference between Japan's global export and import expansion rates. To be more specific, Japan's imports were greater than its exports in Period I (1955-64), and its merchandise trade balance was roughly in equilibrium in Period II (1965-73), except in 1971 and 1972. In Period III (1974-82), because of the two oil crises with soaring oil prices, Japan's trade balance was disturbed and fluctuated in an unprecedented manner. Nevertheless, despite the enormous impact of the two oil crises on the Japanese economy, Japan's merchandise trade balance clearly showed a surplus trend. This was reflected particularly in Japan's trade balance with the United States.

The United States merchandise trade balance showed an approximately opposite trend. The United States maintained trade surpluses until the end of the 1960s; then its trade balance was roughly in equilibrium during the period of 1968-75. After 1976, the U.S. merchandise trade balance showed a clear deficit trend.

We shall be interested in the long-run trends of both America's and Japan's trade shares in the world market. During the period 1955-82, the U.S. share of world exports clearly showed a declining trend. The U.S. export share was approximately one-fifth of the world exports in the middle of the 1950s (19 percent in 1957), but it declined steadily to the level of 12 percent in 1980. By contrast, Japan increased its share almost steadily from 2.4 percent in 1955 to the level of 8.5 percent in 1981. On the other hand, the United States had no such declining trend in its share of world imports, while Japan had a similarly rising trend, though a milder one compared with its export share trend in the same period.

It is striking to observe that, during the period 1955-82, the total of the U.S. and Japanese shares of the world exports remained at a fairly stable level, approximately 21 percent on the average. Judging from this, it appears that the United States was losing its export market share as rapidly as Japan was adding to its share. It is true that Japan raised its export share by increasing exports to the United States by the same expansion rate of 18.6 percent per annum, but U.S. exports to Japan increased at approximately 14 percent annually, much faster than it global exports, which increased only 11.5 percent annually during this period. Therefore, it is simply not true that the decline in the U.S. share of world exports is attributable to a decline in its share of exports to Japan.

Nevertheless, during the period 1955-82 the United States and Japan were competing in world export markets, where the United States share continued to decrease while Japan's expanded to almost the same degree. There must be many factors to explain this, but I shall restrict myself to several empirical observations.

First, as Table 8.1 shows, during this period, U.S. export prices (relative to the Japanese wholesale price index) were rising, while Japan's export prices (relative to the U.S. wholesale price index) were slightly declining. Accordingly, Japan's competitive position vis-à-vis the United States was strengthened steadily in world export markets. In the same period, Japan's real per capita GNP increased about seven times (or at a rate of 7.2 percent per annum), while the U.S. real per capita GNP grew only about 1.8 times (or at a rate of 2.2 percent per annum). This indicates a fundamental difference between the rates of change in value-added labor productivity in the United States and Japan. Furthermore, there was a significant difference between Japan's growth

Table 8.1. Annual Percentage Changes in Production, Wholesale Prices, Wages, and Trade for the United States and Japan

	Period I (1955-64)	Period II (1965-73)	Period III (1974-82)	Total (1955-82)
Real Gross National Product				
Japan	9.8	9.9	4.7	8.3
U.S.	3.2	3.4	2.8	3.4
World GDP[a]	4.3	4.4	2.7	4.0
Industrial Production Index (1980 = 100)				
Japan	15.8	13.6	5.0	10.3
U.S.	3.5	3.5	2.2	3.8
Labor productivity[b]				
Japan	8.3	8.6	3.6	7.1
U.S.	2.1	1.3	0.6	1.5
Wholesale prices (1980 = 100)				
Japan	0.1	2.4	4.6	3.6
U.S.	0.6	3.7	8.7	4.5
Wages (1980 = 100)				
Japan	6.7	13.9	7.9	11.7
U.S.	3.4	5.8	8.6	5.7
Trade (in U.S. dollar value)[c]				
Japan				
Exports	13.1	20.5	14.7	18.6
Imports	12.3	18.8	13.7	17.2
Exports to U.S.	16.5	19.8	17.3	18.6
Imports from U.S.	11.2	16.5	12.1	13.9

(*continued opposite*)

rate, 10.3 percent, and the U.S. growth rate, 3.8 percent, in industrial production. In fact, this difference is more salient in the area of machinery production; Japan's machinery production (index) expanded at a rate of 14.1 percent per year, while the U.S. machinery production (index) grew only at a rate of 4.3 percent per year.

Second, Japan's exports showed a much higher income (or world imports) elasticity than U.S. exports. Indeed, U.S. export elasticity (with respect to world imports) was less than one (0.86), compared to the Japanese export elasticity, which was greater than one (1.36), so that whenever world exports increased 1 percent, U.S. exports expanded less than 1 percent while Japanese

Table 8.1. Cont'd

	Period I (1955-64)	Period II (1965-73)	Period III (1974-82)	Total (1955-82)
Trade (in U.S. dollar value)[c]				
U.S.				
Exports	5.1	11.2	12.6	11.5
Imports	5.1	14.8	14.8	13.6
World				
Exports	6.0	14.2	13.0	13.3
Imports	6.0	13.7	13.5	13.1
Trade (in volume)				
Japan				
Exports	14.7	14.3	7.2	13.9
Imports	14.1	14.8	2.3	10.3
U.S.				
Exports	4.3	6.9	3.9	6.0
Imports	5.5	9.4	3.5	6.8

Sources: International Monetary Fund (IMF); *International Financial Statistics, Yearbook, 1983*; The Bank of Japan, *Economic Statistics Annual* (various years); The Bank of Japan, *Kokusai Hikaku Tokei* (Japan and the World: A Comparison by Economic and Financial Statistics) (various years); U.S. Department of Commerce; *Survey of Current Business (various issues); and Economic Report of the President, February 1984.*

[a]Gross Domestic Product Index (1980 = 100) of the industrial countries, excluding the centrally planned economies.

[b]Real GNP per civilian employed person.

[c]Excludes exports and imports of the centrally planned economies. Japan export data are on f.o.b. basis and imports data are on c.i.f. basis. U.S. export and import data are both on f.a.s. basis.

exports grew more than 1 percent. Because world exports expanded during this period by approximately 13 percent per year, this difference produced a significant gap in the export expansion rates of the two countries.

Third, Japan's export performance was distinctly superior in machinery trade, where world imports expanded most rapidly (at 15.4 percent per year). In contrast to this, the United States had a better performance in food trade, where world imports expanded at the lowest rate (at 10 percent per year). Indeed, at Table 8.2 indicates, the growth rate of U.S. exports was higher than that of world exports only in food trade. During this period, the United States had the highest elasticity of food exports (with respect to world food imports), 1.03, and the lowest elasticity of machinery exports (with respect

Table 8.2. Annual Percentage Growth of U.S., Japanese, and World Trade in Selected Commodities, 1955-82

	World		U.S.		Japan	
Commodity	Exports	Imports	Exports	Imports	Exports	Imports
Food	10.3	10.0	10.6	7.9	8.8	16.6
Raw material & fuel	13.4	13.6	10.2	13.8	12.5	18.6
Manufactured goods	14.1	14.3	11.5	15.9	18.9	18.9
Machinery & transport equipment	15.0	15.4	12.0	21.2	24.6	17.1
Total	13.3	13.1	11.0	13.8	18.6	17.2

Sources: OECD, *Statistics of Foreign Trade*; The Bank of Japan, *Kokusai Hikaku Tōkei*.

Table 8.3. Income Elasticities of U.S. and Japanese Exports for Selected Commodities, 1955-82

Commodity	U.S.	Japan
Food	1.03	0.86
Raw materials & fuel	0.76	0.89
Manufactured goods	0.84	1.29
Machinery & transport equipment	0.83	1.53
Total	0.86	1.36

Sources: OECD, *Statistics of Foreign Trade*; The Bank of Japan, *Kokusai Hikaku Tōkei*.

Note: Estimation on elasticity of export with respect to world import: $\log(EX)$ = Constant + $\eta\log(WI)$; EX: Export of a commodity of each country; WI: World import of a commodity *minus* exporting country's import of that commodity; η: Elasticity of export with respect to world import

to world machinery imports), 0.83. On the other hand, Japan had the highest elasticity of machinery exports, 1.53, and the lowest elasticity of food exports, 0.86. Furthermore, in manufactured goods trade, the United States had also a lower export elasticity, 0.84, while Japan had an export elasticity of 1.29 (see Table 8.3).

Fourth, in world machinery trade, Japan increased its export share from approximately 3 percent in the middle of the 1950s to almost 20 percent in the early 1980s. The United States followed an opposite trend; its market share of world machinery exports decreased from about 38 percent in 1956 to 20 percent in the early 1980s. Thus, in world machinery exports, Japan's export share was less than one-tenth that of the United States in the middle of the 1950s, but it was rapidly approaching equality by the early 1980s. Both the United States and Japan maintained a high proportion of machinery exports to total exports during the period 1955-82. For the United States, the ratio of machinery exports to total exports remained in a stable range of approximately 35 to 45 percent. In contrast, Japan's machinery export ratio increased sharply from about 20 percent in the middle of the 1950s (19.4 percent in 1956) to more than 60 percent in the early 1980s (61.7 percent in 1981). Judging from these results, the difference between U.S. and Japanese export performances appears to reflect a much sharper contrast in machinery export performance.

Fifth, the U.S. share of Japanese imports declined substantially from approximately 34 percent in the middle of the 1950s to less than 18 percent in the early 1980s. On the other hand, the Japanese share of U.S. imports more than tripled during this period, from less than 5 percent in the late 1950s to more than 15 percent in 1982. This marked contrast is certainly one of the contributing factors in producing a significant difference between U.S. and Japanese export performances in the international markets.

Sixth, as noted already during 1955-82, the United States lagged far behind other industrial countires, except the United Kingdom, in export expansion. While Japan's export expansion rate, 18.6 percent per annum, was the highest among the major industrial countries, the corresponding U.S. expansion rate of 11.0 percent was lower than the world export expansion rate, 13.3 percent per annum.

Trade between the United States and Japan expanded rapidly in volume as well as in value during the period 1955-82. In 1955, Japan's exports to the United States amounted to $456 million, which accounted for 23 percent of Japan's total exports. In the same year, Japan's imports from the United States amounted to $774 million, or 31 percent of Japan's total imports. In 1982, the amount of Japan's exports to the United States was more than $36 billion, accounting for 26 percent of total exports, and the amount of Japan's imports from the United States was $24 billion, or 18 percent of total imports (tables 8.4, 8.5, 8.6, 8.7).

The growth rate of Japan's exports to the United States was as high as 18.6 percent per year, equal to the growth rate of Japan's total exports. Japan's imports from the United States also expanded at a fairly high rate of 14 percent per year, which was higher than the growth rate of the United States' total exports in the same period. Until the early 1970s, Japan's export prices remained generally stable and then increased sharply after 1973. During the period 1955-82, Japan's export prices increased at an annual rate of 4.2 percent and Japan's import prices increased at a much faster rate of 6.3 percent. Therefore, in terms of constant export prices at 1980, Japan's (real) exports

Table 8.4. Japan's Exports to the United States for Selected Years (millions of U.S. dollars, percentage)

	1955 ($)	1955 (%)	1960 ($)	1960 (%)	1965 ($)	1965 (%)	1970 ($)	1970 (%)	1975 ($)	1975 (%)	1980 ($)	1980 (%)	1982 ($)	1982 (%)
Food	47	(10.3)	73	(6.6)	84	(3.4)	135	(2.3)	165	(1.5)	245	(.8)	255	(.7)
Raw materials & fuels	25	(5.5)	22	(2.0)	20	(.8)	26	(.4)	30	(.3)	78	(.2)	49	(.1)
Light industry goods	308	(67.5)	653	(59.3)	906	(36.5)	1,408	(23.7)	1,161	(10.4)	2,664	(8.5)	3,437	(9.5)
Textiles	170	(37.3)	288	(26.1)	441	(17.8)	597	(10.1)	432	(3.9)	593	(1.9)	760	(2.1)
Heavy and chemical industry products	76	(16.7)	354	(32.1)	1,446	(58.3)	4,298	(72.4)	9,508	(85.3)	27,956	(89.1)	32,170	(88.5)
Chemicals	6	(1.3)	17	(1.5)	46	(1.9)	160	(2.7)	346	(3.1)	767	(2.4)	918	(2.5)
Metals	41	(9.0)	150	(13.6)	692	(27.9)	1,296	(21.8)	2,499	(22.4)	4,167	(13.3)	4,386	(12.1)
Iron & steel	13	(2.9)	71	(6.4)	509	(20.5)	899	(15.1)	1,845	(16.5)	2,702	(8.6)	2,807	(7.7)
Machinery	29	(6.4)	187	(17.0)	707	(28.5)	2,841	(47.8)	6,664	(59.8)	23,021	(73.4)	26,866	(73.9)
General machinery	14	(3.1)	35	(3.2)	92	(3.7)	408	(6.9)	953	(8.5)	3,368	(10.7)	4,391	(12.1)
Office machines	••		••		••		143	(2.4)	266	(2.4)	779	(2.5)	1,444	(4.0)
Electrical machinery	3	(.7)	106	(9.6)	377	(15.2)	1,328	(22.4)	1,992	(17.9)	5,135	(16.4)	6,880	(18.9)
Radio sets	••		69	(6.3)	104	(4.2)	397	(6.7)	389	(3.5)	783	(2.5)	883	(2.4)
TV sets	••		••		62	(2.5)	265	(4.5)	256	(2.3)	196	(.6)	268	(.7)
Tape recorders	••		••		50	(2.0)	256	(4.3)	256	(2.3)	979	(3.1)	1,510	(4.2)
Transport equipment	••		9	(.8)	158	(6.4)	915	(15.4)	3,239	(29.1)	12,820	(40.9)	13,565	(37.3)
Motor vehicles	••		2	(.2)	34	(1.4)	536	(9.0)	2,281	(20.5)	10,119	(32.3)	11,036	(30.4)
Motorcycles	••		2	(.2)	104	(4.2)	280	(4.7)	577	(5.2)	1,256	(4.0)	1,291	(3.6)
Precision instruments	12	(2.6)	37	(3.4)	81	(3.3)	190	(3.2)	480	(4.3)	1,698	(5.4)	2,029	(5.6)
Total	456		1,102		2,479		5,940		11,149		31,367		36,330	

Sources: Ministry of Finance, *Customs Clearance Statistics*; Ministry of International Trade and Industry, *Tsūshō Hakusho* (White Paper on International Trade) (various years).

Table 8.5. Japan's Imports from the United States for Selected Years (millions of U.S. dollars, percentage)

	1955		1960		1965		1970		1975		1980		1982	
	($)	(%)	($)	(%)	($)	(%)	($)	(%)	($)	(%)	($)	(%)	($)	(%)
Food	178	(23.0)	122	(7.9)	563	(23.8)	812	(14.6)	2,489	(21.4)	5,171	(21.2)	4,965	(20.5)
Raw Materials	327	(42.2)	731	(47.3)	858	(36.3)	1,645	(29.6)	3,144	(27.1)	6,383	(26.2)	4,681	(19.4)
Mineral Fuels	90	(11.6)	178	(11.5)	205	(8.7)	761	(13.7)	1,909	(16.4)	2,098	(8.6)	3,069	(12.7)
Coal	48	(6.2)	92	(6.0)	128	(5.4)	623	(11.2)	1,687	(14.5)	1,581	(6.5)	2,135	(8.8)
Manufactured Goods	177	(22.9)	514	(33.3)	735	(31.1)	2,304	(41.4)	4,011	(34.6)	10,607	(43.5)	11,206	(46.3)
Chemicals	42	(5.4)	148	(9.6)	177	(7.5)	401	(7.2)	775	(6.7)	2,536	(10.4)	3,058	(12.6)
Machinery	93	(12.0)	267	(17.3)	416	(17.6)	1,412	(25.4)	2,195	(18.9)	5,015	(20.5)	5,390	(22.3)
General Machinery	64	(8.3)	159	(10.3)	229	(9.7)	690	(12.4)	986	(8.5)	2,031	(8.3)	2,271	(9.4)
Office Machines	9	(1.2)	31	(2.0)	63	(2.7)	201	(3.6)	228	(2.0)	708	(2.9)	767	(3.2)
Electrical Machinery	9	(1.2)	27	(1.7)	70	(3.0)	341	(6.1)	552	(4.8)	1,489	(6.1)	1,862	(7.7)
Transport Equipment	16	(2.1)	62	(4.0)	95	(4.0)	302	(5.4)	499	(4.3)	1,091	(4.5)	818	(3.4)
Aircraft	3	(.4)	40	(2.6)	78	(3.3)	245	(4.4)	364	(3.1)	890	(3.6)	694	(2.9)
Precision Instruments	4	(.5)	20	(1.3)	22	(.9)	78	(1.4)	158	(1.4)	404	(1.7)	439	(1.8)
Total	774		1,545		2,366		5,560		11,608		24,408		24,179	

Sources: Ministry of Finance, *Customs Clearance Statistics;* Ministry of International Trade and Industry, *Tsūshō Hakusho* (White Paper on International Trade) (various years).

Table 8.6. Japan's Exports for Selected Years (millions of U.S. dollars, percentage)

	1955 ($)	(%)	1960 ($)	(%)	1965 ($)	(%)	1970 ($)	(%)	1975 ($)	(%)	1980 ($)	(%)	1982 ($)	(%)
Food, raw materials, & fuel	250	(12.4)	347	(8.6)	471	(5.6)	847	(4.4)	1,626	(2.9)	2,859	(2.2)	2,440	(1.8)
Light industry goods	1,072	(53.3)	1,893	(46.7)	2,692	(31.9)	4,335	(22.4)	7,220	(12.9)	15,786	(12.2)	16,781	(12.1)
Textile	749	(37.2)	1,223	(30.2)	1,582	(18.7)	2,408	(12.5)	3,719	(6.7)	6,296	(4.9)	6,240	(4.5)
Chemicals	103	(5.1)	181	(4.5)	547	(6.5)	1,234	(6.4)	3,889	(7.0)	6,767	(5.2)	6,364	(4.6)
Metals	387	(19.2)	568	(14.0)	1,718	(20.3)	3,805	(19.7)	12,518	(22.5)	21,319	(16.4)	21,215	(15.3)
Iron & steel	259	(12.9)	388	(9.6)	1,290	(15.3)	2,844	(14.7)	10,176	(18.3)	15,454	(11.9)	15,645	(11.3)
Machinery	249	(12.4)	1,035	(25.5)	2,975	(35.2)	8,941	(46.3)	30,004	(53.8)	81,481	(62.8)	90,514	(65.2)
Radio sets	1	(.0)	145	(3.6)	216	(2.6)	695	(3.6)	1,324	(2.4)	3,009	(2.3)	2,401	(1.7)
TV sets	..		3	(.1)	85	(1.0)	384	(2.0)	783	(1.4)	1,660	(1.3)	1,489	(1.1)
Motor vehicles	6	(.3)	78	(1.9)	237	(2.8)	1,337	(6.9)	6,190	(11.1)	23,273	(17.9)	24,559	(17.7)
Ships & boats	78	(3.9)	288	(7.1)	748	(8.8)	1,410	(7.3)	5,998	(10.8)	4,682	(3.6)	6,870	(4.9)
By Destination														
U.S.	456	(22.7)	1,102	(27.2)	2,479	(29.3)	5,940	(30.7)	11,149	(20.0)	31,367	(24.2)	36,330	(26.2)
Western Europe	..		478	(11.8)	1,093	(12.9)	2,905	(15.0)	8,131	(14.6)	21,503	(16.6)	21,640	(15.6)
Oceanea, Canada, S. Africa	137	(6.8)	344	(8.5)	726	(8.6)	1,595	(8.3)	4,155	(7.5)	8,303	(6.4)	10,225	(7.4)
Developed area	..		1,924	(47.4)	4,298	(50.9)	10,440	(54.0)	23,434	(42.0)	61,172	(47.1)	67,995	(49.0)
Southeast Asia	565	(28.1)	1,307	(32.2)	2,195	(26.0)	4,902	(25.4)	12,543	(22.5)	30,910	(23.8)	31,873	(23.0)
Middle East	..		178	(4.4)	356	(4.2)	634	(3.3)	6,075	(10.9)	14,358	(11.1)	16,946	(12.2)
Developing area	..		2,056	(50.7)	3,672	(43.4)	7,827	(40.5)	27,632	(49.6)	59,480	(45.8)	62,435	(45.0)
Communist bloc	39	(1.9)	73	(1.8)	478	(5.7)	1,045	(5.4)	4,683	(8.4)	9,155	(7.1)	8,401	(6.1)
Total	2,011		4,055		8,452		19,318		55,753		129,807		138,831	

Sources: Ministry of Finance, *Customs Clearance Statistics*; The Bank of Japan, *Economic Statistics Annual* (various years); Office of the Prime Minister, Bureau of Statistics, *Japan Statistical Yearbook* (various years).

Table 8.7. Japan's Imports for Selected Years (millions of U.S. dollars, percentage)

	1955 ($)	1955 (%)	1960 ($)	1960 (%)	1965 ($)	1965 (%)	1970 ($)	1970 (%)	1975 ($)	1975 (%)	1980 ($)	1980 (%)	1982 ($)	1982 (%)
Food	625	(25.3)	548	(12.2)	1,470	(18.0)	2,574	(13.6)	8,815	(15.2)	14,666	(10.4)	14,575	(11.0)
Raw materials	1,263	(51.1)	2,209	(49.2)	3,220	(39.4)	6,677	(35.4)	11,660	(20.2)	23,760	(16.9)	18,911	(14.3)
Textile materials	586	(23.7)	762	(17.0)	847	(10.4)	963	(5.1)	1,524	(2.6)	2,393	(1.7)	2,327	(1.8)
Metal ores	186	(7.5)	673	(15.0)	1,019	(12.5)	2,696	(14.3)	4,417	(7.6)	8,430	(6.0)	6,757	(5.1)
Wood	62	(2.5)	170	(3.8)	493	(6.0)	1,572	(8.3)	2,621	(4.5)	6,909	(4.9)	4,546	(3.4)
Mineral fuels	289	(11.7)	742	(16.5)	1,626	(19.9)	3,905	(20.7)	25,641	(44.3)	69,991	(49.8)	65,618	(49.7)
Coal	56	(2.3)	141	(3.1)	270	(3.3)	1,010	(5.3)	3,454	(6.0)	4,458	(3.2)	5,782	(4.4)
Oils	149	(6.0)	465	(10.4)	1,047	(12.8)	2,236	(11.8)	19,644	(33.9)	52,763	(37.5)	46,274	(35.1)
Petroleum products	84	(3.4)	135	(3.0)	289	(3.5)	550	(2.9)	1,351	(2.3)	5,088	(3.6)	5,135	(3.9)
Manufactured goods	308	(12.5)	992	(22.1)	1,853	(22.7)	5,634	(29.8)	11,521	(19.9)	30,568	(21.8)	30,252	(22.9)
Chemicals	112	(4.5)	265	(5.9)	408	(5.0)	1,000	(5.3)	2,057	(3.6)	6,202	(4.4)	6,824	(5.2)
Metals	..		..		..		1,292	(6.8)	1,664	(2.9)	5,797	(4.1)	5,571	(4.2)
Machinery	132	(5.3)	435	(9.7)	760	(9.3)	2,298	(12.2)	4,286	(7.4)	9,843	(7.0)	9,112	(6.9)
Light industry goods	..		63	(1.4)	254	(3.1)	1,043	(5.5)	3,514	(6.1)	8,725	(6.2)	8,744	(6.6)
By Origin														
U.S.	774	(31.3)	1,545	(34.4)	2,366	(29.1)	5,560	(29.4)	11,608	(20.1)	24,408	(17.4)	24,197	(18.3)
Western Europe	..		394	(8.8)	730	(8.9)	1,962	(10.4)	4,395	(7.6)	10,437	(7.4)	10,149	(7.7)
Oceanea, Canada, S. Africa	311	(12.6)	636	(14.2)	1,091	(13.4)	2,908	(15.4)	7,891	(13.6)	14,275	(10.2)	14,100	(10.7)
Developed area	..		2,584	(57.5)	4,186	(51.2)	10,430	(55.2)	23,894	(41.3)	49,120	(35.0)	48,428	(36.7)
South East Asia	527	(21.3)	915	(20.4)	1,406	(17.2)	3,013	(16.0)	10,586	(18.3)	31,751	(22.6)	29,985	(22.7)
Middle East	..		449	(10.0)	1,112	(13.6)	2,337	(12.4)	16,477	(28.5)	44,500	(31.7)	37,764	(28.6)
Developing area	..		1,782	(39.7)	3,456	(42.3)	7,564	(40.1)	30,962	(53.5)	84,733	(59.9)	76,069	(57.7)
Communist bloc	89	(3.6)	125	(2.8)	527	(6.5)	887	(4.7)	3,006	(5.2)	6,669	(4.7)	7,430	(5.6)
Total	2,471		4,491		8,169		18,881		57,863		140,528		131,931	

Sources: Ministry of Finance, *Customs Clearance Statistics*; The Bank of Japan, *Economic Statistics Annual* (various years); Office of the Prime Minister, Bureau of Statistics, *Japan Statistical Yearbook* (various years).

to the United States expanded at a rate of approximately 14 percent, while Japan's (real) imports from the United States grew at a rate of about 7 percent in constant import prices at 1980.

We shall be interested investigating how the U.S. share and the Japanese share in each country's trade have changed during this period when the world economy as a whole experienced a wave of drastic and painful change: the suspension of the gold convertibility of the U.S. dollar, the transition to a system of floating exchange rates among major currencies, and two oil crises.

First, and most important, Japan's trade dependence on the United States was much greater than the U.S. trade dependence on Japan. This difference is particularly evident with regard to Japan's exports. On the average, the United States accounted for more than 25 percent of Japan's total exports, except in two brief periods at the end of the 1950s and in the middle of the 1970s after the first oil crisis. The U.S. share of Japan's exports continued to be well above the level of 30 percent in the late 1960s. On the other hand, Japan's share of U.S. exports remained stable, below the level of 10 percent, except for the period 1970-74. Thus, on the average, the U.S. share of Japan's exports remained more than twice as high as Japan's share of U.S. exports, though disparity in these two shares was gradually diminishing. There was a mild rising trend in Japan's share of U.S. exports during the period of 1955-82.

Second, the U.S. share of Japan's imports steadily declined while Japan's share of U.S. imports showed a rising trend. The U.S. share of Japan's imports was falling as early as in the 1960s, but this trend accelerated after the first oil crisis of 1974. In 1975 this share reached the level of 20 percent, down from about 38 percent in 1957, and remained below a 20 percent level in Period III (1974-82). Japan's share of U.S. imports also fell substantially during the oil crises, but a rising trend in this share was also observed.

Third, Japan's continued effort to diversify its worldwide import sources of raw materials and a huge increase in the amount of Japan's oil imports since the two oil crises were major causes for the sharp decline in the U.S. share of Japan's imports during the 1960s and the 1970s. On the other hand, a continued increase in Japanese machinery exports, particularly electrical machinery and transport equipment, to the United States was a prime factor in increasing Japan's share of U.S. imports. Machinery accounted for more than 40 percent of Japan's exports to the United States in the early 1970s and for more than 55 percent in the early 1980s.

Fourth, since the U.S. share of Japan's exports was virtually stable, except for two brief periods in the late 1950s and in 1974-75, the gap between a stable level of the U.S. share of Japan's exports and a sharply declining trend in the U.S. share of Japan's imports continued to widen. This widening gap was also reflected in the discrepancy between a relatively stable Japanese share of U.S. exports and an expanding Japanese share of U.S. imports during the same period.

Fifth, Japan's oil import ratio changed dramatically during this period. The value of Japan's oil imports was 9.4 percent of its total imports in 1955, and gradually increased to 17 percent in 1973. The first oil crisis made this ratio jump to 34 percent in 1974 and eventually to 41 percent in 1980. Japan's oil import bill in 1980 amounted to $57.8 billion, which was almost two and a half times the total amount of Japan's imports from the United States in the same year. Nevertheless, we find that the U.S. share of Japan's imports after excluding its oil imports remained remarkably stable with a range of 30 to 40 percent.

During the period 1955-82, the commodity composition of Japan's exports to the United States underwent a drastic change. Starting from a position of exporting mainly foodstuffs and light industry products such as textiles, Japan made a distinct transformation of its trade pattern, exporting machinery and other heavy industry products, which came to account for almost 90 percent of Japan's exports to the United States. In contrast to this, the commodity composition of Japan's imports from the United States remained remarkably stable during the same period.

Tables 8.8 and 8.9 show Japan's principal commodities traded with the United States in 1955, 1970, and 1982. Japan has continued to import foodstuffs (wheat, soybeans, maize), raw materials (cotton, coal), and high technology machinery (aircraft, office machines), and to export mainly manufactured goods (clothing, iron and steel, machinery and transport equipment) since the middle of the 1950s. This trade pattern is basically in accord with the principle of comparative advantage, considering the fact that the United States is a country richly endowed with land, natural resources, and highly advanced technology, while Japan is a country of poor natural resources and little arable land, amply endowed with highly skilled and resourceful labor. A complementary trade relationship between the United States and Japan is principally a reflection of such differences in resource endowments between the two countries. However, from a long-range perspective of two to three decades, the quantity and quality of capital stocks accumulated in each country play a crucial role, determining the rate of technical progress which, in turn, gradually changes the dynamic structure of the trade pattern in each country.

Is is apparent from Table 8.8 that the commodity composition of exports to the United States shows a radical change between 1955 and 1982. Excluding iron and steel and sewing mahcines, the top eight commodities Japan exported to the United States in 1955 consisted of fish and shellfish, silk, and light

Table 8.8. Principal Commodities Exported by Japan to the United States in 1955, 1970, and 1982 (millions of U.S. dollars, percentage)

	1955 ($)	(%)	1970	1970 ($)	(%)	1982	1982 ($)	(%)
1. Clothing	59	(12.9)	Iron & Steel	899	(15.1)	Passenger Cars	9,588	(26.4)
2. Fish & shellfish	42	(9.2)	Passenger Cars	458	(7.7)	Iron & Steel	2,807	(7.7)
3. Raw silk	31	(6.8)	Radio Sets	397	(6.7)	Tape Recorders	1,510	(4.2)
						(VTR)	(1,066	(2.9))
4. Cotton fabrics	30	(6.6)	Metal Products	324	(5.5)	Office Machines	1,444	(4.0)
5. Plywood	27	(5.9)	Motorcycles	280	(4.7)	Motorcycles	1,291	(3.6)
6. Toys	27	(5.9)	Clothing	274	(4.6)	Radio Sets	883	(2.4)
7. Pottery	21	(4.6)	TV Sets	265	(4.5)	Trucks	806	(2.2)
8. Sewing machines	15	(3.3)	Tape Recorders	256	(4.3)	Motor Vehicle Parts	578	(1.6)
9. Iron & steel	13	(2.9)	Office Machines	143	(2.4)	Copying Machines	556	(1.5)
10. Floor coverings	11	(2.4)	Fish & Shellfish	97	(1.6)	Semiconductors	539	(1.5)
Sum (1-10)	276	(60.5)		3,393	(57.1)		20,002	(55.1)
Total exports to U.S.	456			5,940			36,330	

Sources: Ministry of Finance, *Customs Clearance Statistics;* Ministry of International Trade and Industry, *Tsūshō Hakusho* (White Paper on International Trade) (various years).

Table 8.9. Principal Commodities Imported by Japan from the United States in 1955, 1970, and 1982

	1955		1970			1982		
	($)	(%)		($)	(%)		($)	(%)
1. Cotton	121	(15.6)	Coal	623	(11.2)	Coal	2,136	(8.8)
2. Wheat	83	(10.7)	Wood	518	(9.3)	Maize	1,466	(6.1)
3. Soybeans	67	(8.7)	Soybeans	330	(5.9)	Wood	1,371	(5.7)
4. Coal	48	(6.2)	Iron & steel scrap	270	(4.9)	Soybeans	1,108	(4.6)
5. Rice	42	(5.4)	Aircraft	245	(4.4)	Office machines	767	(3.2)
6. Iron & steel scrap	33	(4.3)	Maize	217	(3.9)	Aircraft	694	(2.9)
7. Heavy fuel oils	27	(3.5)	Office machines	201	(3.6)	Fish & shellfish	673	(2.8)
8. Barley	21	(2.7)	Wheat	173	(3.1)	Wheat	650	(2.7)
9. Beef tallow	21	(2.7)	Kaoliang	133	(2.4)	Meat	562	(2.3)
10. Maize	15	(1.9)	Petroleum products	110	(2.0)	Cotton	552	(2.3)
Sum (1–10)	478	(61.8)		2,820	(50.7)		9,979	(41.3)
Total imports from U.S.	774			5,560			24,179	

Sources: Ministry of Finance, Customs Clearance Statistics; Ministry of International Trade and Industry, Tsūshamo Hakusho (White Paper on International Trade) (various years).

industry goods, which accounted for more than 50 percent. The value of these eight commodities declined to 12 percent of 1970 exports and then to less than 2.5 percent in 1982. In 1970, the top seven commodities exported to the United States consisted mainly of heavy industry products and machinery equipment, which accounted for more than 48 percent. In 1982, the top ten commodities exported to the United States were all machinery and transport equipment except for iron and steel. The export of transport equipment (passenger cars, trucks, motorcycles, motor vehicle parts) alone accounted for about one-third of Japan's exports to the United States. (These products were imported mostly from the United States in 1955.) Observe that office machines were traded in both directions between the United States and Japan and were a substantial component in Japan's export and import. Semiconductors are another example of a two-way trade between the United States and Japan in 1982; semiconductors valued at $362 million accounted for 1.5 percent of Japan's imports from the United States.

At the beginning of Period I (1955-64), heavy and chemical industry products were less than 17 percent of Japan's exports to the United States; foodstuffs and other light industry goods accounted for more than 83 percent. Heavy industry products (chemicals, metals, machinery and transport equipment) increased steadily and at a remarkably rapid pace, reaching over 50 percent in 1964 and 85 percent in 1974, while the value of light industry products approached the level of 10 percent of exports. Then, in Period III (1974-82), this trend appeared to reach a saturation level.

In 1966-68, metals (mainly steel) were more than 25 percent of exports, but this share was gradually reduced to the level of 15 percent in Period III. Chemical exports to the United States never exceeded 3 percent except in 1974-75, during the first oil crisis.

In the long-run trends of U.S.-Japanese trade relations, textiles and automobiles played a significant role at critical times for both the United States and Japan. During the period 1955-82, we can observe two entirely opposite trends in Japan's trade in these commodities with the United States: Japan's textile exports, more than 37 percent in 1955, declined to less than 2 percent by 1980; transport equipment, negligible at the beginning of Period I, rose dramatically from 4 percent in 1964 to 30 percent in 1972 and eventually to 40 percent in 1980. In 1982, Japan exported to the United States $13.6 billion of transport equipment, which accounted for 37.3 percent of Japan's exports to the United States. The automobile exports to the United States amounted to $11 billion, which alone accounted for about 30 percent of Japan's exports to the United States in 1982.

The commodity composition of Japan's exports to the United States from 1955 to 1982 shows a steady downward trend in the percentages of foodstuffs, textiles, and other light industry products such as toys and footwear on the one hand, and a rapidly expanding trend in metal goods and machinery, particularly in transport equipment, on the other. The principal commodity exported to the United States was textiles in the middle of the 1950s, then toys and footwear in the early 1960s. These light industry products were replaced quickly by steel in the middle of the 1960s, which was in turn replaced first by electrical machinery, such as radio and television sets and tape recorders, in the middle of the 1970s and then by motorcycles and automobiles in the late 1970s and the early 1980s. This shift in the export ratios of the commodities continued with a gradual expansion of office machines (electronic computers) and more sophisticated electrical machinery and equipment (video tape recorders and semiconductors) in the early 1980s.

In comparison with a drastic change in Japan's export structure, there was a stable commodity composition of imports from the United States during 1955-82. There were cyclical fluctuations in this composition, which largely reflected the cyclical fluctuations of the Japanese domestic economy during the same period. At the time of boom periods (1961, 1964, and 1973), the import ratio of raw materials and fuel increased, while the import ratio of manufactured goods, particularly machinery and equipment, was forced to decline. On the whole, however, a stationary trend was observable especially in the ratio of foodstuffs and machinery imports. On the average in this period, food imports remained at approximately 18 percent and machinery imports at about 20 percent. Fuel (mainly coal) imports were fairly constant, remaining at about 10 percent.

Japan's raw material imports from the United States ranged from about 50 percent in the middle of the 1950s to 35 percent in 1968 and then to approximately 25 percent in the early 1980s. The downward trend in the raw material imports can be contrasted to the upward trend in the import of manufactured goods, particularly chemical products such as medical and pharmaceutical products and electrical machinery. The import ratio of manufactured goods rose from approximately 25 percent in the middle of the 1950s to 40 percent at the beginning of the 1970s and eventually to the level of more than 46 percent in 1982.

The trend in the commodity composition of Japan's exports to the United States seems to have reflected precisely the trend in the commodity composition of Japan's exports to the whole world. This is also true for the United States exports. That is, the trend in the commodity composition of Japan's imports from the United States reflected the trend in the commodity composition of U.S. exports to the whole world. Indeed, the trend in the global exports of the United States showed a strikingly stable structure in this period.

During the period 1955-82, world machinery trade expanded rapidly at a rate of 15 percent, which clearly contributed to accelerating world trade expansion by as much as 13 percent per year. As a result, the commodity composition of world exports changed significantly, increasing the machinery export share from 17 percent in 1955 to around 30 percent at the end of the 1970s. But the growth rates of machinery exports differed significantly among nations during 1955-82. The U.S. growth rate was the lowest, at 12 percent, and the U.K. rate was 13.7 percent. Both these rates were lower than the growth rate of world machinery exports, 15 percent, which was approximately equal to West Germany's. Japan's machinery exports expanded at a rate of 24.6 percent annually, the highest growth rate among the industrial countries. Thus, Japan had the largest elasticity of machinery exports, 1.6, while the United States had the smallest elasticity, approximately 0.8, among the industrial countries.

Japan's impressive performance, particularly in comparison with that of the United States, was brought about by a remarkable expansion of the Japanese machinery industry in the same period. In terms of the industrial production index, Japan's machinery industry production expanded at a rate of more than 14 percent annually, while the production index of the United States machinery industry grew only at a rate of 4.3 percent per year during 1955-82. Furthermore, there was a significant difference in the growth rate of labor productivity between the United States and Japan. Indeed, Japan's labor productivity (measured by real GNP per employed person) increased at a rate of approximately 7 percent annually, while in the United States it remained fairly stable, increasing only at a rate of 1.5 percent per year. During 1967-79, Japan's automobile and electrical machinery industries especially attained a remarkable high growth rate of more than 15 percent annually in terms of value-added labor productivity index, which was three times more than the growth rate of those industries in the United States.[1]

Machinery trade between the United States and Japan expanded very rapidly during the period 1955-82. Japan maintained a remarkably high growth rate, approximately 29 percent per year, in machinery exports to the United States. This was indeed a leading factor in maintaining the high growth of Japan's exports to the United States during this period. On the other hand, the growth rate of Japan's machinery imports from the United States was much lower, about 15 percent per year. As a result, the machinery trade balance between the United States and Japan changed greatly during this period. Until 1963, Japan had a chronic deficit in machinery trade with the United States. After 1964, however, Japan's machinery trade with the United States turned into a surplus, which continued to increase in magnitude.

It is interesting to see how Japan's machinery trade with the United States changed from a deficit to a surplus, indicating the dynamic nature of Japan's evolving comparative advantage in international markets. First in 1956, Japan's trade of electrical machinery with the United States became a surplus which expanded at a rate of more than 20 percent per year in the period 1959-82. Then, in 1964, following the spectacular growth of domestic production and exports of motorcyles and automobiles, Japan's trade balance of transport equipment with the United States turned into a surplus, which expanded at a spectacular rate of more than 38 percent in the period 1965-82. Thus, in 1965, U.S.-Japanese trade relations entered into a new era in which Japan maintained a surplus not only in machinery trade balance but also in overall merchandise trade balance with the United States. Japan's surplus of machinery trade with the United States increased more than seventy times (or at a rate of approximately 29 percent per annum), from less than $300 million in 1965 to more than $21 billion in 1982. Finally in 1976, Japan's trade balance in general machinery with the United States changed from a chronic deficit to a surplus, mainly because of a steady increase in the export of office machines such as electronic calculators and automatic data processing machinery. Thus, Japan continued to have a considerable surplus in most categories of machinery trade with the United States. Indeed, in the period of 1962-82, export expansion (in value terms) was remarkable rapid, at a rate of 26 percent for the machinery industry as a whole, 20 percent for electrical machinery, 22 percent for precision instruments (including cameras, copying mahcines, watches), 27 percent for general machinery (including prime movers and office machines), and 37 percent for transport equipment.

The principle of comparative advantage appeared to be working in machinery trade between the United States and Japan. Japan imported from the United States technology-intensive machinery such as scientific instruments, eletrical measuring instruments, semiconductors, electronic computers, atomic reactors, and aircraft. In return, Japan exported mass-produced and skilled-labor-intensive machinery such as cameras, telecommunications equipment, electronic calculators, motorcycles, and motor vehicles in which Japan had its comparative advantage vis-à-vis the United States.

The machinery trade between the United States and Japan in the period also showed, however, that the commodities constituting Japan's and America's comparative advantages changed gradually as technological progress on and international competition continued.

Japan's balance of payments in the current account fluctuated widely during the whole period 1955-82. There was a long-run tendency, however, toward an increasing surplus in Japan's current account. The trend in Japan's current surplus was mainly a reflection of the surplus trend in its trade balance since the middle of the 1960s. On the other hand, there appeared to be a falling tendency of the U.S. current surplus since the middle of the 1960s, reflecting

Table 8.10. Elasticities of Exports and Imports of the United States and Japan, 1955-82

	Income Elasticity	$\bar{R}^2$	S.E.	DW
log(JEXV) = − 10.423 (−63.899)	+ 3.275 log(WGPDI) (84.270)	0.9962	0.0664	1.169
log(JIMV) = − 10.672 (−36.617)	+ 1.240 log(JGNPR) (49.357)	0.9890	0.0873	1.089
log(USEXV) = − 2.18 (−9.979)	+ 1.444 log(WGDPI) (27.623)	0.9658	0.0893	0.629
log(USIMV) = − 10.731 (−29.373)	+ 1.957 log(USGNPR)[g] (40.241)	0.9836	0.0710	0.550

    JEXV: Japan's exports in volume (1980 = 100)
    JIMV: Japan's imports in volume (1980 = 100)
  USEXV: U.S. exports in volume (1980 = 100)
  USIMV: U.S. imports in volume (1980 = 100)
  WGDPI: Gross Domestic Product Index (1980 = 100) of the industrial countries
          (excluding centrally planned economies)
  JGNPR: Japan's real GNP at 1980 prices
 USGNPR: U.S. real GNP at 1980 prices
Source: IMF, *International Financial Statistics, Yearbook, 1983*.

a sharply declining trend in its trade surplus. In fact, during the whole period, the two countries' current balances went in entirely opposite directions. The magnitude of this opposite imbalance became proportionately large as time went on.

In order to assess such contrasting characteristics, I shall point out three salient features in the basic structures of each country's trade, services, and current balances. First, in the period of 1955-82, Japan's income elasticity of exports, approximately 3, was much larger than its income elasticity of imports, which was about 1.3. For the United States, the income elasticity of exports was approximately 1.4, its income elasticity of imports about 2 (table 8.10). If these estimates are roughly correct, Japan's trade balance tends to yield a surplus as long as Japan maintains the same growth rate of its real GNP as the rest of the world. The opposite will be the case for the United States. In particular, Japan had a much larger income elasticity of exports to the United States than its income elasticity of imports from the United States (table 8.11). Indeed, the difference between export elasticity and import elasticity is much greater in Japan's trade with the United States than in its global trade. Therefore, as long as Japan's GNP grows at the same rate as that of the United States, it is very likely that Japan will continue to increase its trade surplus with the United States.

Table 8.11. Elasticities of Japan's Exports and Imports in Its Trade with the United States 1955-82

	Income Elasticity	Price Elasticity	$\bar{R}^2$	S.E.	DW
log(JAEXR) =	− 12.055 + 3.676 log (USGNPR) (− 6.939) (37.501)	− 1.394 log ($JEXP/USWPI) (− 4.780)	0.9848	0.2358	0.762
log(JAIMR) =	2.569 + 0.953 log (JGNPR) (− 3.647) (25.912)	− 0.929 log (¥JIMP/JWPI) (−5.728)	0.9614	0.1222	1.585

JAEXR: Japan's exports to U.S. at 1980 prices = Japan's exports to U.S. /$JEXP
$JEXP: Japan's export prices on dollar base (1980 = 100)
JAIMR: Japan's imports from U.S. at 1980 prices = Japan's imports from U.S./$JIMP[i]
$JIMP: Japan's import prices on dollar base (1980 = 100)
¥JIMP: Japan's import prices on yen base (1980 = 100)
USWPI: U.S. wholesale price index (1980 = 100)
 JWPI: Japan's wholesale price index (1980 = 100)
USGNPR: U.S. real GNP at 1980 prices
JGNPR: Japan's real GNP at 1980 prices
Sources: IMF, *International Financial Statistics, Yearbook, 1983*; The Bank of Japan, *Kokusai Hikaku Tōkei*; Ministry of International Trade and Industry, *Tsūshō Hakusho* (White Paper on International Trade); Ministry of Finance, *Customs Clearance Statistics*.

Second, since the early 1960s, Japan continued to have a deficit trend in the service account which tended to reduce considerably Japan's increasing trade surplus. In sharp contrast, the United States increased the surplus in its service account, which contributed to mitigating U.S. trade deficits. It is particularly noteworthy that the United States maintained an enormous amount of investment income from abroad which exceeded its trade deficits after 1971, except for 1977, 1978, and 1982. We also note that the United States maintained a strong surplus trend in technological trade (such as patent royalties), in which Japan's payments exceeded it receipts. This was unavoidable because Japan insatiably imported technological services from the United States. Indeed, it was by so doing that Japan succeeded in establishing its comparative advantage, particularly in the machinery industry.

Third, during the whole period of 1955-82, Japan maintained a much higher rate of savings and investment than did the United States. Until the middle of the 1970s, Japan's rate of investment was high enough to offset a considerable portion of the personal sector's savings. Since 1975, however, the net savings ratio (in percentage of GNP) increased gradually, while the business sector's net investment ratio sharply declined. Though the imbalance between savings and investment was diminished by increasing the public sector's deficits, Japan continued to have a trend of increasing excess (domestic) savings, which helped finance the current deficits in the external sector. That is to say,

Hideo Kanemitsu

Table 8.12. Appendix: Japanese and U.S. Merchandise Trade, 1955-82 (millions of U.S. dollars)

	Japan[a]					
Year	Exports	Imports	Balance	Exports to U.S.	Imports from U.S.	Balance with U.S.
1955	2,011	2,471	− 460	456	774	− 318
1956	2,501	3,230	− 729	550	1,067	− 517
1957	2,858	4,284	− 1,426	604	1,623	− 1,019
1958	2,877	3,033	− 156	690	1,056	− 366
1959	3,456	3,599	− 143	1,047	1,115	− 68
1960	4,055	4,491	− 436	1,102	1,545	− 443
1961	4,236	5,810	− 1,574	1,067	2,096	− 1,029
1962	4,916	5,637	− 721	1,400	1,809	− 409
1963	5,452	6,736	− 1,284	1,507	2,077	− 570
1964	6,673	7,938	− 1,265	1,842	2,336	− 494
1965	8,452	8,169	283	2,479	2,366	113
1966	9,776	9,523	253	2,969	2,658	311
1967	10,442	11,663	− 1,221	3,012	3,212	− 200
1968	12,972	12,987	− 15	4,086	3,527	559
1969	15,990	15,024	966	4,958	4,090	868
1970	19,318	18,881	437	5,940	5,560	380
1971	24,019	19,712	4,307	7,495	4,978	2,517
1972	28,591	23,471	5,120	8,848	5,852	2,996
1973	36,930	38,314	− 1,384	9,449	9,270	179
1974	55,536	62,110	− 6,574	12,799	12,682	117
1975	55,753	57,863	− 2,110	11,149	11,608	− 459
1976	67,225	64,799	2,426	15,690	11,809	3,881
1977	80,495	70,809	9,686	19,717	12,396	7,321
1978	97,543	79,343	18,200	24,915	14,790	10,125
1979	103,032	110,672	− 7,640	26,403	20,431	5,972
1980	129,807	140,528	− 10,721	31,367	24,408	6,959
1981	152,030	143,290	8,740	38,609	25,297	13,312
1982	138,831	131,931	6,900	36,330	24,179	12,151

Sources: Ministry of Finance, *Customs Clearance Statistics*; The Bank of Japan, *Economic Statistics Annual*; U.S. Department of Commerce, *Survey of Current Business*.

Table 8.12. Appendix: Japanese and U.S. Merchandise Trade, 1955-82
Cont'd.

	United States[b]					
Year	Exports	Imports	Balance	Exports to Japan	Imports from Japan	Balance with Japan
1955	14,291	11,384	2,907	651	432	219
1956	17,333	12,615	4,718	905	558	347
1957	19,495	12,982	6,513	1,236	601	635
1958	16,367	12,835	3,532	845	671	174
1959	16,407	15,207	1,200	967	1,029	− 62
1960	19,629	15,018	4,611	1,341	1,149	192
1961	20,188	14,714	5,474	1,739	1,055	684
1962	20,973	16,390	4,583	1,415	1,358	57
1963	22,427	17,138	5,289	1,711	1,498	213
1964	25,690	18,684	7,006	2,009	1,768	241
1965	26,691	21,364	5,327	2,080	2,414	− 334
1966	29,379	25,542	3,837	2,364	2,963	− 599
1967	30,934	26,812	4,122	2,695	2,999	− 304
1968	34,063	33,226	837	2,954	4,054	− 1,100
1969	37,332	36,043	1,289	3,490	4,888	− 1,398
1970	42,659	39,952	2,707	4,652	5,875	− 1,223
1971	43,549	45,563	− 2,014	4,055	7,259	− 3,204
1972	49,119	55,583	− 6,464	4,963	9,064	− 4,101
1973	70,823	69,476	1,347	8,313	9,676	− 1,363
1974	97,908	100,251	− 2,343	10,679	12,338	− 1,659
1975	107,130	96,116	11,014	9,563	11,268	− 1,705
1976	115,150	121,009	− 5,859	10,145	15,504	− 5,359
1977	121,150	147,685	− 26,535	10,522	18,550	− 8,028
1978	143,578	171,978	− 28,400	12,885	24,458	− 11,573
1979	181,651	206,256	− 24,605	17,581	26,248	− 8,667
1980	220,549	240,834	− 20,285	20,790	30,701	− 9,911
1981	233,677	261,305	− 27,628	21,823	37,612	− 15,789
1982	212,193	243,952	− 31,759	20,966	37,744	− 16,778

[a]Japanese export data on f.o.b. basis, import data on c.i.f. basis.
[b]U.S. data on f.a.s. basis.

as long as Japan maintains a trend of high savings which cannot be sufficiently offset by domestic deficits such as private investments or public consumption, it is very likely that Japan will continue to increase its current surplus by increasing its capital exports (foreign lending) to the rest of the world.

1. Based on data estimated by Ministry of International Trade and Industry, *Tsūshō Hakusho* (White Paper on International Trade) (1982), 460-63; (1983), 446-49.

9

Internationalization of
Japanese Capital Markets

ROBERT ALAN FELDMAN

This essay describes the regulatory environment of capital account transactions in Japan in the 1950-80 period. The rationale for regulation of such transactions is discussed within a theoretical framework before turning to a discussion of the channels through which payments were made and how proper structuring of such channels could simplify the achievement of national economic goals. Specific rules relating to foreign investment,[1] raising funds in foreign markets, and banking are also discussed.

First, a brief discussion regarding capital market regulation and its relation to foreign exchange is appropriate. To improve welfare, an economy must trade and invest. Without foreign exchange, both trade and investment would be seriously restricted; hence, maintaining access to foreign exchange is essential for normal economic activity. This access is usually maintained by supply and demand in the market, but the flows from the two sides are not always smooth; seasonality and economic shocks can easily disturb foreign exchange markets. In serious cases, such shocks can terminate access to foreign exchange.

Access to foreign exchange has two aspects, price and quantity. Under a fixed exchange rate regime, the price of foreign exchange is guaranteed by the central bank, and access is ensured by quantities of foreign exchange which the central bank buys and sells in the course of normal trade and investment flows.[2] This has the advantage that traders and investors know the price of foreign exchange with certainty (so long as central bank reserves and access to foreign exchange borrowing are sufficient), but the disadvantage that quantities held by the central bank can change drastically in short periods. Under a floating rate system, in which the central bank withdraws from the foreign exchange market, the price is freely determined, and access is guaranteed by the profit motive; holders of foreign exchange will provide quantities so long as the price is right. This system has the advantage that prices are likely to reflect fundamental changes in a more timely fashion and thus be more efficient, but has the disadvantages of uncertainty and susceptibility to short-term disturbances.

Because disturbances in the foreign exchange market inevitably cause distortions in the real economy, it is reasonable for government to provide a regulatory structure to minimize these distortions; capital market regulation is one tool, and it can be used, with modifications, under both fixed and flexible exchange rate regimes. The hard parts are assessing what disturbances are likely, what distortions they will cause, and what regulatory responses are appropriate.

Next, we must consider the actors in the foreign exchange market. The market consists of the authorities (in a fixed rate or managed floating regime), the financial sector, and the nonfinancial sector. Both the latter include resident and nonresident subsectors. Each sector and subsector differs in the composition of its balance sheet, its expertise in asset and liability management, and its tastes for risk and return. Thus, each sector and subsector will react differently to circumstances, so that there is a clear rationale for different regulations for each sector or subsector.

A typical balance sheet is presented in Table 9.1. The instruments available are currency, deposits, loans, bonds, equities, and real assets (e.g., capital equipment, real estate). These may be assets or liabilities to any sector, depending on the nature of its business; for example, deposits are an asset to the nonfinancial sector but a liability to banks. And some sectors will hold different types of an instrument on both sides of the balance sheet. The difference between assets and liabilities is net worth. This balance sheet lists assets denominated in both foreign and domestic currency. The conversion factor is the exchange rate; values of negotiable assets are listed as the product of price and quantity, to emphasize that their values change in the marketplace (e.g., entries for equities are multiplied by the price of equities, but deposits need not be so multiplied, because they are of fixed nominal value). When the exchange rate changes, both asset and liability sides will change; but typically, one will rise by more than the other, the difference being the change in net worth, i.e., profit or loss. When the foreign currency is expected to appreciate (i.e., e is expected to rise), then it is wise to sell foreign currency liabilities and buy foreign currency assets; once the rise occurs, the value of assets will be higher and that of liabilities lower than in the original state, leaving a profit.

But such transactions are complicated by two factors, the risk and return of the instrument being used for such foreign exchange speculation. Between the time of purchasing the foreign asset and the time of selling it to realize

Table 9.1. Typical Balance Sheet

Instrument	Return	Risk	Assets	Liabilities and Net Worth
Currency	Low	Low	C eC^*	
Deposits	Low	Low	D eD^*	D eD^*
Loans	Medium	Medium	L eL^*	L eL^*
Bonds	Medium	Medium	P_bB $eP_b^*B^*$	P_bB $eP_b^*B^*$
Equities	High	High	P_eE $eP_E^*E^*$	P_eE $eP_E^*E^*$
Real Assets	High	High	P_uK $eP_k^*K^*$	P_uK $eP_k^*K^*$
Net Worth				NW

Note: Variables with asterisks are denominated in foreign currency and converted to domestic currency at the exchange rate, e. Negotiable assets are premultiplied by their prices. No entry for currency exists on the liability side because currency is a liability only for the authorities.

the profit, the foreign asset will earn a return. The higher this return, the more attractive is the asset as a vehicle for speculation. But risk is also a factor, particularly for negotiable assets. When the foreign currency price of the foreign asset is highly variable, any gains made on the exchange rate can be wiped out by losses from a lower price.

Authorities take these factors into account when determining the regulatory structure for each sector. If authorities believe that the destabilizing effects of speculation more than outweigh the benefits of efficient resource allocation from free capital movement, then it is reasonable to limit foreign exchange transactions to those for instruments with either low returns or high risk. When the benefits of free capital flows outweigh the risks of destabilization, then reducing these restrictions is reasonable. And because conditions change over time, e.g., because of innovations by institutions or because of technology of funds transfer, it is only natural for the regulatory structure to adapt.

Because the goal of Japan's foreign exchange regulation in the 1950s was prevention of large, sudden outflows, it was logical for the authorities to restrict the number of channels through which capital could flow. This was done by limiting the number of banks allowed to handle foreign exchange transactions. Only certain nonresident accounts held at these banks were deemed convertible to foreign exchange, and even this convertibility was restricted. As time passed and the foreign exchange constraint eased, the conditions of convertibility of these accounts also eased. New types were added and old types abolished.

From the abolition of freely convertible accounts in 1951 through 1959, the main type of nonresident account was the Nonresident Yen Deposit Account (NYDA). Opening a NYDA required approval before 1959 but was made free to any nonresident from 1959 on. In early years, there is no special mention of what types of funds could be credited to such accounts, but they were generally credited with yen earned on trade transactions. The funds in such accounts could be used to pay debts in yen or transferred to other NYDA accounts, but remittance from these accounts in foreign currency was subject to individual license.

Another type of account was the Foreign Investor Deposit Account (FIDA). Inward investment was hard to attract without special remittance rights, and these accounts were a response to that need. In the early 1950s, proceeds of securities sales could be remitted in five equal annual installments, starting two years after the purchase of the security. FIDAs held the funds awaiting repatriation.

A change in regime occurred in 1960, with the establishment of the Free Yen Account (FYA). From 1960 until 1977, the FYA and the NYDA stood together as the two main types of accounts, with the former receiving funds deemed available for immediate repatriation and the latter receiving only partially convertible funds. Over time, as the foreign exchange constraint eased further, the domain of the free yen account enlarged while that of the NYDA shrank.

When FYAs were established, in July 1960, they were thought of as the receptacle for yen earned by nonresidents on trade account transactions. Payments from FYAs were not restricted, but credits to them were. Originally, only proceeds from sales of foreign exchange, transfers from other free yen accounts and "authorized payments"[3] were creditable. But after December 1964, proceeds of securities liquidation could be deposited in FYAs if the equity in question had originally been purchased with NYDA funds and if it had been held for at least three years. From 1965, proceeds from the sale of any security for which acquisition was validated could be deposited in an FYA if the security had been held for six months or more. "Amnesties" of transfer between NYDA and FYA accounts were declared in July 1969, December 1970, and February 1971, allowing transfer of NYDA balances into FYA accounts. These liberalizations occurred at times of upward pressure on the yen—pressure Japanese authorities wished to relieve.

In the 1970s, the authorities influenced FYA accounts through reserve requirement changes. That is, authorities made additions to FYA accounts very expensive for banks, particularly at times of intense upward pressure on the yen. Ceilings on increases in FYA balances on a bank-by-bank basis were instituted in August 1971, just as the Bretton Woods System entered its first crisis. These ceilings were lifted early in 1972. In mid-1972, the Bank of Japan acquired the legal power to set reserve requirements (in force since 1959 on domestic accounts) on FYAs, and in July of that year set a reserve requirement of 50 percent on increases in FYA balances. This requirement was lowered to 10 percent in December 1973 as the yen weakened, and was eliminated in September 1974. Use of reserve requirements on nonresident accounts continued as a tool to affect capital flows after 1977, the year the FYA/NYDA distinction was abolished.

The other main nonresident account in the 1960-77 period was the NYDA, which remained the same in name but changed in character. It was intended for receipt of funds which were only partially convertible, but the rules of repatriation of even NYDA funds eased over the years. In May 1961, NYDA deposits became transferable among holders so that a nonresident wishing to exchange yen for foreign currency could do so if another nonresident were willing to be counterpart in the transaction. No organized market for such transfers existed, but the possibility of conversion through this means did exist. Interest earned on NYDA accounts became freely remittable in June 1961. NYDAs also became the receptacle for fixed asset liquidation proceeds and for proceeds of sales of any nonvalidated investments. When securities liquidation proceeds became creditable to FYAs in 1965, the importance of NYDAs declined. The amnesties of 1969-71 further reduced the importance of these accounts, and they were finally abolished in 1977.

Since 1977, there has been essentially one type of account for nonresidents, the nonresident deposit account (NDA). (For a few years it was still called a free yen account, but because all yen became free, there was no need to retain the name.) Any proceeds of any transaction can be credited to these accounts, and they can be used for any purpose. The main tool of control continues to be reserve requirements. A basic level of 0.25 percent of total balances was imposed in May 1977, with changes at the discretion of the Bank of Japan. In November 1977, as the climb in the yen steepened, a marginal rate of 50 percent was imposed. In March 1978, with the yen rapidly approaching ¥200/US$—an unheard of strength—the marginal rate was set at 100 percent. This rate was reduced in January 1979, after the dollar rescue measures of late 1978 were announced by the Federal Reserve, and the NDA reserve requirement was lowered to 50 percent. With the oil crisis of late 1979 and consequent weakening of the yen, the reserve requirement on increases in NDAs was eliminated completely (February 1980).

In summary, the types of accounts available in Japan to nonresidents varied over the years; in the early period, convertibility was severely restricted through limits on the proportions of balances convertible to foreign exchange in any year and limits on the types of proceeds creditable to accounts with repatriation rights. Gradually, these restrictions were eased and new types of fully convertible accounts established. As Japan's very strong reserve position emerged in the late 1960s, the importance of the distinction between convertible and nonconvertible accounts waned and quicker response to yield differences across countries became possible for nonresidents.

In the late 1970s, the chief method of regulating capital flows shifted from control of conditions affecting demand for nonresident accounts to control of conditions affecting their supply by banks. By this time, the distinction between trade and capital transactions was essentially eliminated, and overall flows became the important factor. Even 100 percent reserve requirements on nonresident deposits failed to have a noticeable effect on the course of the exchange rate. The general commitment to internationalization and the apparent lack of success in using regulatory changes to affect the exchange rate may well account for deregulations codified in the 1980 foreign exchange law and for the fewer changes of rules since then in response to market developments.

We now change focus from the accounts through which nonresidents' payments were made to the types of instruments used by all investors. These instruments differ in risk and liquidity, and the differences make them more or less attractive as avenues for foreign investment, whether resident or nonresident. For example, a low risk, highly liquid security is best for foreign exchange speculation, as the risks of speculation are not compounded by repayment and liquidity risks inherent in the security. The basic types of instruments of foreign investment were direct investment, equity purchase, and bond or other fixed income (security) purchase. We begin with direct investment, and investigate the regulatory environment surrounding each type of asset in turn.

One might wonder why a country such as Japan in the early 1950s, hungry for capital and for foreign exchange, would regulate nonresidents wishing to bring foreign exchange to build factories. The major reason seems to have been the fear that capital brought in would wish to exit quickly at an inconvenient time. In fact, Japanese authorities did not view themselves as being restrictive toward foreign direct investment but rather as giving it special repatriation privileges. Reflecting this concern, the system for direct investment recognized two types, validated and nonvalidated investment. The former, to which special foreign exchange conversion rights were granted, required approval; the latter, with no conversion rights other than those for nonresidents, did not require approval.

It is sometimes said that the reason for direct investment controls was to prevent foreign competitors with better technology from entering the Japanese market and dominating it. Although application of approval procedures for validated investments may have given some support to this hypothesis,[4] the existence of the nonvalidated investment category at least shows that the concerns of authorities were not entirely about protection of resident-owned industry.

The concept of direct investment itself developed over the years. In earlier years, all stock purchases, whether for participation in management or for portfolio, were treated identically. There were two types of controls, one on the total share held by nonresidents and one on the amount of stock any single nonresident could own. There were also, for the purpose of this regulation, two types of industries: restricted ones (including electricity and gas utilities, waterworks, banking, transportation, and retail trade), and nonrestricted ones. Before 1960, automatic approval was given to equity ownership by nonresidents if the total foreign share was less than 8 percent, or for nonrestricted industries if the size of the block purchased by a single resident was less than 5 percent. (Limits were slightly lower for restricted industries.) Purchases above these limits required approval. These limits were raised in 1960 to 15 percent and 10 percent.

The concept of distinguishing direct investment from portfolio investment emerged in the early 1960s, and a new system for direct investment was implemented in July 1963. The category of nonvalidated investment was abolished, and income on nonvalidated investments was made freely remittable. (Principal, if repatriation was desired, had to be deposited in a NYDA and remitted from there.) New direct investments were freely remittable for both principal and interest as long as the original validation requirement had been fulfilled. Moreover, the 1963 reforms simplified screening procedures, even though an escape clause (allowing delay in repatriation or allowing denial of investment right if an "adverse effect" on the Japanese economy were foreseen) was inserted.

Another liberalization of direct investment procedures was announced in 1967, to be implemented in four steps. Two lists were constructed, the A list and the B list. For industries on the A list, automatic approval for direct investments (with management participation) was given if less than 50 percent of the firm was foreign owned. For those on the B list, automatic approval was given up to 100 percent foreign ownership. The stages of implementation saw the A list grow to 160 and the B list to 44 industries in 1969, and to 448 and 79, respectively, in 1970. In 1971, a negative list of seven industries (in which no direct investment was permitted) was established, with the B list expanded to 228, and the A list expanded to all others. Through the 1970s, industries were removed from the negative list, with retail trade removed in

1975 and data processing in 1976, leaving only agriculture and forestry, petroleum, mining, and leather as restricted.

The foreign exchange law of 1980 further clarified the definition of direct investment. Acquisition of shares of unlisted companies, acquisition of more than 10 percent of equity in a firm by a single nonresident, or acquisition of long-term loans or privately placed securities is treated as direct investment. A negative list of "designated" industries still exists, on which ministries concerned may place industries where foreign ownership is judged likely to have adverse impact on the economy.[5] Direct investment regulations may be applied to such industries if the total foreign share rises above 25 percent. Application of direct investment regulations means that prior approval must be obtained in certain cases; most will require prior notice with a twenty-day waiting period for comments (and potential objections) by competent ministries.

Although direction of the liberalization program was clear, the degree of discretion in implementation was not always clear. It is somewhat confusing to investors to require approval which is given automatically. In practice, this appeared to be only a reporting requirement but still left investors with doubts. Particularly, given the changes in the automatic nature of approval of other categories of transactions, the system itself, until the foreign exchange law of 1980, could still appear confusing. Until data on the ratio of applications to approvals is available, no definite conclusion is possible about when regulation of direct investment was tight and when weak.[6]

Outward direct investment by Japanese residents was controlled much more strictly than inward direct investment by foreigners. Indeed, in the 1950s, residents were required to declare all foreign assets and to liquidate and repatriate proceeds if authorities so ordered. Approval was required for any foreign investment. Gradually, however, approval became easier. By late 1969, approval was automatic for direct investments of less than US$200,000, except by financial sector firms. This limit was raised to US$1 million in September 1970 and abolished in July 1971. The timing here is interesting; the big liberalizations occurred just as pressure on the Bretton Woods exchange rate was growing.

After 1972, the official attitude toward direct investment became one of active encouragement; public sector financial institutions were authorized to lend up to 70 percent of the total value of any direct investment overseas in late 1972, and the limit was raised to 90 percent in May 1973. Under the foreign exchange law, outward direct investment requires prior notice, with a twenty-day waiting period for official comment.

Equity investment has been the easiest way for nonresidents to invest in Japan in the postwar years. Although the attitude was restrictive in the 1950s, this changed in the early 1960s and made equities the easiest of Japanese securities to buy and sell, with proceeds remitted freely after 1963. A series of restrictions was imposed in the early 1970s, not on purchasers but rather on securities firms. These were eliminated fairly rapidly, and automatic approval of equity purchase returned. At present, equity acquisition for portfolio investment requires only notification of purchase.

The rules on equity purchase in the 1950s did not restrict the purchase of equities so much as sale and repatriation of proceeds, although equities of certain industries (see above) required prior approval before purchase, even if repatriation rights were not desired. If an investor wished to liquidate a position in an equity and remit the proceeds, these proceeds had first to be deposited in a NYDA or FIDA; if two years had elapsed from the original purchase of the stock, 20 percent of the liquidation proceeds became eligible for repatriation in each year thereafter. The 20-percent-per-year-over-five-years rule was relaxed to a 33.33-percent-per-year-over-three-years rule, and then to a 100-percent-in-one-year-rule in 1961, but the two-year waiting period from original purchase remained.

There were also limits on total foreign ownership below which approval was automatic; these were 8 percent for most industries and 5 percent for restricted ones (see above). These ratios were raised to 15 percent and 10 percent in 1960. Approval was also required for any individual to own more than 5 percent.

A major change occurred in 1961, when income on equities became freely remittable, and another major change occurred in 1962, when the two-year holding period was reduced to six months. Even this six-month rule was abolished in 1963, making rapid movement of funds in and out of Japan possible if the funds were invested in the stock market. Here, equities had a distinct advantage over other securities, to which the six-month rule still applied. In 1967, the automatic approval limits were raised from 15 percent and 10 percent for unrestricted /restricted industries to 20 percent and 15 percent, and the limit for any individual was raised to 7 percent. The unrestricted industry limit was raised to 25 percent in 1970. With these changes, Japanese equities became the most liquid investments for foreigners, a liquidity which continued throughout the 1970s when the Japanese stock market seemed most sensitive to movements in the yen.

There were, however, some restrictions in the early 1970s, as part of a general package of capital flow restrictions aimed at defending the Bretton Woods System. After October 1972, each securities dealer in Japan was required, until November 1973, to avoid net sales of Japanese securities to nonresidents. Any given nonresident customer could acquire Japanese equities, but only if another nonresident were willing to sell. It is interesting that this regulation continued well past the advent of floating in February 1973; it was only rescinded when the yen began to weaken after the first oil crisis. Again, the regulatory structure appeared to reflect concerns about the exchange rate.

But since 1973, regulation of nonresident purchases in the equities market has been progressively eased to the point of virtual elimination. With the change in the direct investment law in 1973, the 25 percent and 15 percent limits on portfolio acquisitions were eliminated, and after 1976 stock purchases were given automatic approval. Moreover, equities retained an advantage over other securities, because proceeds of liquidation of equities could go directly into the foreign exchange market, while proceeds of liquidations of other securities had to be deposited in bank accounts before conversion to foreign exchange. Under the 1980 foreign exchange law, nonresident acquisition of Japanese equities requires notification but no wait, so long as the acquisition is not in the nature of direct investment.

Residents were treated far more strictly than nonresidents with respect to equities purchase in early years. Equities, like other foreign assets, were subject to the declaration and liquidation-at-request requirement of the old foreign exchange law, and each equity investment required approval until 1971. In general, only investment trusts were allowed to purchase foreign equities, and this only on a case-by-case basis. But official attitudes changed in mid-1971, as the exchange crisis approached. From July 1971, all residents except mutual funds were permitted to purchase foreign equities in any amount. This treatment changed abruptly with the oil crisis; case-by-case approval was required after November 1973. The Ministry of Finance also issued a directive to securities dealers not to encourage residents to buy foreign equities (or other securities); this directive was not revoked until June 1975. After that, however, foreign equity purchase by residents became fully free. Under the 1980 law, it is fully free if executed through one of twenty-six designated dealers (who notifies authorities) and requires notice, but no wait, if executed through a nondesignated dealer.

The rules applying to nonresident purchase of securities other than equities were similar to those for equities in the 1950s but were relaxed at a slower pace. The 20-percent-per-year-over-five-years rule with the two-year holding period applied to most, but the rule on debentures was even tighter. Principal was remittable only at maturity and the shortest maturity available was five years. In effect, there was a buy-and-hold-until-maturity requirement. Moreover, proceeds of securities sales (other than equities) could not even be reinvested in Japan; proceeds had to be held in appropriate bank accounts to await repatriation.

These rules were eased in the early 1960s, and the holding period was shortened to six months in August 1962. In 1965, the remittability of securities investments rose when proceeds of sales became payable into FYAs if the six-month holding period had passed.

Regulations were apparently tightened in 1971, with a prohibition "in principle" of nonresident purchase of short-term government securities. Apparently these securities had become a vehicle for pro-yen speculation. These rules were tightened again in 1972, because foreign exchange for securities purchase was required to be deposited in special accounts at foreign exchange banks or securities dealers, with conversion to yen not permitted until an actual contract for the purchase was written. From October 1972, proceeds of sales of securities had to be reinvested or remitted within a month after liquidation, presumably to prevent a pool of highly liquid funds from accumulating. This rule was imposed along with the prohibition of net sales of securities to foreign customers by authorized dealers, mentioned above. These rules were rescinded in December 1973—after the oil crisis.

In fact, the oil crisis appears to have brought a complete turnabout in the official treatment of foreign purchase of securities. After August 1974, nonresident purchase of short securities was given automatic approval, even for unlisted securities, though a six-month hold rule was also enforced.

The rules changed again when the yen started appreciating sharply in 1977-78. In March 1978, an outright ban of nonresident purchase of securities of less than five years and one month in remaining maturity was enforced.[7] This lasted to January 1979, when the period was reduced to thirteen months to maturity; it was abolished in February 1979. A major liberalization of 1979 was the grant of automatic approval status for *gensaki* (bond repurchase) transactions. The *gensaki* market is one of the largest and most free of the Japanese money markets, and nonresident participation has in fact become an important link between Japanese interest rates and the world money market.

Thus, liberalization of nonequity security markets to nonresidents proceeded more slowly than liberalization of the equity market but was virtually complete by 1980. The 1980 foreign exchange law approves all nonresident purchases of securities (unless of a nature to make them subject to direct investment laws—see above) with only notification. In actual practice, authorities have not used even the available power to restrict flows as a tool to affect the value of the yen. Many rule changes of the 1970s were aimed at influencing the exchange rate, but fluctuations were still very wide. This experience apparently convinced authorities that markets had grown beyond the point where regulation could be effective in controlling captial flows and that basic macroeconomic policies, not capital market regulations, are more important in achieving external targets.

As with equities, resident purchase of foreign nonequity securities required approval, which was not granted freely, throughout the 1950s and 1960s. Also as with equities, only investment trusts were permitted to purchase foreign securities before 1971, and even this amount was subject to a global ceiling (of US$100 million per firm in 1970).

Deregulation began in early 1971, with life insurance firms granted approval for up to US$100 million on nonequity foreign securities. Total liberalization of purchase of foreign securities (except for mutual funds) occurred in July 1971, and foreign securities firms were allowed to open branches from September—to make such purchase easier. Trust banks were allowed unlimited purchase of foreign securities after February 1972, and in April of that year private placement of foreign bonds in Japan was allowed if less than 50 percent of total subscriptions came from Japan. Mutual fund purchase was approved in November 1972.

The oil crisis brought tightening of rules on resident purchases of short-term foreign bonds, with approval put on a case-by-case basis. The Ministry of Finance directive to dealers and banks not to encourage purchase of foreign securities applied to nonequities as well as to equities. A turnabout occurred in 1977, when the yen started strengthening rapidly; from May 1977, automatic approval was given to resident purchases of foreign securities. Free acquisition continues under the 1980 foreign exchange law; such purchases require only notification.

Overall, both residents and nonresidents were strongly restricted in their ability to buy and sell nonequity securities through the 1950s and 1960s. For nonresidents, liquidity of such investments was low compared to that of equities, while for residents approval was difficult to obtain. Around a trend of overall liberalization, regulations in the 1970s were affected by the state of the currency market; inflows were encouraged when the yen was weak and outflows when the yen was strong. But the endogenous regulatory behavior of authorities did not appear to substantially alter the value of the yen. Since the implementation of the foreign exchange law of 1980, the regulatory environment has been highly free and highly stable.

The issue of nonresident borrowing in either equity or securities markets hardly was mentioned in the 1950s and 1960s. Nonresident equity was first issued in Japan in October 1972; part of the delay here was because of different institutional situations, such as par value issue, market value issue, and disclosure rules. Nonconsolidation of balance sheets was the rule in Japan in the early 1970s and, at first availability of such balance sheets, was made a condition of equity flotation in Japan. But in September 1973, the Ministry of Finance agreed to accept foreigners' consolidated balance sheets if accounts were in accordance with home country rules. In March 1974, even this was eased, and disclosure requirements were made equivalent to those of the issuing firm's home country. Despite these liberalizations, Tokyo does not appear to have become a thriving market for foreign issues, perhaps because the purpose of some foreign flotations is to avoid domestic disclosure requirements.

Bond issue by nonresidents in Tokyo was liberalized over the 1970s, though not suddenly. First permission for foreign issue was given in 1971, but only to international organizations (e.g., the IBRD and the Asian Development Bank). Guidelines for nonresident issue were presented in April 1972 and required case-by-case authorization. But the list of acceptable issuers was widened to include individual governments in that year. The issue guidelines changed with the value of the yen; for example, after August 1972, 90 percent of the proceeds of flotations had to be converted to dollars and remitted immediately after issue. This rule was relaxed in November 1973; one way to help stem capital outflow was to cease requiring it of foreign flotations. But authorities simultaneously ceased approving nonresident issues at all, to reduce the pool of potential outflow.

Approvals of nonresident issue resumed in July 1975, and frequent approvals began in 1976. The timing and size of issues were determined by agreement among borrowers and the underwriters' association (*kisaikai*), in consultation with the Ministry of Finance. There were eighteen issues in 1977 worth a total of ¥326 billion and forty issues in 1978, worth a total of ¥827 billion.[8] Tax privileges on nonresident issue expanded in 1977, with interest income on the first ¥3 million of holdings becoming tax free for foreign-government guaranteed bonds as well as foreign government bonds themselves. This accorded nonresident bonds equal treatment with Japanese government bonds.[9]

Another factor, in addition to worries about capital flows and the exchange rate, affected regulatory decisions on nonresident issues. This was the potential for competition between Japanese government bonds and nonresident bonds. With its own debts accumulating, the Japanese government was forced to grant concession after concession to financial institutions to maintain the bond underwriting syndicate, with its many benefits for the government.[10] Nonresident bonds were direct competitors for government bonds; the willingness of the Japanese authorities to allow expansion of nonresident issues seems remarkably liberal. (One hypothesis is that the expansion of foreign issues was a concession to syndicate members, eager for foreign business, granted in return for favorable treatment of government issue by the syndicate.) Domestic securities such as financial institution debentures, which also compete with government bonds, were not given such consideration.

With the 1980 foreign exchange law, nonresident issues require prior notice and a twenty-day wait. In practice, however, nonresident issues have been relatively free, at about 2 percent of total domestic bond issue since 1981.

Very little is mentioned in available sources about resident issues in foreign markets in the 1950s and 1960s, but such issues must have occurred, because a ban on conversion of their proceeds into yen was enforced in April 1971. Licenses were necessary for issuing bonds abroad through the 1970s, though such licenses were granted freely after 1977. In fact, free license of issues by trading companies was the practice after December 1973 if the funds were to be primarily used abroad. After November 1974, licenses were issued on a case-by-case basis if funds were to be converted to yen. Approval was required until 1980.

Even with the 1980 law, prior notice with examination is required for such issues. This caution is probably because of two factors, the ability of firms to use foreign issue to circumvent domestic monetary policy and the fear that large numbers of foreign issues might occur at one time, causing unwelcome disruption in foreign markets and friction with foreign governments.

Most of the discussion above has considered transactions by the nonfinancial sector, whether resident or nonresident. Financial sector transactors, however, have also been critical actors throughout the postwar period, particularly since they are the primary traders of foreign exchange. They had special privileges, such as the right to engage in forward transactions without underlying trade transactions,[11] but were also subjected to special regulations at times. We next consider regulation of both asset and liability sides of balance sheets of both foreign and domestic banks, regarding foreign exchange transactions.

The major function of foreign banks in Japan through the 1950s and 1960s was trade financing, but some capital account business did occur. Foreign banks became a source of capital for domestic firms when money became tight, resulting in the invention of the impact loan, a six-to twelve-month loan for operating funds, denominated in foreign currency. Such loans were given official recognition and subjected to official guidance and quotas, at least from late 1960. These quotas appear to have been responsive to official attitudes about the value of the yen; e.g., the quotas for impact loans were raised in January 1974, when capital inflows were being encouraged.

But the critical area of control over foreign banks was on the liability side, in the form of yen conversion quotas. Foreign banks had continuous difficulty in raising yen to carry out their normal business, and special yen conversion rights were the means by which authorities accommodated this need. But in periods of intense pressure on the yen, there was the temptation to convert one's entire quota very early in the quota period (quarterly) and thus augment pressure on the currency. In December 1971, conversion quotas were put on a monthly basis, and prior approval for conversions was strictly enforced. Instructions not to exceed quotas were reissued in March 1972, suggesting that enforcement of the rules was difficult—particularly when incentives to break them were strong.

With the oil crisis, the yen conversion quotas were raised, as capital inflow was to be encouraged in this category as elsewhere. An expansion occurred in November 1973, another in December, two in August 1974, two more in December 1975, and one in January 1976. (No documentary evidence was available on how quotas were determined.) The problem changed in nature after the CD market began in 1979, a market in which foreign banks too could issue yen-denominated CDs; foreign banks now had an alternative source of funding.

Moreover, foreign banks were affected by a change in 1977 in the target of regulation from the total quantity of foreign currency converted to the net position of a bank in foreign currency. Foreign banks were permitted short positions in the dollar from 1977, even when their Japanese counterparts were not. But the competitive environment for foreign banks also stiffened, because domestic banks were permitted to make long-term impact loans after June 1979 and short-term ones after March 1980.

Although foreign banks have at times complained about regulations, Japanese authorities have pointed out certain privileges enjoyed by foreign banks— e.g., sole rights to make impact loans for so long. And one privilege not often mentioned is the nonparticipation of foreign banks in the government bond underwriting syndicate. The rise in the number of foreign banks with branches in Japan from twenty-one in 1969 to seventy-five in 1983 suggests that the restrictions have not been too onerous.

Japanese banks were intimately connected with all aspects of foreign exchange in the postwar period, through the "authorized foreign exchange bank" system. The largest banks were authorized to deal in foreign exchange, and to execute all foreign exchange transactions. Hence, these banks became the actual implementors of foreign exchange regulations. Here, however, we will limit consideration of the banks' role to regulations affecting own-account capital transactions and the net foreign exchange position of the banks.

The first major move of Japanese banks away from pure trade financing transactions came in late 1960, when nonimport-related borrowing in foreign currency from nonresident banks was permitted, along with a relaxation of controls on banks' overall exchange position. Japanese banks continued acquiring foreign currency-denominated liabilities throughout the 1960s, as Japanese trade grew and as Japanese participation in foreign investments rose. One prudential rule was imposed, that 15 percent of total foreign currency liabilities be held as foreign currency assets. But in 1970 and 1971, dollar borrowing grew as part of speculation against the dollar. Along with other controls imposed at the time, a freeze on Japanese banks' foreign currency borrowing was imposed from August to December 1971. But in 1972, the growing importance of dollar funding to Japanese banks helped encourage regulatory evolution. Issue by Japanese banks of dollar-denominated CDs in London began on a limited basis in September 1972, and limits were removed in December of that year. Similar issues in Singapore were permitted from May 1975 and in the United States from June 1975.

Prudential regulation on the net foreign exchange position of banks began in 1974 (in the wake of the Herrstadt collapse). These replaced yen conversion quotas (which were also applied to Japanese banks, though they were not so important relatively) as the main regulatory tool in May 1977. When these new rules were promulgated, Japanese banks were not permitted to be short on the dollar, suggesting a desire by authorities to constrain pro-yen speculation at the time. But the intention to relax this control was announced along with the control itself. The rule was in fact relaxed in January 1979. Under the 1980 foreign exchange law, these prudential regulations on net foreign exchange position remain.

On the asset side, Japanese banks faced a similar development of regulation, with loans abroad requiring official approval through the 1950s. But the limit on nontrade-related credit was eliminated in August 1960, along with the corresponding one on borrowing. Once again, regulations tightened in 1971 as speculation against the dollar mounted; ceilings on Japanese banks' foreign branches' loans to nonresidents and to Japanese firms were imposed in May 1971, along with ceilings on loan guarantees by such branches. These restrictions were lifted in January 1972. In early 1973, encouraging outflow by foreign lending became official policy, and government financial institution loans abroad were a means of accomplishing this. Blanket approval to all foreign loans began in mid-1978, though the approval procedure was kept. A major concern of authorities at this time was the mismatch of maturity structures on the balance sheets of banks; from January 1979, a 60 percent long-term liability match for long-term loans in foreign currencies was imposed. Under the foreign exchange law, there is a formal requirement for notice and a twenty-day wait on foreign loans, but no wait has been imposed in fact since 1982.

Overall, the internationalization of Japanese banks' capital account transactions began in earnest in the late 1960s and grew quickly in the 1970s. Although some attempts to control lending and borrowing in foreign currencies were made in times of crisis, the banks were mostly allowed to pursue their international interests as they wished. Perhaps continued good relations with the underwriting syndicate at home informed the regulatory choices made vis-à-vis the banks' international activities. Prudential regulations do remain, but there do not appear to be strong complaints about them.

The institutional history given in this essay suggests two major turning points in capital market internationalization in the postwar period in Japan. The first was in the mid-1960s. By this time, it was clear that Japan's high growth strategy, aimed partly at easing the foreign exchange constraint, had succeeded. The regulations once needed to protect the economy from the dangers of that constraint became more costly. The benefits of foreign capital inflow could now be acquired at lower cost, and the costs of domestic capital outflow could now be offset by higher benefits. Although deregulation was never abrupt, the intent and direction were clear. Still, in times of crisis, regulatory structure did respond to market pressures; but constraints were always lifted once crises passed—especially becasue many attempts at regulatory control appeared to be ineffective.

The second major turning point was in the late 1970s, and the changes are codified in the foreign exchange law of 1980. More types of transactions were authorized for automatic approval, and there emerged the new principle of freedom of transaction unless specific prohibition exists. In practice, discretionary use of capital market regulation as a tool for achieving external equilibrium has virtually ceased; that is, since the 1980 law, the regulatory structure has ceased to be highly endogenous to the system.

1. The main source of information is the IMF's *Annual Report on Exchange Arrangements and Exchange Restrictions*, which includes pages on Japan from 1952 to present. For a description of the new foreign exchange law and discussion of the differences with the old, see *Atarashii gaikoku kawase kanri hō no kaisetsu* [An Explanation of the New Foreign Exchange Control Law], edited by Fukui Hiroo (Tokyo, 1980).

2. In a fixed rate regime, it is usual to require legally that all foreign exchange transactions be implemented through the central bank or through authorized foreign exchange dealers under the central bank's jurisdiction.

3. Sources are unclear on the exact definition of this term, but the nuance is restrictive.

4. The Dow Chemical case of the early 1970s comes to mind.

5. For example, a debate occurred in 1983-84 over whether to place data communications switching equipment (computer linking equipment, etc.) on the restricted list. Under one proposal, foreign ownership of over 20 percent in any firm would have been prohibited. The Ministry of Posts and Telecommunications favored the restriction on infant industry protection grounds, while MITI opposed it on grounds of encouraging competition. The MITI viewpoint prevailed.

6. For the period before 1980, data are available only on approvals, not on applications.

7. In sources available, no mention was made of a requirement that securities so purchased be held to maturity, or that the six-month holding period had been extended. Without such

regulations, it is unclear how restricting the maturities available to nonresidents would prevent capital flows. So long as the long-maturity securities could be sold, the holding period for new purchases would be the critical matter, not the maturity of the security itself.

8. These amounts are equivalent to 1.1 percent and 2.6 percent of all domestic bonds floated in these years.

9. The importance of withholding taxes was demonstrated in the summer of 1984, when German authorities reacted immediately to the United States' cancellation of the 30 percent withholding tax in the United States on foreign bondholders. The Japanese withholding tax rate on foreign bondholders' interest income is 20 percent.

10. For a description of the syndicate, see Kitamura Kyōji, ed. *Kokusai* (Tokyo, 1979).

11. Nonfinancial firms were permitted to engage in such transactions from April 1984.

PART THREE

Global Awareness

The three essays in this part underscore the extent to which Japanese define themselves in relation to the United States, whereas Americans perceive Japan more in terms of changing American values than in terms of Japanese realities. As an international political economy, the American system may be disintegrating, but it appears to persist culturally. On the other hand, Japan is only now, in the 1980s, beginning to have any influence on America's self-image as quality is identified with Japanese industry and Americans strive to meet Japanese standards. At the same time, Japanese seem confused by the responsibilities of the power that Americans seek to thrust upon them.

Iriye (chapter 10) examines the changes in American perceptions of Japan's role in international politics beginning with the 1931-45 image of a warlike nation, as dangerous as any in the world. He notes the grave concern with which Americans undertook to eradicate Japanese militarism during the occupation and Japanese acceptance of a constitution which left their country the only one in the world unable to resort to war. To the astonishment of many Japanese, their new pacifism was condemned as naïve and selfish by Americans who, conditioned by the Cold War, now concluded that preparedness offered the only path to peace. Iriye sees the Japanese as continuing to oppose rearmament but lacking a coherent view of their role in maintaining world peace.

Homma (chapter 11) remarks upon the persistent American image of the impenetrable Japanese but is not unaware of the great surge of Japanese studies in the United States—the mounting effort to understand. He is bemused by American contempt for the Japanese Socialist party, which he suggests is more committed to American democratic values than are the Liberal Democrats. He is concerned more, however, with Japanese efforts to understand the United States and to find cultural autonomy as they outgrow American political and economic dominance. Homma sees the "Pacific Age" of the late 1980s as a crossroad in the quest for mutual understanding. He wonders how Japan can accept the responsibilities of power and share its burdens without fighting the world, including Americans. Should Japan lead—or is it still better to respond and adapt?

Yamamoto (chapter 12) has had enough of Japan's leaving the initiative to the United States or any other nation. He sketches the cycles of friction that have dominated media accounts of relations between Japan and the United States since the mid-1960s:

American complaints and demands, followed by Japanese concessions and settlement, followed by a new round of friction. He sees Japan constantly on the defensive, forced to respond, relying on damage control. Choosing one of the alternatives in Krasner and Okimoto, he calls upon the Japanese people to play a more activist, global role, to prevent fires rather than perpetually having to put them out.

Again and again these essays, like those that precede them, confront Japan's dilemma. Japan, perhaps more than any other nation today, can make choices, define its role, its partnership with the United States. Is this possible for what Chie Nakane has called the "vertical society"? Do Japanese leaders have the necessary courage and wisdom? Are Americans ready to enter into a real as opposed to nominal partnership with Japan?

10

War, Peace, and U.S.-Japanese Relations

AKIRA IRIYE

During the 1930s and throughout World War II, few ideas were more prevalent in the United States than the notion that Japan was a warlike nation: militaristic, aggressive, brutal, and bent on committing atrocities wherever its soldiers went. As early as 1934, Nathaniel Peffer was describing Japan in the following fashion, using words and concepts that would remain essentially constant until 1945:

> That the country is completely under the rule of the military caste is self-evident, and that the people would follow the army into any adventure, however fantastic, is equally clear. It is the combination of national centralization with feudal loyalty, of mysticism with technical efficiency, of medievalism with tanks and airplanes, that make the Japanese incalculable by twentieth-century criteria and beyond understanding by the modern mind, as well as peculiarly dangerous in a world at least somewhat rationalist. They dwell in a no-man's zone of time: their springs of action in the Middle Ages, their instruments of action out of the twentieth century.[1]

That Japan combined "medieval mysticism with twentieth-century efficiency and organization," as Peffer put it, became the accepted framework in which Japanese behavior in Asia and the Pacific was comprehended. Such a combination made Japan extremely dangerous, for "the romanticism of samurai chivalry," when coupled with "twentieth century imperialism," created "an uncontrollable lust for conquest." The country was "anti-social and inimical to the hope of an ordered, civilized world."[2]

The rape of Nanking, the bombing of the Panay, the Pearl Harbor attack, the Bataan death march, the brutal treatment of indigenous populations in Southeast Asia—all these confirmed such an image of Japan. Few words were applied to it with greater regularity than "warlike." Given such a perception, it is not surprising that in 1945, when Japan's defeat was merely a matter of time, opinion polls in America should have expressed serious doubt that it would ever become peace loving, or that more than one out of eight Americans interviewed should have called for the annihilation of the Japanese race as the only guarantee for postwar peace. The dropping of atomic bombs needed no justification: a country made up of fanatical warriors had to be brought to its knees by whatever means was available.

Within a few years of Japan's defeat, however, the country was being described in very different terms. Almost as soon as he got to Tokyo, General Douglas MacArthur decided that the Japanese were capable of becoming a peace-loving people. In March 1947, he told reporters in Tokyo that the country had undergone the greatest "spiritual revolution" in history, and that it posed no threat to neighboring countries. It now entrusted its security to the goodwill of mankind, and to its own "advanced spirituality."[3] In 1950, he praised the Japanese for taking the lead in dedicating "all energy and all resource to peaceful progress." In due course, he said, "other nations will join you in this dedication, but meanwhile you must not falter."[4] Japan was now depicted as the most peace-loving nation on earth!

The idea that the Japanese are more committed to, or interested in, peace than war, has remained more or less unchanged since then. American opinion has in fact been critical of Japan for not doing enough for its own defense, for spending barely 1 percent of its income for military purposes, and for not being more cooperative with its allies in the global confrontation with the Soviet bloc. It is as if Japan today were being accused of not being belligerent enough, of being too preoccupied with peaceful pursuits.

What does such a reversal of American perceptions reflect? Does it indicate that the Japanese have in fact changed? Or, alternatively, have they remained essentially the same, but have American views of them been transformed? If so, how should one account for it? Have Americans themselves changed? If neither Japanese nor Americans can be expected to have changed so drastically in a few decades, what are the variables that we should look for in explaining the shifts and turns in American attitudes toward Japan?

I would argue that American perceptions of Japan are linked to ideas about war and peace. Japan is judged to be warlike or peace loving according to certain accepted definitions of these terms, but the definitions have changed significantly since the 1930s. To put it simply, before World War II, peace was considered a normal and normative state of affairs among nations: to accuse a country of being bellicose was to ostracize it as unworthy of membership in the community of nations. To regain the respect of the world, it would have to demonstrate its pacific orientation. This was what MacArthur was doing as he argued for a speedy end to the occupation of Japan. By then, however, something had happened to the vocabulary of war and peace, so that his declamations sounded naïve and, according to officials in Washington who were formulating a different policy toward Japan, even disloyal. In a changed environment after 1945, it was no longer an unqualified virtue for a nation to be pacifistic. If the ideas that Peffer expressed had continued to provide a basic ideological framework, it would have made sense to characterize postwar Japan as MacArthur did. Japanese opinion, in fact, would continue to be strongly influenced by those ideas. In the United States, in contrast, new formulations of international affairs steadily undermined earlier views, so that gaps inevitably developed between Japanese and American conceptions.

This essay will trace this transformation by examining postwar American ideas about war and peace, as expressed in books and magazine articles in the 1940s and the 1950s. By the end of the 1950s, it would appear that the most influential of such ideas had already been expressed, so that writers in the subsequent decades would merely be rephrasing them. Japan was hardly mentioned in the bulk of these writings, but this in itself is an interesting phenomenon, for the failure to fit Japan into a discussion of war and peace is illustrative of the state of uncertainty in U.S.-Japanese relations.

When Peffer characterized Japan as bellicose in the 1930s, he assumed that peace was a normal condition of modern life and war an aberration, a product of medieval romanticism or feudal mentality. Although fewer and fewer writers retained their faith in that view, at least until 1939 it remained the most orthodox idea in the United States and Western Europe regarding international affairs. According to this orthodoxy, which may be termed Spencerian, the more advanced a country became economically (and therefore politically—another Spencerian legacy), the less reason there was for it to engage in war. Economic development was conducive to peace as it generated an environment and a mentality for rationalism and liberalism, conditions favorable to peaceful pursuits. Only in less developed, premodern societies were people driven irrationally to war, exalting the martial spirit and finding glory in physical violence. As these premodern societies, or premodern classes in a modern society, were replaced by a more advanced variety, war would become obsolete. This was what Peffer undoubtedly had in mind when he wrote that the premodern ethos of Japan was "dangerous in a world in which the nexus is made by intricate economic ties and which at least hopes to substitute the rule of reason for war in international relations."

Such ideas were identical to what Joseph Schumpeter and Thorstein Veblen had written about Japan, all in the Spencerian tradition; despite its technological modernization, Japan had barely emerged out of the feudal past, and must therefore be considered less rational and more warlike than Western democracies. These views said more about the writers' ideas of war and peace than of Japan, or of any country. If a country such as Nazi Germany appeared bent upon aggression, it was because it, too, contained premodern elements or, alternatively, because its leadership was revolting against modern civilization. In all such analyses, peace and war were sharply differentiated; they were dichotomized in terms of rationality and irrationality, modernity and feudalism, or civilization and chaos.

The situation changed in the late 1930s and altered, perhaps forever, the Spencerian formula. There are two aspects to this change. First, war was no longer an irrationality or an evil when it was waged against warlike nations like Germany, Italy, or Japan. War against aggressive powers was justifiable because, without it, they would dominate the world and crush the values that underlay modern civilization: peace, order, rationality. As Norman Angell, an erstwhile Spencerian, wrote in 1939, "the principle on behalf of which Britain has declared war is in truth the fundamental principle of all organized society and of orderly civilization."[5] Agreeing with such a justification of war, Reinhold Niebuhr asserted in 1940 that now peace was the greater evil, for there could be no peaceful compromise with "modern tyrannical States" that engaged in acts of brutality."[6] The title of the theologian's book, *Christianity and Power Politics*, exemplified his argument: in order to defend their values, Christians must be prepared to practice power politics. They could no longer afford to be pacifists, for peace would only abet more brutality and more war. As the *New Republic* editorialized in July 1941, "It is just as true as it ever was that the best defense, the only defense, is to attack. . . . All over the world people have come to see in the recent past that if a democracy is not prepared to be militant, it is not prepared to survive."[7]

Such views suggested that war and peace were no longer viewed as opposites, representing sharply contrasting compartments of human action. This was the second aspect of the change. More and more came to see war as always a possibility in a peaceful world and, on the other hand, peace as part of an act of war. "When the most fundamental values of life are at stake," wrote G.T. Robinson, a Columbia University historian in 1941, "there is only one thing to do about it, and that is to do something about it." Americans could not indulge in peaceful pursuits when the values that sustained them were in danger of annihilation elsewhere. They must be prepared to go to war. But they must recognize that "the most fundamental thing at issue is not the present . . . but the future contained in the present—in the freedom of the people to plan boldly and to act democratically in the realization of their plans."[8] Even as they went to war, Americans should not lose sight of the future. The antifascist conflict was a total war, enveloping past, present, and future. Put another way, war and peace were comprehended as simultaneous occurrences; war was necessary to enjoy the fruits of peace, while visions of peace were part of the war effort.

Justification of war, and the view of war as always a possibility even in peace, amounted to the blurring of traditional distinctions between war and peace. This was not entirely a new phenomenon, as I have suggested elsewhere.[9] But it clearly emerged as a main feature of international affairs in the late 1930s and remained so during and after the war. In contrast to World War I, in which President Woodrow Wilson maintained that the war was being fought "to end wars" and civilians were asked to volunteer for national service to meet the emergency—with the understanding that once the fighting was over they would all go back to "normal" living—wartime and postwar life became much less distinguishable after 1941. As early as August of that year, the *New Republic* noted that "the kind of peace that will emerge after the war will not be a theoretical or ideological construction, imposed on the world when the fighting is over, but will result from the institutions created during its course. Hitler is now shaping his New Europe. If his enemies are to create a democratic internationalism, they must do so to win the war as well as to organize the peace."[10] This type of thinking called forth an enormous amount of writing during the war about the shape of the peace; virtually all of these publications assumed that wartime arrangements, whether domestic or external, would be carried into the postwar period.

Although there was no consensus, a significant theme in these writings was "realism." This reflected the far more sober state of mind during World War II than World War I. It rejected pacifism as naïve and suggested that another war could be avoided only through preparedness. As Charles E. Wilson, the businessman who was appointed vice chairman of the War Production Board, insisted in 1944, the American economy would never resume purely peaceful activities when the war ended, for "the tendency to war is inevitable." To survive in modern world conditions, the line between peacetime and wartime pursuits must be obliterated. "Instead of looking to disarmament and unpreparedness as a safeguard against war . . . let us try the opposite: full preparedness according to a continuing plan."[11]

The stress now was on preparedness and on the need to base national policy on the realities of power, not on human goodwill or idealism. Appeasement, connoting peace at any price, was considered a greater sin than war. Instead of peace and appeasement, the sacred concepts after 1945 were security and national interest. Less a durable peace than a state of uncertainty was expected to prevail in international relations. Whereas before 1939 writers had tended to view problems of war and peace as fundamentally socioeconomic and published numerous treatises on such topics as the nature of mass politics, the future of democracy, and the relationship between social reform and world peace, after 1945 they were more concerned with military and strategic issues. International relations were seen in interstate, rather than domestic, contexts. It is not surprising that this led to, or reflected, an emphasis on power, for it is easy to see interstate relations as power relations, whereas in domestic affairs one has to pay heed to ethical, religious, social, cultural, and other nonpower factors.

The acceptance of power politics thus was a main characteristic of American ideas of international relations after 1945. This continued the wartime tendencies, but there is little doubt that it was reinforced by the emergence of the Soviet Union as a formidable power, and by nuclear weapons. The two were combined insofar as the Soviet was expected soon to possess its own atomic arms. Any discussion of postwar international affairs had to start by coming to grips with these developments. War and peace came to mean neither war nor peace in the traditional sense. Instead, a state of war-and-peace was envisaged between the United States and the Soviet Union.

There were several aspects to the concept of war-and-peace. One was preparedness, or Daniel Yergin's idea of the "national security state." It was not so much that a third world war was an immediate prospect, as that peace would not be possible without preparing for such a conflict. As one writer put it, "Peace through preparedness for war is the promise that is now being held out to the American people by our elected officials and military leaders."[12] If the United States reverted to peacetime normalcy, this would only increase chances of a future war. Peace and war, in such a view, were no longer clearcut alternatives, but represented a simultaneity, a definition of the prevailing condition of world affairs in which the two superpowers confronted one another. To cite but one example, in the May 1947 issue of the *Atlantic*, a professor of physics at the University of Pennsylvania wrote an article entitled "The Scientist Fights for Peace." The article actually discussed how scientists should prepare for war. "I regard it as deplorable," he said, "that our nation is preparing for war . . . but so long as it is the policy of our nation to prepare for war, I shall certainly not attempt to impede such preparations." It was, he continued, "deplorable but understandable that this country, while desiring and working toward peace, feels it necessary to be strong in a military sense." He fully recognized that "the desirable freedoms of the individual" would be submerged in the event of another war, but felt confident that they would be restored "if we had a succeeding peace." It was not clear how such a peace was going to be achieved, especially as the author justified the development and use of atomic weapons, a "relatively insignificant matter of improving the means of murder."[13]

That the next war would be a nuclear one was assumed by virtually all writers in the immediate postwar years. Americans, a writer noted, were living "in justifiable terror of an atomic attack that can devastate our cities and industries at a single blow."[14] It was not clear, however, that such a war should be avoided at all cost. Memories of the interwar years seemed to indicate that it would not do merely to try to avoid war. In the words of Robert E. Osgood, the interwar fear of war had blinded nations to "the complex conflicts of power that lie at the roots of war." Moreover, it had "made the avoidance of war rather than the achievement of the national interest the indispensable requirement of foreign policy."[15] Such "lessons" persuaded postwar writers not to succumb to the temptation of condemning all wars. Some, in fact, would argue that World War II had not brought about peace, but that another war had already begun. The Cold War, according to numerous National Security Council memoranda, was "in fact a real war," to be waged until victory was achieved.[16] Many commentators echoed the theme and warned their readers that America would "lose the war against communism" unless they stepped up their preparedness.[17] Even those who did not go to such extremes argued that "the fear of these atomic weapons" was a vital instrument for preventing war, as Reinhold Niebuhr pointed out. The theologian was one of the prominent postwar realists who defended the continued production of atomic bombs as necessary for prevention of nuclear war.[18]

There was a danger, of course, that an arms buildup by the superpowers might in fact increase chances of war. But such a risk had to be taken, for the only alternative might be an unacceptable accommodation with communism, which could lead to Soviet domination of the world and extinguish liberty, democracy, and all those values in defense of which the country had just fought a colossal war. There was now a greater willingness than in the 1930s to consider war a lesser evil if the only alternative were submission to totalitarian rule. As Archibald MacLeish said, the United States must try "to avoid world war on the one hand and Communist domination of the earth on the other."[19] Or, as Niebuhr put it in 1953, "we face two problems in our generation rather than one: the avoidance of war and resistance to tyranny. The 'pure' idealists are always tempted to war against communism in the name of justice or to come to terms with it in the name of peace." Both alternatives must be rejected and replaced by "a wisdom which is more relevant to our two-pronged predicament." Such wisdom would try to avoid war with communist states but would also build up "our defenses even though the peril of conflict always confronts us."[20]

The war that these writers had in mind was, at least until the mid-1950s, a nuclear conflict between the United States and the Soviet Union. Horrible as it was to contemplate—as early as 1947 Arnold J. Toynbee had written that in a global atomic war the only survivors might be "Negrito Pygmies of Central Africa"—it would be even more disastrous not to be prepared for it.[21] Preparedness meant deterrence, it was hoped, so that the experiences of the 1930s would never again be repeated.

As in the 1930s, however, arms buildups provoked a fierce opposition. Although pacifism and neutralism were much less vocal and far more limited after 1945, there was an essential continuity in their ideological assumptions. In 1936, for instance, Aldous Huxley had written, "In the war industry technological progress is being made at the rate of ten per cent per annum. In these circumstances can we possibly afford to go on using war-like means to preserve peace?" In order to defend democratic societies against totalitarian states through military means, he argued, "one must be militarily efficient, and one cannot become militarily efficient without centralising powers, setting up a tyranny, imposing some form of conscription or slavery on the state. In other words, the military defence of democracy in the contemporary circumstances entails the abolition of democracy even before war starts."[22]

The idea that war and war preparedness were incompatible with democracy was a Spencerian legacy, and it lingered on after 1945. One of the earliest expressions of this was a celebrated article by Cord Meyer in the June 1947 issue of the *Atlantic*. A former marine who had been engaged in battles in the Pacific, Meyer argued that the policy of deterring war through preparedness necessitated the buildup of arms for an effective counteroffensive. "Not only must this retaliatory force be capable of immediately destroying the cities of all possible opponents, but it must be so distributed and organized as to be able to deliver its blows after our own cities and factories have been leveled by the enemy's initial assault. Preparedness to defend the nation must be supplanted by preparedness to endure the loss of our urban industry and population and to preserve from the wreckage the ability to strike back in equal force." This would call for the maintenance of "the world's largest arsenal of atomic bombs, radioactive poisons, disease-producing germs, and long-range rockets and bombers." In addition, it would be necessary to disperse people and factories of the nation to prevent their destruction, and governmental leaders, arms production works, and other essential personnel would have to be housed in underground shelters. "When this program has been put into effect, the country may be able to fight on though its cities lie in ruins and the majority of its people are maimed, dying, or dead."

As if to anticipate George Orwell's depiction of a nation in a constant state of preparedness, Meyer wrote that the government would drastically restrict the rights and movements of its citizens, who would be subjected to a system of efficient intelligence so as to prevent sabotage. They would become ideologically indoctrinated; "the leaders of the only two nations capable of waging such a war tend to exaggerate the points of difference in the two societies as a means of persuading their respective populations of the moral value of their sacrifices. The noblest principles of freedom become fraudulent propaganda when they are used to disguise an amoral competition for brute force and to lash masses of men into a crusading fury against each other." Echoing Huxley, Meyer concluded, "Total preparedness means totalitarianism for American citizens."[23]

This was a lone voice. Unlike Huxley in England in 1936, Meyer had few supporters in America in 1947. (He himself would soon change his views and embrace "realism.") The bulk of writings on war and peace made a sharp distinction between democracy and communist totalitarianism even as both prepared for war. This was the legacy of the antifascist war. At the same time, it should be noted that there was essentially no difference between the images of future war visualized by Meyer and those of his opponents. They only differed about the implications of preparedness and deterrence for freedom and democracy. Moreover, neither side had a clear vision of peace. For the Cold Warriors and the realists, peace was at best a state of uneasy co-existence with the Soviet Union, at worst a deceptive calm that hid the realities of power politics in the world. In either case, peace was not an ultimate value to be pursued through nonmilitary means. For critics like Meyer there also was a failure to articulate just what a peaceful state of international affairs would entail. In the above article, he wrote that the two superpowers should have been willing, in 1945, to "confer sufficient power and authority on an international organization to make it a reliable instrument for the preservation of peace." The idea that the United Nations should have been the enforcer of peace was shared by a number of writers, but this idea was vague and assumed that the United States and the Soviet Union should have been able to work together in the world body. Because obviously they had not, peace would have required much more than a reaffirmation of faith in the United Nations. It would be more correct to say that no vision of peace existed in the immediate aftermath of the war comparable to earlier definitions of it, Spencerian or otherwise.

The situation seems to have begun to change in the mid-1950s. That the Korean War had not led to a war between America and Russia made a profound impression on American observers. In retrospect, it is clear that for the first time since 1945 they began to think that perhaps a mutually devastating war between the two superpowers could be avoided, and that they could possibly expect to coexist more or less indefinitely. This slight optimism was buttressed by the death of Joseph Stalin, the Geneva summit of 1955, and the subsequent series of high-level contacts between American and Soviet leaders. Peace now came to be defined as peaceful coexistence—not a permanent state of affairs but at least a détente, a word that appeared in American writings as early as 1951. At the same time, ideas about war, too, underwent change. On one hand, much came to be written about limited, rather than total, war. On the other hand, another type of war, the national liberation conflict in underdeveloped areas of the world, began to be noticed.

A few examples will suffice to illustrate the emergence of such ideas about war and peace. A Gallup opinion poll in late 1954 asked the question, "What do you think the people of this country have the most to be thankful for this year?" Peace led the list of answers with 57 percent.[24] This certainty reflected the end of the hostilities in Korea and Indochina. Even *Life* magazine recognized the change in the atmosphere when it noted in November, "It may well be that, for the moment, the struggle for the world, and men's minds, is shifting away from one of mere military might to one of economic and political rivalry." The new rivalry that would replace military confrontation would call for America's initiative in world economic expansion, development of underdeveloped areas, and raising the level of world prosperity.[25] The idea that peace must be taken seriously, not just in terms of creating a military deterrence but in nonmilitary ways as well, seems to have echoed the détente of the Eisenhower-Khrushchev era. In an editorial entitled "Peace Must be Waged," *Collier's* pointed out in 1955 that "One can paraphrase Clausewitz and say that peace is but the extension of national policies, of competition with other powers, by means other than war." Americans must wage peace through "even greater energy, even greater creative thought, even greater faith than war."[26] Vannevar Bush, the scientist who had been involved in the wartime development of atomic weapons and who had advocated a nuclear strategy against the Soviet Union, declared in 1956, "We can have peace. . . . We look forward to living in a new sort of world. The flowering of science, which has rendered a war absurd, is also giving us wealth, comfort, and freedom from disease of the body or the mind."[27]

Lest such ideas should sound too complacent, realists such as Robert E. Osgood and Henry Kissinger began writing of limited war. Total nuclear war, they argued, was now less likely because neither America nor Russia would gain from it. Instead, in the future there might be a small-scale conflict between them that might involve the use of tactical nuclear weapons or consist entirely of conventional forces.[28] Such a war would not devastate the world, and for this very reason it was more likely to occur. The Korean War, as Kissinger pointed out, was a precursor of the new generation of wars. Actually, it was also an old-style conflict for specific objectives, and the United States had intervened in it to restore the balance of power, not to menace Soviet sovereignty. Both Osgood and Kissinger asserted that the United States would be amiss if it concentrated on nuclear armament, for it would then be incapable of waging limited war. Agreeing with such thinking, Bernard Brodie wrote in an article entitled, "How War Became Absurd," that, because an unrestricted thermonuclear war was in the interest of no nation, "we and our opponents will have to adapt ourselves mutually to ways of using military power which are not orgiastic."[29]

Predictably, the limited-war doctrine provoked fierce debate in the late 1950s. On one hand, some viewed limited war as no more acceptable than total war. As Matthew Josephson put it, "Is it to be, then, limited war? This is improvement, indeed! Up to now we had only a stunning picture of a total war that would destroy civilized life in Eurasia, while leaving us with (an estimated) 68 million dead or maimed. Now that there are to be only 'small' wars, with but three or four million sacrificed here and there, we may breathe more easily."[30] On the other hand, hardcore Cold Warriors held on to the view, in the words of Robert Strauss-Hupé, that "Communist doctrine . . . has never been . . . a theory of limited war but of protracted war." Such being the case, the limited war doctrine was nothing but "a nostalgic protest." It sought "to reduce the life-and-death struggle of two vast systems to a reasonable proposition all reasonable men are bound to understand and to accept." This was a liberal Western concept, "as remote from the Communist concept of protracted conflict as Montesquieu is from Mao." The United States should not succumb to such fantasy but continue to strengthen its "capability for all foreseeable types of war."[31] One ironical result of the debate on limited war may have been the general acceptance of both atomic and conventional war. As Mark S. Watson noted, "preparation for atomic warfare, either restricted or unrestricted, or for conventional warfare, is not enough. There must be first-class preparation for both, wasteful as that may appear—all war being wasteful."[32]

Why, given the "armistice" in the Cold War, as Walter Lippmann called it, the nation should continue to accept such "waste" was a question that fascinated observers. Many writers anticipated President Dwight D. Eisenhower's thesis about a "military-industrial complex." Josephson, for instance, asserted in 1957 that "expansion-minded military bureaucrats" and "the technical-war industries" were allied to press for more expenditure of money for arms. Instead of joining forces to work for peaceful compromises with the Russians, they were enjoying the benefits of continued armament. Pushing the thesis still further, C. Wright Mills wrote, also in 1957, that in both the United States and the Soviet Union, "science and loyalty, industry and national canons of excellence are in the service of military metaphysics. . . . Both the Russian and the American elite have fought the cold war in the name of peace." They were aware that war was becoming obsolete, and yet "in both, virtually all policies and actions fall within the perspective of a third world war." It was because "small ruling circles" in the two countries were possessed by a "whole supporting ethos of an overdeveloped society geared for war."[33] This was nothing but madness. A few years later, Lewis Mumford, in *The Pentagon of Power*, brought this type of critique to an extreme by castigating the American elite as morally bankrupt: "So far . . . from [Hitler's] megamachine's being utterly discredited by the colossal errors of its ruling 'elite,' the opposite actually happened: it was rebuilt by the Western allies on advanced scientific lines, with its defective human parts replaced by mechanical and electronic and chemical substitutes. . . . [In] the very act of dying the Nazis transmitted the germs of their disease to their American opponents: not only the methods of compulsive organization or physical destruction, but the moral corruption that made it feasible to employ these methods without stirring opposition."[34]

For critics like Josephson, Mills, and Mumford, peace defined as a temporary truce in the Cold War was unacceptable, as it assumed continued armament and preparedness. Rather, they would call for a restructuring of society to liberate it from military-oriented interests and "the inhuman features of the overdeveloped," in the words of Mills. In calling America, Russia, and other military powers "overdeveloped monstrosities that now pass for human societies," the sociologist was anticipating the radical movements of the 1960s with their emphasis on communal harmony, small-group encountering, and disarmament as bases for peace.

Ideas about war and peace were enlarged in another sense during the 1950s, which saw conflicts and crises in underdeveloped areas of the world. The Korean War was in a sense a precursor of the new type of struggle, as was the French war in Indochina. These were followed by conflicts in the Middle East, on the China-India border, and in Africa. Soon, in the 1960s, the United States itself would become involved in Vietnam. Wars in areas that came to be called the Third World, or wars of national liberation as indigenous ideologues preferred to define them, necessitated concepts and a vocabulary that had not been available in the early phase of the Cold War. Conversely, Third World commotions compelled reconsideration of ideas about peace.

In August 1945, Pearl Buck had predicted that unless the United States understood and dealt adequately with "the peasant mind" in Asia, "we must prepare for endless wars." It was clear to her that Americans could "still win" only by understanding "the mighty peasant peoples" that made up four-fifths of Asians.[35] The idea that the United States faced, in addition to Soviet military power, social revolutions throughout the Third World was not hard to accept, but for a while after 1945 predictions about a future war almost invariably concerned a nuclear conflict between the superpowers, not colonial struggles. Among the first to stress the latter was Robert S. Lynd, the Columbia sociologist, whose essay "Whose Wars?" was published in a 1952 issue of the *Nation*, suggesting that the United States was becoming involved "in a rapidly broadening counter-war against the long overdue world colonial revolution." Although the people were told that they were fighting against Soviet communism, they might actually be engaged in "twentieth-century colonial wars."[36] Agreeing, Edgar Snow pointed out in 1955 that "the very knowledge that the major atomic powers dare not use their thermonuclear thunderbolts" seemed to be encouraging "a new crop of conventional wars"—rebellions, civil wars, and national colonial revolutions. Nationalism was a "major threat" to world peace. But it was now far more self-confident and widespread than ever before. The world system of states had been fundamentally transformed when "1,200,000,000 brown men inhabiting about 7,000,000 square miles of territory have attained full national independence and political equality with the West." The United States must reckon with this fact as it continued to face the Soviet challenge. The only policy it should pursue was to give aid to underdeveloped areas and support their self-determination. Snow was convinced that the rivalry with the Soviet Union would now largely take place in the Third World. "The metamorphosis of Cold War I into competitive coexistence," he concluded, "does not and cannot end ideological rivalry. It intensifies its continuation by other means."[37]

By the late 1950s, the idea that the Cold War involved a global question of development had become commonplace. A good summation of that phase of the Cold War was offered by Reinhold Neibuhr in an article he published in the *New Republic* in 1956:

> Naturally it is necessary to resist Communism whenever it presents itself in terms of military aggression, as in Korea, and to prevent the Communist movement from gaining supremacy in weapons, nuclear and otherwise, with which modern warfare is bound to be conducted. Military force is always the *ultima ratio* in the contest between nations. But this ultimate form of logic in international relations cannot obviate the significance of competition on all other levels—moral, political and economic. . . . The long ardors of competitive coexistence to which we will be subjected perhaps for a century, cannot be understood at all or borne with patience, if we do not realize that the contest between a free society and a tyranny is one in which the tyranny has all the immediate advantages in the colored continents, while we have all the ultimate ones. That is why time is on our side, however much the battle may run against us for decades.[38]

Niebuhr entitled this essay "A Qualified Faith." It was the same faith that yielded an increasingly voluminous literature on "nation-building" during the 1950s and the 1960s. A product of traditional American utopianism combined

with the postwar vogue for social engineering, it seemed to be a perfect answer
to the problem of coping with the challenge of communism in underdeveloped
parts of the world. By encouraging the nation-building efforts of Third World
peoples, it was confidently expected, the United States would ultimately win
the Cold War. Until the faith was severely tested by the Vietnam war, de-
velopmentalism provided a weapon as important as military arms.

It may be noted, however, that while the strategy of nation-building was
clear within the context of the ongoing struggle with Soviet communism, it
did not produce an easily formulatable idea of peace. It was one thing to say,
as Stewart Alsop did in 1960, that "we must . . . find the means and the will
to give poor countries and poor people a practical alternative to Communism."[39] There was no assurance that the poor countries, once given aid,
would not bestir themselves even further and create pockets of instability. In
the mid-1950s, it is true, the "spirit of Bandung" (after a conference of Asian
and African nations held in 1955) defined a vision of peace as formulated by
Asian and African countries. That definition—based on such principles as
respect for sovereignty, noninterference in internal affairs, and nonviolation
of territorial integrity—would have been acceptable to the United States. But
the Bandung doctrine was soon superseded by a far more violent view of
world affairs, with advocates of "peace" openly calling for guerrilla warfare
against colonial regimes and turning anticolonial struggles into revolutionary
movements. They added to the vocabulary of war through their conception
of "people's war" which, as Raymond Aron has pointed out, made no distinction between civilian and military activities, or between civil and external
wars.[40] Moreover, even when they were not engaged in a war of national
liberation, Third World countries' conceptions of international order conflicted
with the idea of a peaceful coexistence among military powers. They viewed
such a peace as involving the freezing of the status quo, keeping them in a
state of dependency on the rich and powerful nations. "Peace with justice"
for them must involve a global redistribution of wealth so that the anomaly
of three-fourths of mankind enjoying only one-quarter of the world's income
could be rectified. They would demand preferential access for their primary
products, which comprised 90 percent of their export in 1955, into markets
of advanced countries, both capitalist and socialist.

Given such developments, it became more than ever difficult to define
peace. In 1973, as the Vietnam conflict was winding down, Henry Kissinger
remarked, "Today, when the danger of global conflict has diminished, we
face the more profound problem of defining what we mean by peace."[41] He
had no easy answer, nor, it would seem, has there emerged in the past fifteen
years a workable definition of peace. On the other hand, Kissinger's optimism
has not been borne out. The danger of global conflict has not diminished,

and many types of wars have been waged in the meantime. The distinction between war and peace appears to be as blurred as ever, as if to suggest that the world today approximates George Orwell's in which "war is peace."

In examining American views of war and peace since 1945, one notices that Japan is hardly mentioned. This is in sharp contrast to the situation before 1945, when it was impossible to discuss world affairs without considering U.S. relations with Japan. A key question that concerned Americans before 1941 was whether there would be war with Japan, and after Pearl Harbor they were determined to punish the Japanese so that the latter would never again launch a "sneak attack" on the United States. After the war, many books and articles were written about the American occupation of Japan, dealing with measures that were taken to prevent the resurgence of militarism. Apart from the initial spate of such writings, however, discussions of international affairs would appear to have begun to bypass Japan. It was as if Japan had ceased to matter. And this was probably the case.

It was not that the memories of the war were erased; Pearl Harbor was always remembered, the *New York Times* writing an editorial on its anniversary every year until the early 1960s. The event and the subsequent war clearly formed an important basis for American perceptions of Japan. Such memories and images, however, did not serve to structure ideas about Japan in the context of the developing conceptions of war and peace. Pearl Harbor was mentioned in discussions about nuclear strategy, to consider how to respond to "an atomic Pearl Harbor," or "a sneak atomic attack." Clearly, the Pearl Harbor precedent had made Americans sensitive to "sneak attacks," but these possibilities would arise in the context of American tensions with the Soviet Union, not with Japan. If Walter Lippmann is to be believed, moreover, few in the 1950s thought the Soviet Union would launch an atomic Pearl Harbor on the United States. "The equivalent of a 'Pearl Harbor' today," he wrote, "would have to be a sudden, annihilating blow not at our cities but at the Strategic Air Command. That would not be an easy thing to do, and it is something that can be made increasingly difficult to do."[42] During the Cuban missile crisis in 1962, the Kennedy administration considered and then discarded the option of a sneak attack on the missile sites on the island, fearing that an American Pearl Harbor would not be acceptable to the people. The point is, however, that such discussions had nothing to do with Japan or U.S.-Japanese relations.

The same holds true of mentions of Hiroshima and Nagasaki. For most of the period through the 1960s, the atomic bombings of these cities were remembered less to illuminate postwar Japanese attitudes toward peace and war than to imagine what a future war would look like. This was true even of those who were highly critical of the postwar atomic strategy. An editorial in the *Christian Century*, for instance, noted in August 1951, "All the signs . . . indicate that the nations are hastening toward the next world war, which is to be the First Atomic War. And the common man has concluded that there is nothing he can do but wait in dumb resignation. So we come to Hiroshima—plus six years. Each of the recurring anniversaries of that dreadful day has seen the hope of lasting peace a little more dim than it was the year before."[43]

That Japan ceased to be a factor in discussions of war is not surprising. The country was clearly not a hypothetical enemy, nor was its potential military power to be feared. Japan would be incorporated into a regional system of mutual security through which Soviet and, after 1949, Chinese power would be contained. Japan was not expected to play a military role in American strategy. Instead, it would function as a showcase of political stability and economic development, as an alternative to revolutionary upheaval. In this sense, Japan fitted into the "nation-building" strategy of the 1950s and the 1960s. Although not a "new nation," postwar Japan seemed to exemplify how a country could undertake modernization and, in the process, avoid falling prey to the allure of communism.

What role Japan would play in world affairs, however, was by no means clear. If Spencerianism had retained its influence, postwar Japan might have been held up as an example of an industrializing country that had shed its feudal past and had entered the phase of peaceful economic development. Such an image would have been fitted into a liberal internationalist conception of world affairs and defined a positive role for Japan as a nonmilitaristic nation making use of its economic resources for global interdependence and peace. If liberal internationalism had not been overshadowed by geopolitical realism, the kind of idealism underlying MacArthur's image of Japan, quoted earlier, would have received wider acceptance and might have established itself as a postwar orthodoxy.

A few remained committed to those ideals. For instance, Stanley I. Stuber, executive secretary of the International Christian University of Japan, wrote in September 1951 that the will of the Japanese people, as reflected in the new constitution, must not be "flouted by American military strategists who are thinking only in terms of another Spain in the Far East. . . . While military strategists are trying to make a fortress of Japan, and while certain businessmen are aiming to supply Japan with the raw products from which the materials of war can be produced, let the Christian church do everything possible to develop the new Japan as a peace-loving nation."[44] This was a theme that was sustained throughout the next two decades, but "a peace-loving nation" became more and more at variance with American strategy.

Both the disasters of the Vietnam War and the failure of the détente have induced the United States to call upon other countries to cooperate more actively with the United States in maintaining the global status quo, which is how peace has continued to be defined. If American power were insufficient to match the increasing might of the Soviet Union, then others would have to be brought into the equation. To stand outside of power calculations would be naïve and selfish. Today, the image of the Japanese as naïvely pacifist and selfish in pursuit of economic objectives seems to have replaced the earlier emphasis on their bellicosity and sneakiness.

Such a transformation in American perceptions of Japan is a corollary to the more fundamental changes in conceptions of war and peace. Basic to the "perception gaps" between the two countries is the fact that, whereas Americans have been willing to embrace geopolitical realism to add to, if not entirely replace, their traditional internationalism, the opposite trend has characterized postwar Japanese thought. The Japanese have tended to view war and peace as domestically generated, much as earlier generations of American writers did. There would be no peace unless the countries of the world were themselves peaceful, and a key assurance that Japan remained peaceful, according to Japanese thinking, would be its refusal to undertake rapid armament expansion. Beyond this, however, they have not been very helpful in defining how they propose to promote peace in the world. They have failed to develop a coherent image of a peaceful international community, and peace research has been fragmented along ideological lines. Although the Japanese government has promoted the idea of "an international state" as a goal for the nation, the concept has included everything from balance of power to trade liberalization. What both Americans and Japanese need as they approach the end of the century would be a serious collaborative effort to come to grips with the contemporary world's existential problems—not just wars, but population explosion, deforestation, pollution, disease—and to develop an agenda for a new kind of peace, a peace that assumed the basic unity of humanity even while recognizing diversity. Not old-fashioned internationalism, nor conventional power politics, but the internationalization of consiousness would be the way to peace.

1. *Harper's* 168 (March 1934): 398-403.
2. *Harper's* 169 (Aug. 1934): 257-69.
3. Michael Schaller, *The American Occupation of Japan* (New York, 1985), 68-70.
4. Quoted in *Christian Century* 68 (5 Sept. 1951): 1009-11.
5. Norman Angell, *For What Do We Fight?* (London, 1939), 1.
6. Reinhold Niebuhr, *Christianity and Power Politics* (New York, 1940), 16-17.

7. *New Republic* 105 (21 July 1941): 73.

8. *New Republic* (4 Aug. 1941): 153.

9. Akira Iriye, "War as Peace, Peace as War," in Nobutoshi Hagihara, et al., eds., *Experiencing the Twentieth Century* (Tokyo, 1985), 31-54.

10. *New Republic* 105 (25 Aug. 1941): 238.

11. Richard Pollenberg, *War and Society* (Philadelphia, PA, 1972), 236.

12. *Atlantic* 179 (June 1947): 27.

13. *Atlantic* 179 (May 1947): 80-82.

14. *Atlantic* 179 (June 1947): 28.

15. Robert E. Osgood, *Ideals and Self-Interest in America's Foreign Relations* (Chicago, 1953), 333.

16. Thomas H. Etzold and John L. Gaddis, eds., *Containment* (New York, 1978), 442.

17. *American Mercury* 78 (Jan. 1954): 4-5.

18. *New Republic* 125 (31 Dec. 1951): 15. For a detailed examination of postwar America's "nuclear consciousness," see Paul Boyer, *By the Bomb's Early Light* (New York, 1985).

19. *Atlantic* 188 (Aug. 1951): 42.

20. *Christian Century* 70 (Dec. 2, 1953): 1386-88.

21. *Atlantic* 179 (June 1947): 34-38.

22. Grover Smith, ed., *Letters of Aldous Huxley* (London, 1969), 401, 407, 411.

23. *Atlantic* 179 (June 1947): 27-33.

24. *Christian Century* 71 (8 Dec. 1954): 485-87.

25. Quoted in above article.

26. *Collier's* 136 (23 Dec. 1955): 28-31.

27. *Atlantic* 197 (Feb. 1956): 35-38.

28. Robert E. Osgood, *Limited War* (Chicago, 1957); Henry Kissinger, *Nuclear Weapons and Foreign Policy* (New York, 1953).

29. *Harpers* 211 (Oct. 1955): 33-37.

30. *Nation* 185 (31 May 1957): 90.

31. *Reporter* 17 (28 Nov. 1957): 30-34.

32. *Nation* 181 (24 Dec. 1955): 547.

33. *Nation* 185 (7 Dec. 1957): 419-24.

34. Lewis Mumford, *The Pentagon of Power* (New York, 1964), 242, 251, 253.

35. *Asia and the Americas* 45 (Aug. 1945): 365-68.

36. *Nation* 175 (27 Dec. 1952): 601-03.

37. *Nation* 181 (22 Oct., 29 Oct., 12 Nov., 1955): 333-34, 353-55, 409-11.

38. *New Republic* 134 (13 Feb. 1956): 14-15.

39. *Saturday Evening Post* 19 (16 July 1960): 233.

40. Raymond Aron, *Pensez la guerre, Clausewitz*, vol. 2 (Paris, 1976), 103-16.

41. Henry A. Kissinger, *American Foreign Policy*, 3d. ed. (New York, 1977), 118.

42. *Look* 18 (9 Feb. 1954): 70-71.

43. *Christian Century* 68 (1 Aug. 1951): 883.

44. *Christian Century* 68 (5 Sept. 1951): 1009-11.

11

America in the Mind of the Japanese

NAGAYO HOMMA

In recent years, the postwar period in Japanese history has been interpreted and reinterpreted. Controversies—both academic and nonacademic—have surrounded issues such as the meaning of Japan's surrender, the significance of the American occupation, the character of the "New Constitution," and the importance of the Japan-U.S. security system. Behind these issues lies the fundamental problem of the relevance of the United States to Japan and the Japanese people—the United States as a nation, a power, a party in economic relations, a positive or negative model, a civilization, and, above all, an object of identification.

Recent trends in reconsideration of what America has meant to Japan and to Japanese people point to a kind of impasse in our effort to adjust ourselves to forces of Americanization and to understand America and Americans. As the following examples show, the meaning of "Americanization" has become increasingly ambiguous and the concept of "understanding" less and less clear.

In an article written in January 1984, Matsuyama Yukio, editor-in-chief of the *Asahi* newspaper, uses the metaphor "twist in the intestines" to describe Japanese-American relations. He contends that the Liberal Democratic party embodies elements that are incompatible with American democracy and laments that an increasing number of people whom the American founding fathers would not find congenial have come to pass as "pro-American." For Matsuyama, Japan's identification with the United States is twisted.[1]

To take another example, Kiuchi Nobutane, an influential senior economist, calls for a reexamination of the term "internationality" in a December 1983 article. He asserts that the Japanese people suffered after the war from a kind of "internationality complex" and embraced internationalism uncritically. Whereas the substance of postwar internationalism was Americanization, Kiuchi considers the change in Japanese business ways into American ways to be undesirable; he insists that a new view—"to be American is not necessarily good"—is replacing the old one. He argues that the Japanese people must, therefore, discard their "Americanization complex" and recognize the inherent internationality of Japan itself.[2]

Isoda Kōichi's *Sengoshi no kūkan* provides a third recent example of reconsideration of the U.S.-Japanese relationship. Isoda, a literary critic, attempts to reconstruct the historical meaning of the postwar period through various works of literature. Isoda includes topics such as the image of defeat, the double structure of the occupation, the 1960 upheaval against the revision of the Japan-U.S. security treaty, and the end of *ryūgaku* (studying abroad). His fundamental concern is Japan's national identity, illustrated, for example, in his discussion of the occupation. He argues that, although initially Japan's democratization was identified with pro-Americanism, the growing awareness among the Japanese people of "the national" gradually transformed pro-Americanism into anti-Americanism. In the last chapter of his book, Isoda observes the ambiguity in Japan's economic growth and prosperity. Economic nationalism, supported by the machismo of the work ethic, is closely related to Japanese nationalism vis-à-vis the United States. Yet the pervasion of Americanism in the whole area of Japan's culture of consumption, as described so effectively in the novel *Nantonaku, kuristaru* (Passively, Chrystal), by Tanaka Yasuo, symbolizes the feminine acceptance of the occupation and nostalgia for Japan's dependence on the United States during the occupation. The psychology of manliness leads to exhortations such as "Japan! Be a state!" In contrast, the feeling of feminine passivity, Isoda suggests, could make it possible for the Japanese people to play with a fantasy in which Japan becomes the fifty-first state of the United States. Isoda's book expresses, in a sophisticated and sometimes tortured way, the feeling shared by many Japanese that we are still caged within a space of protection and dependence guaranteed by America's power. He concludes by arguing that only with the establishment of the "individual" will the Japanese people finally be liberated from the limitations of the postwar period.[3]

The above cursory look at a few samples of recent thinking—or rethinking—about the postwar period of Japanese history may tempt us to simplify the major intellectual trend in Japan during the period as one changing "from dependence to autonomy" or "from acceptance to self-assertion" or "from Americanism to post-Americanism." The issue is not so easily resolved, however, because the postwar period is filled with ambiguous and contradictory currents in the attitudes, feelings, and calculations of Japan's leaders and people toward the United States as a power and a civilization.

A three-volume study of the impact of American culture on postwar Japan entitled *Amerikan karuchā* (American Culture) edited by Ishikawa Hiroyoshi et al. proposes a challenging periodization. According to Fujitake Akira, one of the three editors, the first period from 1945 through the 1950s can be called the period of love-hate feelings toward America. During this period, Japanese identification with America as a model of democracy and assimilation of American popular culture went hand in hand with anti-Americanism on a political level.

The second volume discusses the 1960s, characterized again by permeation of Japanese society by the American life style. The American way was still the goal for the Japanese people, but as Fujitake analyzes the trend, America remained Japan's model not from a desire to be "American" but as an inevitable consequence of economic growth. The leitmotif of this period, then, was the realization of the American way in Japan without a clear awareness of its being American.

In the 1970s, the Japanese people experienced changes in their value system, represented by the then popular commercial, "from hardworking to beautiful." New concerns and movements in America about ecology and its related problems found their counterparts in Japan almost simultaneously; Fujitake therefore contends that Japanese and Americans came to share common problems of contemporary civilization. Particularly for the youth in Japan, the United States had come to serve as the source of information so that young people regarded America not as a foreign country but as their cultural fatherland. The new generation of Japanese grew up in Japan but breathed American air, Fujitake explains, and wonders whether the Japanese people today discover their birthplaces not only in the ancient cities of Nara or Kyoto but also in the United States in various places such as Atlanta, Georgia, home of Scarlett O'Hara in the fictional world of *Gone with the Wind*, with which a vast number of Japanese identify themselves by way of the original novel as well as its film version.[4]

If Fujitake's interpretation of the general trend in the Americanization of Japanese society and life-style is valid, what are we to make of those Japanese whose identification with American culture is so advanced that they are not conscious of it as a foreign culture? Is it possible that these people have achieved a kind of autonomy of culture or life style, or should we regard them as a case of complete subservience? With such slices of Americana as McDonald's, Kentucky Fried Chicken, Mister Donut, and Seven-Eleven becoming an inescapable part of any Japanese city, the American way appears to be conquering Japanese society, on one hand, while on the other, this can be construed as an indication of successful Japanization of American culture. If the younger generation today is free from an inferiority complex, it may have acquired that freedom at the expense of its sense of nationality.

Evaluations of political and economic relations between Japan and the United States all show that the facile generalization of "from dependence to autonomy" is misleading. After the war, the goals of Japan were maintaining relations of mutuality with the United States and achieving a sense of equal partnership. In the 1960s, the terms partnership and equal partnership were used to describe the relationship between Japan and the United States. Partnership was a euphemism for alliance, but the very fact that it functioned that way reflects precisely the reluctance among the Japanese people to accept the full connotation of the term alliance.

Part of the problem was not unique to the alliance relationship between Japan and the United States. Theodore Draper's characterization of the relationship between the United States and Western European countries as a *mésalliance* applies equally to the U.S.-Japanese alliance. Recalling President Kennedy's remark that "real partnership is possible only between equals," Draper argues that "real partnership is not the only thing possible between equals; independence and antagonism are not only possible—they are probable," and he may well be right.[5] The meaning of the alliance with the United States is becoming less and less clear in the minds of the Japanese people. According to Nagai Yōnosuke, those political realists among Japanese specialists in international relations are now discredited by American politicians as being harmful to U.S. strategic thinking. In their place the so-called military realists in Japan seem to be gaining the confidence of American policymakers, we are told. In Nagai's view, some of the military realists are latent Gaullists of Japan, aiming at real autonomy rather than at strengthening the alliance relationship. The whole picture is confusing, making us wonder who are genuine realists and who are pseudorealists.

The emergence of the Nakasone administration in November 1982 further complicated the situation. At the time of his visit to the United States in January 1983, he reportedly uttered provocative expressions, such as linking Japan and the United States under common fate (*unmei kyōdōtai*, a phrase that evokes dark memories of Japan's fatal tie with Nazi Germany) and calling Japan an "unsinkable aircraft carrier." Thanks to his articulate opinions, Nakasone apparently succeeded in establishing his reputation as a hawk and a close collaborator with President Reagan. This stance was supposed to have earned Nakasone an aura of an equal partner to the highest American political leader, but Shimizu Tomohisa, an independent leftist historian, asserts that the Nakasone administration deliberately chose, from among many possibilities, subservience to the United States at the very time when, because of the relative decline of American power, Japan could have avoided that choice.[6]

Policymakers in charge of Japanese-American relations seem to be aware of the danger of simplistic appraisals of the political and economic relationship between Japan and the United States. For example, a published discussion among three high-echelon officials of the Ministry of Foreign Affairs aims at a review of past and present relations between the two countries, but their attempt is at times confusing. For example, although Okazaki Hisanhiko notes that Japanese-American relations have been remarkably amicable since the time of Commodore Perry, with the sole exception of the period between 1930 and 1945, that there is something inherently good about the relationship, and that, because of the geopolitical advantages they share, the two countries make natural allies, he cautions that Japan must make some sacrifices and try hard to maintain friendly relations with the United States. Kitamura Hiroshi agrees with Okazaki, saying that, although Japanese-American relations are basically good, they should not be taken for granted. The three officials agree that equality in the relationship between the two countries was achieved in the middle of the 1970s, but, on problems of economic frictions and defense, Murata Ryōhei argues that economic frictions can be contained as long as the crucial issue of defense is dealt with satisfactorily. A little later, however, he qualifies his view by saying that Americans see the two issues as intertwined.

All three officials lament the deficiency in understanding between Japanese and Americans, pointing out the lack of a sufficient number of America specialists even within the Ministry of Foreign Affairs and hoping that the American policymakers study and understand the realities of Japanese politics and society.[7] But before we take up the problem of perception and understanding, we should recall what George Kennan has said about the nature of Japanese-American relations and compare his views with those of the three officials. In *The Cloud of Danger* (1977), written hastily as an overall analysis of the realities of the world and as a prescription for a new administration's foreign policy, Kennan explained why Japan should be the cornerstone of American policy in the Far East. The first reason is geographic or geopolitical and the second is that Japan's industrial power is so tremendous that it could constitute a force either for great good or for great evil. But the most important point about Japan, according to Kennan, is what he calls a kind of moral obligation or moral opportunity. Without the Pacific war, Kennan would have advised, as he does about China, "Let us not push an unnatural intimacy too far and too fast." But the war and the subsequent occupation of Japan threw the United States into the closest contact with the Japanese, and there came "an intimacy born of conflict and much agony." Clearly Kennan regards the newly formed intimacy as a crucial factor in Japanese-American relations.[8]

We may assume that Kennan's views about the American relationship with Japan have been consistent throughout the postwar period. The question is how much emphasis Japanese policymakers have put on the war and the occupation as contributive factors in the intimacy the country enjoys with the United States. The view that the wartime period was an aberration from the naturally amicable relationship between Japan and the United States may or may not be compatible with Kennan's theory, but the concepts of natural allies and unnatural intimacy are in conflict. In this respect, the increasing interest in studying the Pacific war and the American occupation of Japan might give birth to a new identity crisis among Japanese. There is a possibility, for instance, that a highly critical reinterpretation of occupation policies may offer grounds both for a hawkish view of Japan-U.S. strategic collaboration and for an identification with the antinuclear movement.

We need a new perspective, particularly in the cultural area. Hirakawa Sukehiro, the controversial specialist in comparative literature and comparative culture, recently published a long essay analyzing the autobiographies of Benjamin Franklin and Fukuzawa Yukichi. In this well-researched essay, Hirakawa points out the remarkable resemblance between the two great men: both were self-made men, advocates of the so-called work ethic and fathers of capitalism, masters of foreign languages, orators, deists, interested in science and technology, coiners of new words, political and social reformers, writers of clear style and felicitous phrases, and both were endowed with pleasing humor. Moreover, Franklin and Fukuzawa disliked impractical intellectuals (*"Interi,"* with a special Japanese derogatory connotation). As Hirakawa explains, Franklin's writings influenced Fukuzawa—and, for that matter, a great many Japanese people in the Meiji period knew the name of Franklin—but the degree of likeness between the two men of such different times and different places is simply amazing.[9] It is of course debatable whether this discovery of historical affinity between Japanese culture and American culture in the personalities of Fukuzawa and Franklin could provide the younger generation of each country with a new basis for a sense of mutuality. It is more likely that young people of both countries will share many things with each other in the world of consumption culture. Even so, a healthy sense of balance between the search for uniqueness and the pursuit of commonness will become more and more important.

What is most disturbing about mutual understanding between Japan and America is that specialists—at least in Japan—do not seem to be functioning effectively. The urgent need for the study of American society was proclaimed by Nitobe Inazō in 1919, and today the same plea continues to be repeated. Tokutomi Sohō, an influential journalist whose long career covered the three periods of Meiji, Taisho, and Showa, stressed in 1920 that Japan was misunderstood by Americans partly because of the Japanese themselves.[10] Kiyosawa Kiyoshi, another journalist whose wartime diaries are highly valued, said in 1938 that Japan was misunderstood by foreigners; in his opinion Japan was at that time the most unpopular nation in history.[11] According to Tokutomi, pro-American Japanese, anti-Japanese Japanese, and those despicable politicians and military people who served them were to blame. Kiyosawa criticized the ignoranace and lack of communication that generated misunderstanding. But the point is that even today complaints are heard that foreigners do not—some people say cannot—understand Japan.

Specialists have made serious efforts to improve our understanding of the United States. Even during the war some research was done, and there were publications about American society and culture that were not blatant propaganda. For example, in January 1944, at the critical stage of the war, Taiheiyō Kyōkai, a society dedicated to the study of the problems of the Pacific region, published the first volume of a projected ten-volume study of the United States. Judging from the plan of the project, it was an ambitious attempt at a systematic understanding of American power. The ten volumes were to deal with topics such as the American national character, American world hegemony, American national character as seen by foreign observers, American power of economic mobilization, American religious ideals and religious organizations, foreign missionary activities, American organizations of investigation and the methodology of investigation, recent trends in American scientific research, physics and chemistry, and American heavy industries. The contributors to the first volume on American national character included Tsuru Shigeto who, returning from the United States in 1942, wrote a chapter on the philosophical vulnerabilities of the American national character. Another contributor, Sakanishi Shiho, who had worked for the Library of Congress in Washington, D.C., until 1942, wrote a chapter on the contradictions hidden in the American national character. Apparently this ambitious project was disrupted by Japan's defeat, although the volumes on American national character were published after the war.[12]

This endeavor was symbolic of the seriousness of Japanese specialists' interest in grasping the essential characteristics of the American people. Takagi Yasaka, who gave lectures on American politics at the Tokyo Imperial University even during the war, wrote a small book on American political culture, based on the lectures, and identified Puritanism and the frontier spirit as the sources for American democracy.[13] Takagi was the intellectual pillar of the academic study of America, and, together with Matsumoto Shigeharu, who later established the International House of Japan, founded an organization for American studies that grew into the present Japanese Association for American Studies.

Takagi had studied in the United States in the early 1920s. He identified with what might be called "WASP Americanism" and built the orthodox view of the United States for Japanese specialists. In contrast, Hasegawa Kaitarō (also known as Tani Jōji, Maki Itsuma, and Hayashi Fubo), who also lived in the United States in the early 1920s, wrote popular fiction and depicted the ethnic United States of the Jazz Age. In his own ragtime style, he discussed an America of movies, horse racing, dancing, saxophones, speeding, sky-scrapers, and a world record of divorces. Tani created a fictitious type of "*Meriken-Jappu*, American-Jap," a kind of caricature of the Issei immigrant from Japan. In one of Tani's short stories, a *Meriken-Jappu* appears as a very skillful and cunning gambler from the West Coast who succeeds in a smart way in taking from a white American of Louisiana not only $10,000 but also his wife.[14] His America was poles apart from Takagi's, and it is very doubtful that either was aware of the other's image of the United States; but, looking back, we may say that they represent two contrasting ways of identifying America: one is academic, orthodox, frequently idealizing, and WASP-oriented; the other is nonacademic—journalistic or literary—antiestablishment, debunking or muckraking, and ethnic-oriented.

Ironically, the development of American studies in the postwar period moved in the direction of increasing reluctance to generalize, undermining the belief of such people as Matsumoto Shigeharu that one reason for the Pacific war was the appalling ignorance of the Japanese—both the policymakers and the public—about the United States, so that knowledge of the country should be disseminated widely for the cause of lasting peace.[15]

In recent years Americans themselves have emphasized the regional and ethnic diversity of American society, and academic discussions of national traits seem to be unfashionable. With the vastly improved access to information, journalists can provide detailed stories on segments of the American political and social scene. American studies specialists in Japan are caught in a dilemma; they are faced with a hard choice of either pursuing a specialization at the expense of meaningful generalization, or trying desperately to influence both policymakers and the general public by the force of their expertise.

As of the mid-1980s, Japan's problem of self-identity is increasingly discussed vis-à-vis the ambiguous concept of the Pacific Age. The Japanese people, like Americans, are dreaming a dream of the Pacific Age, forming organizations, holding conferences, and issuing reports. For instance, in October 1984, Fukukawa Shinji of the Ministry of International Trade and Industry (MITI) delivered an address before the U.S.-Japan Council, Aspen, Colorado, on the Pacific Rim idea. Fukukawa recalled that Prime Minister Ohira had advanced the Pacific Rim concept five years earlier and that Fukukawa himself participated in drafting a report on it. Using the phrase "the advent of the Pacific Age," he emphasized that "one fact that speaks plainly about the arrival of the Pacific Age is the tempo at which trade has been expanding . . . The vast Pacific region is developing the conditions needed to become an increasingly interdependent 'regional society,' " Fukukawa noted, adding that "the political and economic ties between the United States and Japan . . . will only work to the benefit of the region's development."[16]

Another recent example of the Japanese interest in the Pacific region is the activity of the Pacific Basin Study Team of the Kansai Keizai Dōyūkai, an influential organization of businessmen chiefly in the Kansai area of Japan with the city of Osaka as its home. The members of the study team visited seven countries and eleven cities in the Pacific region in October and November 1984, and the report of the team noted that "the Pacific Basin has the potential to launch a new economic era in the 21st century," and that understanding each other's societies and cultures within the region is "essential for effective economic cooperation." The economist Rōyama Shōichi, one of the members of the study team, stressed his view that the Pacific Age should be basically an "economic age" in which economic interests should play a central role, and strategic concerns should be subordinate. Rōyama maintained that the Pacific Basin Community, if it is to materialize, should be multicentered with countries such as the United States, Japan, Indonesia, and Australia being more salient than the rest of the member countries rather than having just one country of overwhelming influence.[17] A somewhat similar idea was expressed by Fukukawa in his Aspen address, in which he urged that Japan and the United States "must construct and manage a free and vigorous 'Pax Consortis' in the international economic community." The age of Pax Americana has gradually changed, Fukukawa contended, and "roles must now be shared not only by Europe and Japan but also by newly industrialized countries."[18] The idea of the absence of a single dominant power and the need for partnership between leading powers is common to both Rōyama's and Fukukawa's arguments.

In terms of the partnership between Japan and the United States, the whole concept of the Pacific Age is still very vague, perhaps conveniently so, leading to a variety of views in addition to the ones already mentioned. In an article in the *Nippon keizai shinbun*, Kodama Kōji of the MITI summarizes the present stage of progress toward what he calls "Pax Pacifica." He emphasizes economic and cultural cooperation among the nations in the Pacific region and warns against setting military and political targets for cooperation. Second, Kodama insists that the development of the ASEAN nations is essential. Third, he contends that the form of economic cooperation must be open to countries outside the Pacific region. Finally, Kodama advises that a joint project format should be adopted to enable countries in the region to participate in those cooperative programs that attract their particular attention. Kodama presumably speaks for the Japanese government, and his counsel is to go slowly about advancing the idea of the Pacific Basin Community. Comparing the job of regional cooperation in the Pacific Basin to that of a gardener rather than a mechanic, Kodama stresses that the process of the development of the Pacific countries ought to be regarded as an organic one.[19]

Amaya Naohiro, who left MITI several years ago and has been active as an opinion leader, looks at the Pacific Age from a historical perspective. Starting with the beginning of human civilization, he quickly follows the westward movement of European civilization from Italian city states to Spain, Portugal, and then on to the New World; compares the Mediterranean civilization with the Atlantic civilization; and poses the questions, "Why did the industrial civilization of North America not advance southward but westward across the Pacific? Why does the region of the western Pacific bustle with vigor in its economic activities amidst general stagnation in the rest of the world?"[20] Amaya's own answer is that in countries of vitality, such as Japan, the separation of the sacred and the secular, or to put it differently, the rational and nonideological order of business, has been established. Moreover, he asserts, the very heterogeneity of the region in climate, race, religion, economy, politics, the way of life, will be the fountains for the vigor to produce a civilization of impressive magnitude.

Amaya's grand theory may be more intriguing than convincing. Whether American civilization has been distinct in its separation of the sacred from the secular is highly problematical, and on the other hand, it may not be so easy for many nations in the Pacific region to make the logic of the secular prevail. Yet it is interesting to note that Amaya thinks, unlike Kodama who seeks organic growth of a cooperative system, that the clashes of heterogeneous factors will generate the energy for creating a new civilization. He even ascribes the stagnancy of Europe in recent years to the lack of heterogeneous factors within European civilization. His thesis serves as a caveat against assuming casually that homogeneity leads to better mutual understanding, which in turn will sustain stability and development.[21]

Still another example of theorizing on the concept of the Pacific Age is offered by Ishikawa Yoshimi, a freelance writer who has lived in California for several years. Although his arguments sound rather farfetched, he has been a frequent contributor to influential opinion magazines in Japan, and he seems to be convinced that the coming of the Pacific Age is a kind of manifest destiny. Ishikawa asserts that Japan must not be a bridge across the Pacific Ocean but should be a "stepping island" between the Pacific Ocean and the Japan Sea. Ishikawa seems to suggest that Japan should not aspire to become a rival of the United States for hegemony in the Pacific Ocean but rather should do its best to bring prosperity to Asian countries in the Pacific Age.[22]

There are other variations on the theme of the Pacific Rim Community, but the examples mentioned illustrate that the process of mutual understanding between Japan and the United States is at a crossroad. The crucial question is whether mutual understanding between the two countries has reached a stage where bilateral problems requiring the refinement and revision of facile generalizations about Japan and the United States can be solved, and where, at the same time, we can cooperate in the Pacific Rim.

All too often the dialogue between Japan and the United States in the mass media centers on the political and economic aspects of our relationship and on crude comparisons between Japanese and American cultures. There may be a trap for those who are engaged in the study of a foreign culture, or even the study of culture in general. The American poet Robert Penn Warren gave lectures on democracy and poetry in 1976 in which he referred to Bertrand Russell's distinction between "power knowledge," the knowledge given by science, and "love knowledge," the knowledge that comes from the intuitive and imaginative grasp of nature and man. The poet's question is, "Will the continual presence of abstraction in man's thought dry up, as Santayana once suggested, the old spring of poetry?"[23] With the accelerating development of high-tech industry, the poet's question is of increasing relevance.

A 1985 essay written by a Japanese mathematician on the American character argues that Americans excel in logical thinking but are deficient in emotions and that they should think seriously about the importance of emotions in value judgment.[24] Kawai Hayao, a Japanese Jungian psychologist, who lives in Los Angeles, has focused on the differences between Japanese and Americans. Lecturing on the feminine consciousness in Japanese folk tales, he suggested the symbolism of marriage in the Japanese psyche and observed that marriage as symbolism had been lost in America. Thereupon, someone in the audience asked him what he thought of nature as symbolism in today's Japan, and Kawai interpreted it as a penetrating question hurled at the Japanese people today.[25]

We must address ourselves to the realm of the humanities, and we should be free from cultural nationalism, pernicious symptoms of which are now found in Japan. The Japanese people can be legitimately concerned about their own economic interests. But that does not necessarily mean that we can neglect the problem of perception, particularly the image of Japan as a closed and inaccessible country. After all, in *Moby Dick*, Herman Melville wrote "The same waves wash the moles of the new-built California towns, but yesterday planted by the recentest race of men, and lave the faded but still gorgeous skirts of Asiatic lands, older than Abraham; while all between float milky-ways of coral isles, and low-lying, endless, unknown Archipelagoes, and inpenetrable Japans."[26] The awareness of the deep-rooted image of Japan's impenetrability held by Americans should serve as a guiding factor for Japanese policymakers when coping with problems of economic frictions between Japan and the United States.

However nebulous the concept of the Pacific Age may be, it points to a new stage of historical consciousness of the passing of Pax Americana or the "American Century." This implies, on the part of Americans, a radical reexamination of the character of American identity. It is, indeed an index to the seriousness of the task of reconstructing American historical consciousness that John Diggins has to conclude his searching reinterpretation of the American politicocultural tradition by such statements as, "The problem facing liberal America is the problem of its uniqueness," or ". . . an understanding of Machiavelli and Lincoln might help us face the world without the dangerous self-deceptions of innocence."[27]

As for the Japanese people, the passing of the American century provokes them into reviewing the double process of the Americanization of Japanese culture and the Japanization of American culture since the end of the Japanese-American war. Underlying the endless discussion of America today in books, magazine articles, and TV programs in Japan, one can detect both conscious and unconscious searching for a new Japanese cultural identity in the post-industrial, high-technology age. If we can admit that the dominance of the American cultural impact in the twentieth century has been supported by what may be called mass consumption culture, then the Japanese people must ask themselves whether they can make a breakthrough in changing their way of life in a new technological environment, or whether they should again wait for an American initiative. When the Japanese people ask the question, "Is America really back?" or "Does America really have potentialities for revitalization?" they are simultaneously asking what the role of Japan should be.

Modern Japanese history seems to favor a Japanese posture of response and adaptation rather than initiation of a leadership role. Mitani Taichirō draws an intriguing parallel between the Taisho democracy in Japan as a response to Pax Americana in its formative phase and the post–World War II democracy as a response to Pax Americana in its prime. According to Mitani, this parallel leads to an ominous prospect for the future of Japanese-American relations, because in the first case the democratic response to Pax Americana led to an aspiration for a hegemonic nation with strong military capabilities. Thus we are warned that the end of Pax Americana has in part been caused by the rebirth of Japan as a leading power in the world, if not in terms of its military strength then certainly in terms of its economic influence.[28] Ironically, as a consequence of our responsive behavior, the Japanese people are now faced with the paradoxical challenge of living up to American expectations in sharing burdens on the one hand and of refraining from becoming so strong and disturbing as to be called an "orphan of the world."

Both in the bilateral relations between Japan and the United States and in the multilateral concept of the Pacific Basin Community, the key word is still partnership. The vital question for both nations is whether they will let their partnership degenerate into retaliation, or whether they will be able to work out a constructive relationship of mutual stimulation in cultivating the spirit of liberal-mindedness, deprovincialization, and the desire for understanding.

1. Matsuyama Yukio "Shitatakana gaikō" (Resilient diplomacy), *Asahi Shinbun* (8 January 1984): 1.

2. Kiuchi Nobutane, "Kokusaisei' wa, itsumo iikoto towa kagiranai" (Internationality does not always spell good), *Keizai Rondan* (January 1984): 12-21.

3. Isoda Kōichi, *Sengoshi no kūkan* (The spatiality of the postwar history of japan) (Tokyo, 1983).

4. Ishikawa Hiroyishi et al., eds., *Amerikan karuchā* (American culture), 3 vols. (Tokyo, 1981).

5. Theodore Draper, *Present History* (New York, 1983), 51-114.

6. Shimizu Tomohisa and Wada Huruki, eds., *Kindaichū-shi tachi to tomoni* (Tokyo, 1983), 124-27.

7. Kitamura Hiroshi et al., *Nichibeikankei o toitsumeru* (Exploring Japanese-American relations) (Tokyo, 1983).

8. George F. Kennan, *The Cloud of Danger* (Boston, 1977), 107-11.

9. Hirakawa Sukehiro, "Shinpo ga mada kibō de atta koro" (When progress meant hope), *Shinchō* (February 1984): 6-105.

10. Tokutomi Sohō, *Taisengo no sekai to Nippon* (Japan and the postwar world) (Tokyo, 1920), 678.

11. Kiyosawa Kiyoshi, *Ōbei wa Nippon o ikani miteiruka* (How do western nations view Japan?) (Tokyo, 1938), 46.

12. Taiheiyō Kyōkai, ed., *Amerika kokuminsei no kenkyū* (Studies in American national character) (Tokyo, 1944), 1-52.

13. Takagi Yasaka, *Amerika* (America) (Tokyo, 1969), 1-32.

14. Tani Jōji, *Merkien-Jappu shōbai ōrai* (American Jap's business dealings) (paperback edition, Tokyo, 1975), 6-57, 202-240. Also see Muro Kenji, *Odoru chiheisen: Meriken-Jappu Hasegawa Kaitarō den* (Dancing horizons: The life of Hasegawa Kaitarō, an American Jap) (Tokyo, 1985).

15. *Matsumoto Shigeharu-sensei ni kiku* (An interview with Mr. Matsumoto Shigeharu), Oral History Series, vol. 9 (Tokyo, 1980), 41-42.

16. Fukukawa Shinji, "Ties over the Pacific: Solving Common Problems," *Speaking of Japan* (February 1985): 15-22.

17. Kansai Keizai Dōyūkai, *Shin-Taiheiyō jidai no tōrai to wagakuni no yakuwari* (Japan's role in the new Pacific age) (Tokyo, 1985).

18. Fukukawa, "Ties over the Pacific."

19. Kodama Kōji, "Taiheiyō no jidai" (The age of the Pacific), *Nippon keizai Shinbun* (February 6, 1985): 17.

20. Amaya Naohiro, "Bunmei no seizen to Taiheiyō no jidai" (The westward march of civilization and the coming of the Pacific age), *Tsūsan Jyaanaru* (MITI Journal) (February 1985): 56-57.

21. Ibid.

22. Ishikawa Yoshimi, "Taiheiyō: Nichibei hakenkōsō no jidai" (The Pacific ocean: The Japanese-American struggle for diplomacy), *Voice* (March 1985): 212-33.

23. Robert Penn Warren, *Democracy and Poetry* (Cambridge Mass. 1975), 48.

24. Fujiwara Masahiko, "Amerika no tsumazuki" (America stumbles), *Gakushi kaihō* (January 1985): 17-21.

25. Kawai Hayao, "Nichibei no Aidentitī" (Japanese and American identities), *Tosho* (January 1985): 2-7.

26. Herman Melville, *Moby Dick* Library of America ed. (New York, 1983), 1308.

27. John P. Diggins, *The Lost Soul of American Politics* (New York, 1984), 345.

28. Mitani Taichirō, "Futatsu no sengo: Pakusu-Amerikana to Nippon no 'demokurashī'" (Two dimensions of postwar history: Pax Americana and Japanese 'democracy'), *Chūōkōron* (April 1985): 100-110.

12

Beyond the Pressure-Response Cycle

MITSURU YAMAMOTO

Since the late 1960s, trade and economic frictions of a serious nature requiring government-to-government negotiations and consultations have continued to reoccur between Japan and the United States. The now familiar sequence of events typically begins with the United States filing complaints and demands, which then lead to drawn-out negotiations, and eventually the two sides arrive at an arrangement to alleviate the particular problem. A brief period of tranquility follows, only to be disrupted by the outbreak of a new friction. This cycle of developments has established itself more or less permanently, introducing a discordant note into relations between the two Pacific allies. Invariably Japan is driven to the defensive. When protectionism flares up in an industrial sector, among trade unions or farmers, and in Congress, the American administration responds by asking Japan to reduce export pressure on the U.S. market and improve access for U.S. products to the Japanese market. Japan nearly always tries to meet American demands by piecemeal concessions.

Economically, trade friction can hardly be considered an unmanageable dispute between the two allies when it is approached within the entire context of their relations, though finding a solution is by no means easy. A recurrence of friction has had the effect of rapidly developing intensive communication between the two nations. It has also led to a proliferation of opportunities for nongovernmental dialogue, apart from the discussions carried on between their official representatives. For example, in a 1983 symposuim in Washington cosponsored by Japan's National Institute of Research Advancement and the Brookings Institution of the United States, there was little, if any, American criticism of the basic features of the Japanese economy and policies.[1] The symposium addressed a broad theme—the "Future Course of U.S.-Japan Economic Relations." According to a Japanese organizer of the project, discussion was conducted in a coolheaded manner and with a willingness among the American participants to rethink their own problems and to put Japan-U.S. issues in a broad perspective. Ushiba Nobuhiko, former external economic affairs minister who was among the Japanese participants, shared this observation and said he was encouraged by the impassioned and analytical manner in which discussions were conducted at the gathering. He nevertheless wondered whether and to what extent the American participants in that particular symposium represented the political climate in Washington and, for that matter, in the United States.[2]

A mature attitude seems to be developing today among economists and informed people in Japan and the United States. It is based on the belief that economic friction can be dealt with far more productively as an amalgam of economic, political, and even psychological problems, to be tackled by the two nations together, than as a clash of fundamental national interests. Unfortunately, no such change in perception or approach is found outside the quiet conferences of informed persons. Although the U.S. public decries the Japanese for taking unfair advantages, the Japanese retort that their economic success has been attained through hard work and increased competitiveness. Whether in the United States or in Japan, public opinion is more easily influenced by simplified images and symbols than by complicated discussions of international trade and foreign exchange.

The unproductive habit of focusing debate on which side is being unfair and which party is more industrious or better qualified to win the trade competition needs to be reconsidered. Arguing over who is morally superior only exacerbates the problem and could even trigger an unwanted crisis in Japan-U.S. relations. If the United States and Japan cannot hope to remove the sources of economic friction in a given time span, perhaps of five or ten years, then it is all the more urgent today for leaders of the two countries to find a new definition of the issues involved and change the focus of debate.

Japan should switch to a more activist and globalist approach in coping with trade and economic problems with its largest trading partner. Attention ought to be directed to developing a preventive policy conceived from a longer-term and multilateral perspective and not preoccupied with the day-to-day handling of bilateral frictions with the United States. Prevention of fire is more important today than fighting fires after they have broken out; Japan's economic diplomacy should be reoriented in light of the need for such a change in the focus of concern.

Although specific instances of Japan-U.S. economic friction are outside the immediate concern of this essay, the basic categories of conflict must be noted. Trade and economic conflicts already include at least three types. The first irritant relates to specific Japanese export products to the Unites States, including textiles, steel, color TV sets, and automobiles. A rapid increase in the export of some Japanese products at a particular point in time marks each cycle of product-centered friction. The second concerns the closed nature of the Japanese market. Falling into this area of friction are (1) quantitative restrictions on agricultural imports; (2) product standards and certification, the complex distribution system, and a plethora of alleged nontariff barriers in Japan; (3) government procurement (e.g., Nippon Denshin Denwa Kosha, the Telegram and Telephone Public Corporation, and Nippon Senbai Kosha, the Salt and Tobacco Public Corporation); and (4) the opening of the credit and capital markets and of other service sectors including the insurance business and data processing. The third major source of friction is the American irritation over Japan's sizable bilateral current account surpluses. Beginning in 1965, the payments imbalance became a chronic problem between the two nations. It underlies the first two types of friction. In this connection, the controversy often extends to macroeconomic policies in Japan. Added to all this is the notion of Japanese unfairness, or the concept of industrial targeting.

Inasmuch as the Japan-U.S. economic friction stems from multiple sources, one must caution against easy generalization. Yet these different types of friction are so closely intertwined that they present the symptoms of a compound malaise having several causes. Further, the problem of burden-sharing in a common defense effort under the Japan-U.S. security treaty—a noneconomic factor—also tends to be linked inseparably to the economic issues.

I have argued in favor of shifting the emphasis in Japanese policy from fighting fires to preventing them. It would seem unrealistic to think that we can eliminate friction entirely. Prevention here means that Japan and the United States must prevent future trade and economic problems from becoming unduly exaggerated either by design or by the uncontrolled momentum' of events. The United States and Japan must also see to it that they will deal with future friction without sacrificing their longer-term interests or allowing themselves to be overly swayed by short-term motivations. At the same time, they should seek a solution from a multilateral perspective, embracing not just themselves but all trading nations.

The proposed redirection of Japanese policies is made necessary by these considerations. First, the reactive measures regularly used by Japan to date will inevitably produce diminishing returns after the successive reductions in the tariff and nontariff barriers implemented under American pressure. Second, the recurrent process of American pressure, resulting in Japanese concession, followed by renewed American pressure has brought about a vicious circle of cumulative emotional effects among the people of both Japan and the United States. In April 1983, when the Nakasone cabinet was preparing to submit to the Diet a bill to amend sixteen statutes on product standards and certification with clauses that allegedly discriminated against imports, a Tokyo dispatch of the *New York Times* quoted William Piez at the American embassy in Tokyo as saying that trying to move the Japanese on trade was like peeling an onion; "You start taking the layers off, but you are never sure if there will be anything inside at the end—the whole thing is a rather zen experience, what is an onion anyway?"[3] Indeed, the decisions of the Japanese government very often are more cosmetic than substantive. There are also more than a few instances where high-level official decisions are drained of content through collusion between lower-echelon bureaucrats who skillfully control front-line operations and interest groups.

Japanese politicians, government officials, and interest groups, for their part, like to think that they have offered major concessions to accommodate American demands, in spite of political, economic, and other constraints at home. They react with frustration and bitterness when they discover that their sacrifices are not appreciated in the United States but are met instead by additional complaints and demands. They are driven to wonder whether Americans are determined to find something unfair behind the Japanese economic success, or whether they are simply eager to blame whatever difficulty they have on the "unfair Japanese competitor," closing their eyes to their own problems, such as a relative decline in U.S. industrial productivity and an inadequacy of effort to develop exports.

Elections and mass media contribute to the cumulative process of emotional interaction both in Japan and in the United States. A popular maxim among Japanese parliamentarians says, "When a monkey falls from a tree it remains a monkey, but when a legislator falls in an election, he is reduced to a nobody." Japanese politicians are too vulnerable to speak out for what they believe. Their powerlessness is compounded by pressure from the mass media. Compared with electronic media, print media enjoy more room for presenting complex realities as they actually are. The electronic media must explain everything, however complicated, in a thin slice of time sandwiched between commercial messages. In the face of this relentless pressure for oversimplification and compression, the gap widens inexorably between realities and the public perception of them.

Third, economic friction between Japan and the United States must be considered as a more or less permanent feature of their bilateral relationship, which is rooted in not only cyclical but also structural factors. Underlying the friction is a more fundamental problem—the changing pattern of the world trade environment and the growing inability of the conventional thoughts and rules of the game to catch up with it. These two considerations—the structural roots of friction and the conceptual inability to cope with the changed environment, both political and economic, of the world economy and trade— make it all the more clear that the conventional formula used by Japan and the United States to alleviate economic friction is but an improvisation.

Finally, it is important to recognize that voluntary export restraint on individual products, a major means of fire fighting employed together with market-opening measures, tends to be self-prepetuating and self-multiplying. Its effect is to feed rather than curb protectionism. Sectoral adjustments by other means than voluntary export restriction are no different. An attempt to protect any one industrial sector is bound to weaken the competitiveness of its downstream (allied) industries, which in turn prompts the latter to seek protection, and in a democratic political system, protection can hardly be denied to those demanding it after it already has been given to many other groups.

Quantitative import restrictions imposed under the cloak of voluntary export restraint functions as a sort of international cartel enabling producers in both the exporting and importing countries to raise prices in the importing market to the detriment of consumer interests. This is illustrated by the Japanese program to "voluntarily" limit automobile exports to the United States. In 1982, when the program was forced on Japanese automakers, they even threatened to sue the Japanese government for damages. In a complete turnaround, they came to welcome the restraint arrangement as a system under which they could reap profits without exertion.[4] The same arrangement was not without advantages to the Ministry of International Trade and Industry (MITI). It afforded MITI an opportunity to regain some of the power and influence it had lost in the process of trade liberalization.

Tolerating the political and psychological rather than the economic justifications for voluntary export restraint as a short-term, emergency palliative to economic friction is, admittedly, a practical necessity in view of the current situation. One must be aware, however, that, although this medicine can ease the symptoms, it cannot cure the illness. There is even a danger that its abuse can cause serious poisoning.

In Japan and the United States, politicization of the economy has affected international economic friction. Politicians, their parties, branches of bureaucracy, various industrial sectors, and other interest groups become so engrossed in defending their own vested interests as to seriously endanger the economic rationale and interfere in the definition of public interest. The so-called residual import restrictions applied in contravention of the General Agreement on Tariffs and Trade (GATT) number twenty-seven in the case of Japan, of which twenty-two are accounted for by agricultural items. The name of one or another influential member of the ruling Liberal Democratic Party is associated with each item.[5] To give an example, the main production center of *konnyaku* roots (devil's tongue roots) happens to be in Gunma Prefecture where the constituency of former Prime Minister Fukuda Takeo and present Prime Minister Nakasone Yasuhiro is located.

An economic policy package was adopted by the government on October 21, 1983, in time for President Ronald Reagan's visit to Japan. In the course of shaping this program, different government departments, as usual, contributed measures that they thought could help ease the trade friction. Each departmental concession is carefully measured so that the existing distribution of powers and influences among ministries and agencies, either legal or administrative, is not upset. In doing this, "each of them accepted a small share of the pain and shed tears together."[6] This interagency formula of sharing the pains and tears is also applied among different bureaus in each ministry and agency and among different sections of each bureau. The low-level politicization of the economy is also evident in the United States. In light of these experiences, it is noted that the trade friction phenomenon is in large measure a manifestation of the failure to integrate, or define, national interests within the countries concerned.

We are, therefore, in need of a higher level of politicization of economic relations among states. This must be considered, for Japan, in three dimensions. First, a strategy must be adopted with a view to facilitating the redefinition of the long-term, enlightened, forward-looking, and integrated national interests in the domestic political process of the major trading partner. Raymond Vernon speaks of two constant strands of U.S. trade policy, a long-term commitment to the principle of open markets and a tendency to stray from that commitment in individual cases. The central principles of GATT, reflecting U.S. ideological preferences, are nondiscrimination, the continuous reduction of trade barriers, and the mediation of trade disputes on the basis of multilaterally established rules and regulations. Although Vernon observes that there is no serious possibility of restoring the strength of these key principles that have gradually been worn away by a stream of legitimated exceptions, he rightly stresses the necessity of retaining the institution itself as an important instrument for talking out trade disputes and as a potential launching pad for new initiatives when such initiatives again become feasible.[7]

No doubt the future of the debate in the United States over international trade and economic policy will be a matter of serious concern for Japan, and the coming of new initiatives is what Japan, together with other trading nations in the world, should strive for. Future Japanese behavior in the game of Japan-U.S. economic friction must not be governed by day-to-day tactics to reserve the existing sectoral interests or to fend off American pressure with one small concession at a time. Instead, Japanese policy must be guided by strategic considerations to encourage the revitalization of the more positive one of the two conflicting strands in U.S. trade policy. Stemming the global spread of protectionism and preserving an open trading system are in the vital interests of Japan. It is decidedly important to prevent the United States, still the most weighty presence in the world economy, from abandoning the open-market principle. The guiding principle for Japan's response should be to focus on enhancing the above-mentioned basic goal rather than the perceived intensity of pressure the United States brings to bear on Japan from time to time. This kind of response demands political insight beyond economics or lower-level politicization.

Second, we do not live in a world of untainted free trade where the forces of competitive markets are at work. Nor are members of the international trading community interested in finding a theoretical settlement of the controversy between advocates of free trade and of protectionism. If these assumptions are valid, then any vigorous advocacy by Japan of the free-trade principle from its present position of strength would be of little use to solving actual problems it faces in world trade. A mature political approach is needed here. A deficit country would ask for an improvement in the bilateral current account imbalance with a surplus country. The surplus country replies that balance of payments problems cannot be usefully discussed on a bilateral basis and that the multilateral equilibrium is what counts. The deficit country insists that, whatever the logic of economics may be, it must seek an improvement in the bilateral balance. This was the pattern of exchange repeated every time the ministerial-level Japan-U.S. Joint Committee on Trade and Economic Affairs sat in its annual meeting in the first half of the 1960s, when Japan ran a deficit more or less regularly in current transactions with the United States. The two trading nations have since changed places, and Japan now uses the line of argument then used by U.S. representatives. The episode shows that the logic of a nation's trade policy changes when its international economic position changes. What matters is an ability to understand and appreciate the other's position and difficulties and the political and psychological impact of these difficulties.

Third, the process of Japan's adjustment to the rapidly changing world must be made more endogenous rather than exogenous. It must be initiated and carried out regardless of whether pressure is applied from outside. Japan urgently needs to transform its export-led pattern of economic growth if it is to enjoy prosperity in harmony with other countries on the world economic scene. It must also shift from the intensive industrialization of the past quarter century toward a new pattern of growth more compatible with the quality of the environment, social welfare, increased leisure for the people, and other nonindustrial values. Moreover, as the world's second largest market economy, Japan must widen its own domestic market not just to domestic but to foreign producers so that it can contribute to the economic stability and development of an interdependent world. Japan's international economic policy must be guided by a new, internally motivated attitude, recognizing that Japan must change the policy inertia of the past for the sake of its own interest, not because it faces external pressure for change.

Japan's gradual transition since the 1960s from a closed system to an open economic system has proceeded often in timid responses to U.S. guidance, demands, and sometimes outright pressure. Liberalization occurred in the

absence of any strong free-trade ideology in Japan. Each new round of liberalization in the areas of trade, payments, and inward foreign investment
gave rise to alarms over the coming of "a second black ship" and "a third
black ship." (The first black ship panic was triggered by the arrival in 1853
of Commodore Perry's Pacific fleet and the American demand for access to
Japanese ports.)

Intensified American demands for liberalization of farm imports have pitted
a minority group (e.g., Keidanren—Japan Federation of Economic Organization—MITI, etc.) against the numerically dominant alliance of farmers'
organizations, the Ministry of Agriculture, Forestry and Fisheries, Diet members of all ideological hue ranging from the LDP to the Communist party,
labor unions, and consumer organizations. This standoff, however, has never
developed into a national debate on how to direct the evolution of Japanese
agriculture, be it in the direction of liberalization or permanent maintenance
of the existing protection, and how to define the future status of that industry
in the nation's economy as a whole. This seems another notable instance of
the Kurofune (black ship)-style reaction that simply deals with shocks from
the outside. For Japanese agriculture, step-by-step liberalization in one way
or another will have to be introduced if it is to become more productive.
Unfortunately, the debate so far has been focused solely on whether or to
what extend a concession is to be made to U.S. pressure.

One sees little chance of the Japan-U.S. friction being reduced or eliminated
in the near future. It is clear, however, that both sides must and can change
the formats and foci of debate. Too often we have seen the problems of
bilateral trade and economic friction defined entirely by the United States,
with Japan merely responding. To change this pattern, endogeneous moti-
vation should be developed in Japan's decision making as well as in public
debate.

1. Yoshida Shigenobu, "Nichibeikankei—Netsu dewa naku hikario" [Japan-U.S. Relations—Not Heat, but Light Wanted], *Gekkan NIRA* (August 1983):5.

2. Yoshida, "Nichibeikankei," 31.

3. *New York Times*, international weekly edition (April 17, 1983): 5.

4. *Asahi Shimbun*, evening edition (October 19, 1983): 3. See also, Shimokawa Kōichi,
"Jidōsha yushitsu jishu-kisei no ketsumatsu" (The results of voluntary export restraint of the
automobile), *Keizai Hyōron* (November 1983): 32-33.

5. *Mainichi Shimbun* (February 7, 1982): 7.

6. Funabashi Yōichi, "Fukugō bōeki masatsu no seijikeizaigaku" (Political economy of a
complex trade friction), *Sekai* (January 1984): 153.

7. Raymond Vernon, "International Trade Policy in the 1980s," *International Studies Quarterly* 26 (December 1982): 483.

Contributors

Tadashi Aruga, Professor of Law, Hitotsubashi University
Warren I. Cohen, Professor of History, Michigan State University
Robert Feldman, Research Associate, International Monetary Fund
Robert G. Gilpin, Professor of Government, Princeton University
Nagaya Homma, Professor of American Studies, Tokyo University
Chihiro Hosoya, Professor of International Relations, International
  University of Japan
Akira Iriye, Professor of History, University of Chicago
Hideo Kanemitsu, Professor of Economics, Sophia University
Stephen Krasner, Professor of Political Science, Stanford University
Walter LaFeber, Professor of History, Cornell University
Daniel Okimoto, Professor of Political Science, Stanford University
Akio Watanabe, Professor of International Relations, Tokyo University
Mitsuru Yamamoto, Professor of Politics, Hitotsubashi University

Index